PHP 5 For Dummies®

Creating Arrays

Method for Creating an Array	*Example Code*	*Result*
Using empty brackets	`$colors[] = "red";` `$colors[]= "blue";`	`$colors[1]=red` `$colors[2]=blue`
Using keys	`$paint['house'] = "blue";` `$paint['barn'] = "red";`	`$paint[house] = blue` `$paint[barn] = red`
Using `array` function	`$colors = array( "blue", "red");`	`$colors[1]=blue $colors[2]=red`
Using `array` function	`$colors = array( 5 =>"blue", "red")`	`$colors[5]=blue $colors[6]=red`
Using `array` function with keys	`$paint = array( "barn"=> "red","house"=>"green");`	`$paint[barn] = red` `$paint[house] = green`

Multidimen-sional array	`$paint['house']['tall'] = "yellow";`
	`$paint['barn']['tall'] = "white";`
	`$paint['house']['short'] = "blue";`
	`$paint['barn']['short'] = "red";`
		`$paint[house][tall] = yellow`
		`$paint[house][short] = blue`
		`$paint[barn][tall] = white`
		`$paint[barn][short] = red`

Comparison Operators

Operator	*What It Means*
==	Are the two values equal in value?
===	Are the two values equal in both value *and* data type?
>	Is the first value larger than the second value?
>=	Is the first value larger than or equal to the second value?
<	Is the first value smaller than the second value?
<=	Is the first value smaller than or equal to the second value?
!=	Are the two values not equal to each other in value?
!==	Are the two values not equal to each other in either value or data type?
<>	Are the two values not equal to each other in value?

PHP Variable Name Rules

Start with a dollar sign ($)
Can be any length
Include letters, numbers, and underscores
Begin with a letter or an under-score, not a number
Uppercase and lowercase letters not the same

For Dummies: Bestselling Book Series for Beginners

PHP 5 For Dummies®

Special Characters Used in Patterns

Character	*Meaning*	*Example*	*Match*	*Not a Match*
^	Beginning of line.	`^e`	exam	math exam
$	End of line.	`m$`	exam	exams
.	Any single character.	`..`	up, do	I, a
?	The preceding character is optional.	`ger?m`	germ, gem	geam
( )	Groups literal characters into a string that must be matched exactly.	`g(er)m`	germ,	gem, grem
[ ]	Encloses a set of optional literal characters.	`g[er]m`	gem, grm	germ, gel
[^]	Encloses a set of non-matching optional characters.	`g[^er]m`	gym, gum	gem, germ
-	Represents all the characters between two characters.	`g[a-c]m`	gam, gbm, gcm	gdm, gxm, gal
+	One or more of the preceding items.	`bldg[1-3]+`	bldg111, bldg132	bldg, bldg555
*	Zero or more of the preceding items.	`ge*m`	gm, geeem	germ, grm
{*n*}	Repeat *n* times.	`ge{5}m`	geeeeem	geeeem, geeeeeem
{*n1*,*n2*}	The starting and ending number of a range of repetitions.	`a{2,5}`	aa, aaaa	1, aa3
\	The following character is literal.	`g\*m`	g*m	gem, germ
(| |)	A set of alternate strings.	`(Sam|Sally)`	Samuel Go Sally	Sarah Salmon

Item 4166-8.
For more information about Wiley Publishing, call 1-800-762-2974.

PHP 5 FOR DUMMIES®

by Janet Valade

WILEY
Wiley Publishing, Inc.

PHP 5 For Dummies®

Published by
Wiley Publishing, Inc.
111 River Street
Hoboken, NJ 07030
www.wiley.com

Published by Wiley Publishing, Inc., Indianapolis, Indiana

Published simultaneously in Canada

For general information on our other products and services or to obtain technical support, please contact our Customer Care Department within the U.S. at 800-762-2974, outside the U.S. at 317-572-3993, or fax 317-572-4002.

Wiley also publishes its books in a variety of electronic formats. Some content that appears in print may not be available in electronic books.

Library of Congress Control Number: 2003105680

ISBN: 0-7645-4166-8

Manufactured in the United States of America

10 9 8 7 6 5 4 3 2 1

1B/RQ/QZ/QT/IN

About the Author

Janet Valade is the author of *PHP & MySQL For Dummies.* In addition, she has authored and revised chapters for several Linux books and for a Webmaster certification book.

Janet Valade has 20 years experience in the computing field. She worked as a Web designer/programmer for an engineering firm. Prior to that, Janet worked for several years in a university environment as a systems analyst. During her tenure, she supervised the installation and operation of computing resources, designed and developed a data archive, provided technical support for faculty and students, wrote numerous technical papers, and developed and presented seminars and workshops on a variety of technology topics.

Dedication

This book is dedicated to anyone who finds it useful.

Acknowledgments

I wish to express my appreciation to the entire Open Source community. Without those who give their time and talent, there would be no cool PHP for me to write about. Furthermore, I never would have learned this software without the PHP lists where people generously spend their time answering foolish questions from beginners. Many ideas have come from reading questions and answers on the lists.

Publisher's Acknowledgments

We're proud of this book; please send us your comments through our online registration form located at `www.dummies.com/register/`.

Some of the people who helped bring this book to market include the following:

Acquisitions, Editorial, and Media Development

Project Editors: Kala Schrager, Christopher Morris

Acquisitions Editor: Terri Varveris

Senior Copy Editors: Kim Darosett, Teresa Artman

Technical Editor: Szemir Khangyi

Editorial Manager: Kevin Kirschner

Media Development Manager: Laura VanWinkle

Media Development Supervisor: Richard Graves

Editorial Assistant: Amanda Foxworth

Cartoons: Rich Tennant (`www.the5thwave.com`)

Production

Project Coordinator: Maridee Ennis

Layout and Graphics: Andrea Dahl, Joyce Haughey, Stephanie D. Jumper, Michael Kruzil, Heather Ryan, Jacque Schneider

Proofreaders: Carl Pierce, TECHBOOKS Production Services

Indexer: TECHBOOKS Production Services

Publishing and Editorial for Technology Dummies

Richard Swadley, Vice President and Executive Group Publisher

Andy Cummings, Vice President and Publisher

Mary C. Corder, Editorial Director

Publishing for Consumer Dummies

Diane Graves Steele, Vice President and Publisher

Joyce Pepple, Acquisitions Director

Composition Services

Gerry Fahey, Vice President of Production Services

Debbie Stailey, Director of Composition Services

Contents at a Glance

Table of Contents

Introduction

Because you're here, you must be interested in writing PHP scripts. Perhaps you just want to learn to program and you heard that PHP is one of the easiest languages to learn. You're right; it is. PHP is a good choice for your first programming language.

Perhaps you're developing an interactive Web site and you heard that PHP is particularly good for Web site development. You're right; it is. You can be interacting with users at your Web site in no time at all.

Perhaps you have an application to write and you have a short timeline. You heard that PHP is easy to learn. You're right; it is. It was designed with *easy to learn* as a specific design goal.

Perhaps you have some system administration, file manipulation, or data handling tasks to perform and you heard that PHP can handle these tasks. You're right; it can. PHP can do almost anything that you can think of, although it draws the line at asking your boss for a raise. Well, wait a minute, PHP *can* send e-mail. . . . Hmmm.

About This Book

Think of this book as a friendly introduction to programming in PHP. This book is both an introduction to programming and an introduction to PHP. The book starts with the basics of PHP, including how to tell whether you need to install it. (Full installation instructions are included in Appendix A.) The book describes the basic features of PHP with examples of their use. If you have experience with programming, you can probably just skim this section, but if you don't, all the programming basics are here.

The book goes on to describe the most common uses of PHP. It shows how to write scripts for Web sites, file manipulation, databases, and other common tasks. It provides techniques and shortcuts and warns against common errors. Both beginners and experienced programmers can write useful scripts for many common applications in a very short time by using the information in the application section (Part IV) of the book.

How to Use This Book

This book is designed as a reference, not as a tutorial, so you don't have to read this book from cover to cover unless you want to. You can start reading at any point in the book — in Chapter 1, Chapter 8, wherever. I divide the world of PHP programming into manageable chunks of information, so check out the Table of Contents and locate the topic that you're interested in. If you need to know information from another chapter to understand the chapter that you're reading, I reference that chapter number.

This book includes many examples of PHP programming statements, ranging from a line or two to complete PHP programs. PHP statements in this book are shown in a different typeface that looks like the following line:

```
A PHP program statement
```

In addition, PHP is sometimes shown in the text of a paragraph. When it is, the PHP in the paragraph is also shown in a different typeface. For example, `this text` is an example of a PHP statement within the paragraph text.

In examples, you will often see some words in italics. Italicized words are general types that need to be replaced with the specific name appropriate for your data. For example, when you see an example like the following

```
echo number1,number2
```

you know that *number1* and *number2* need to be replaced with real numbers because they are in italics. When you use it in your script, you may use it in the following form:

```
echo 3,127
```

In addition, you may see three dots (. . .) following a list in an example line of code. You don't need to type the three dots. The three dots just mean that you can have as many items in the list as you want. For example, when you see the following line

```
echo number1,number2, . . .
```

you don't need to include the three dots in the statement. The three dots just mean that your list of numbers can be as long as you want. You can include *number3*, *number4*, and so on, as follows:

```
echo number1,number2,number3,number4
```

Foolish Assumptions

First, I assume that you know enough about computers to understand terms like files, directories, path names, and other basic operating system concepts. I assume that when I tell you to put a file in a specific directory, you know how to do that.

Next, I assume that you know how to create files. You need to know how to create a file and edit it by using a basic editor, such as Notepad in Windows. You need to know how to save the file, copy it, and move it around.

I assume that you are using an operating system that PHP runs on, which included almost every operating system. Your operating system needs to be reasonably current. For example, Windows 95 is too old, as is Mac OS 9. Even Windows 98 is a little old, although some people do run PHP on it.

If you're using PHP for the Web, you need to use HTML (HyperText Markup Language) statements. I assume that you know HTML. Consequently, although I use HTML in many examples, I do not explain the HTML. If you need to use PHP for a Web site and you do not have an HTML background, I suggest that you first read a book on HTML — such as *HTML 4 For Dummies,* 4th Edition, by Ed Tittel and Natanya Pitts, or *HTML 4 For Dummies, Quick Reference*, 2nd Edition, by Deborah S. Ray and Eric J. Ray (both by Wiley Publishing, Inc.) Then build some practice Web pages before you start this book. However, if you're the impatient type, I won't tell you that it's impossible to proceed without knowing HTML. You may be able to glean enough HTML from this book to build your particular Web site. If you choose to proceed without knowing HTML, I would suggest that you have an HTML book by your side to assist you when you need to figure out some HTML that isn't explained in this book.

Also for PHP for the Web users, I assume that you have created at least a static Web page, probably one or more static Web sites. I assume that you know where you need to put files so that your Web pages are available to your Web site users and that you know how to put the files in the appropriate place by using `copy`, `ftp`, and so on.

I do *not* assume that you know anything at all about writing computer programs in any language. This introductory book provides the needed instructions for anyone to write PHP scripts. So, if this is your first programming language, you should be fine. If you have a background in another programming language, particularly C, you may find this book to be a quick reference to learning how to do things in PHP. However, those who have no background in programming will find all the information that they need.

How This Book Is Organized

This book is divided into six parts. The content ranges from an introduction to PHP basics to common applications for PHP.

Part I: Say Hello to the PHP Scripting Language

This part provides an overview of PHP, including how it works and its many uses. You discover how to set up your environment for using PHP. Finally, this part shows you how to create your first PHP program.

Part II: Variables and Data

Variables are the fundamental feature of PHP. This section shows you how to create variables and use them. It also describes the kind of data that you can store in a variable as well as how to handle the various types of data. Then, you find out how to create and use complex variables called *arrays*.

Part III: Basic PHP Programming

This part shows you how to program PHP scripts. You find out about the basic features of PHP and the details of how to use them to create your scripts. This part also introduces you to object-oriented programming.

Part IV: Common PHP Applications

Part IV provides the techniques needed to write scripts for the most common PHP applications. You find out how to write scripts for use in your Web site, such as how to display HTML forms and how to process information that users type into forms. You find out how to use PHP to interact with databases. Using PHP to perform system tasks, such as writing files on your hard disk and executing operating system commands, is also described.

Part V: The Part of Tens

This part provides some useful lists of things to do and not do when writing PHP scripts, as well as a listing of PHP resources.

Part VI: Appendixes

This part provides detailed instructions for installing PHP for those who need to install it themselves. Appendix B is a list of functions available in PHP, intended to be a useful reference while you write your scripts.

Icons Used in This Book

Icons are provided to help you identify information in this book. The following icons point out types of information for your notice.

Tips provide extra information for a specific purpose. Tips can save you time and effort, so they're worth checking out.

This icon is a Post-It note of sorts, highlighting information that's worth committing to memory.

You should always read and pay attention to warnings. Warnings emphasize actions that you must take or must avoid to prevent dire consequences.

This icon flags information and techniques that are more technical than other sections of the book. The information here can be interesting and helpful, but you don't need to understand it to use the information in the book.

Part I

Say Hello to the PHP Scripting Language

"You're a great geek, Martin. You're just not my geek."

In this part . . .

I provide an overview of PHP. I describe PHP, how it works, and what it is useful for. After describing your tools, I show you how to set up your working environment. I also present options for accessing PHP and point out what to look for in each environment.

After describing the tools and options for the development environment, I provide an overview of the development process. I show you how to write your first script and discuss a few simple output statements.

Chapter 1

Getting to Know PHP

In This Chapter

- Taking a look at PHP
- Understanding how PHP works
- Understanding PHP as open source software

So, you want to get to know PHP. Perhaps this is your first adventure in programming, and you chose PHP because your techie friend told you it's easy to understand. Well, your friend is right. PHP is one of the easiest programming languages to understand. The developers of PHP strive constantly to keep it easy to use.

Perhaps you already know how to program in another language. You've decided to study PHP because it's the best language for your new Web application project. It's a good decision because PHP is well suited for writing dynamic Web applications. PHP is easy to get started with, but it also has many advanced features for seasoned programmers. If you know C, you have a great head start because PHP syntax is similar to C syntax.

In this chapter, I discuss what PHP is, what it can do, and how it does it.

Getting Familiar with PHP

PHP is a widely used open source, general-purpose *scripting language*. It was originally designed for use in Web site development. In fact, PHP started life as Personal Home Page tools, developed by Rasmus Lerdorf to assist users with Web page tasks. PHP proved so useful and popular, it rapidly grew to become the full-featured language that it is today, acquiring the name PHP Hypertext Preprocessor along the way to represent its expanded abilities — processing Web pages before they're displayed.

The popularity of PHP continues to grow rapidly because of its many advantages:

- **It's fast:** On Web sites, because it is embedded in HTML code, the time to process and load a Web page is short.
- **It's free:** PHP is proof that free lunches do exist and that you can get more than you paid for.
- **It's easy to use:** The syntax is simple and easy to understand and use, even for non-programmers. For use in Web sites, PHP code is designed to be included easily in an HTML file.
- **It's versatile:** PHP runs on a wide variety of operating systems — Windows, Linux, Mac OS, and most varieties of Unix.
- **Technical support is widely available:** You can join one of several e-mail discussion lists offered on the PHP Web site (`www.php.net`), which cover topics such as general PHP, PHP on Windows, or databases and PHP. In addition, a Web interface to the discussion lists is available at `news.php.net`, where you can browse or search the messages.
- **It's secure:** As long as your scripts are designed correctly, the user does not see the PHP code.
- **It's customizable:** The open source license allows programmers to modify the PHP software, adding or modifying features as needed to fit their own environments. PHP provides significant control over the environment, reducing chances of failure.

Considering the Various Uses for PHP

PHP is a general-purpose language that can be used to write general-purpose scripts. Scripts are computer files containing instructions in the PHP language that tell the computer to do things, such as display `Hello` on the screen or store some specified data in a database. Most scripts contain a series of instructions that can accomplish tasks from designing Web pages to navigating your file system. Because PHP began life on the Web, it has many features that are particularly well suited for use in scripts that create dynamic Web pages. Currently, you find PHP most often hard at work in Web pages, but its use for other purposes is growing.

PHP is very popular for Web sites. According to the PHP Web site (`www.php.net/usage.php`), over 11 million domains are using PHP. Yahoo!, which is probably the world's most visited site, recently decided to change from its own proprietary language to PHP.

Using PHP for Web applications

In the beginning, Web pages were static — they just presented documents. Users went to Web sites to read information. Documents were linked together so that users could easily find the information they sought, but the Web pages didn't change. Every user who arrived at a Web page saw the same thing.

Soon Web page developers wanted to do more. They wanted to interact with visitors, collect information from users, and provide Web pages that were customized for individuals. Several languages have developed that can be used to make Web sites dynamic. PHP is one of the most successful of these languages, evolving quickly to become more and more useful and rapidly growing in popularity.

PHP is a server-side scripting language, which means that the scripts are executed on the *server* (the computer where the Web site is located). This is different than JavaScript, another popular language for dynamic Web sites. JavaScript is executed by the browser, on the user's computer. Thus, JavaScript is a client-side language. Web servers and the interaction between servers and clients are discussed in the section "PHP for the Web," later in this chapter.

Because PHP scripts execute on the server, PHP can dynamically create the HTML code that generates the Web page, which allows individual users to see customized Web pages. Web page visitors see the output from scripts, but not the scripts themselves.

PHP has many features designed specifically for use in Web sites, including the following:

- **Interact with HTML forms:** PHP can display an HTML form and process the information that the user types in.
- **Communicate with databases:** PHP can interact with databases to store information from the user or retrieve information that is displayed to the user.
- **Generate secure Web pages:** PHP allows the developer to create secure Web pages that require users to enter a valid username and password before seeing the Web page content.

PHP features make these and many other Web page tasks easy.

PHP is only server-side, meaning it can't interact directly with the user's computer. That means PHP can't initiate actions based on the status of the user's computer, such as mouse actions or screen size. Therefore, PHP alone can't produce some popular effects, such as navigation menus that drop down or change color. On the other hand, JavaScript, a client-side scripting language, can't access the server, limiting its possibilities. For example, you can't use JavaScript to store data on the server or retrieve data from the server. But wait! You don't have to choose. You can use JavaScript and PHP together to produce Web pages that neither can produce alone. See Chapter 11 for details on using JavaScript and PHP together.

Using PHP for database applications

PHP is particularly strong in its ability to interact with databases. PHP supports pretty much every database you've ever heard of and some you haven't. PHP handles connecting to the database and communicating with it, so you don't need to know the technical details for connecting to a database or for exchanging messages with it. You tell PHP the name of the database and where it is, and PHP handles the details. It connects to the database, passes your instructions to the database, and returns the database response to you.

Major databases currently supported by PHP include the following:

- dBASE
- Informix
- Ingres
- Microsoft SQL Server
- mSQL
- MySQL
- Oracle
- PostgreSQL
- Sybase

PHP supports other databases as well, such as filePro, FrontBase, and InterBase. In addition, PHP supports ODBC (Open Database Connectivity), a standard that allows you to communicate with even more databases, such as Access and IBM DB2.

PHP works well for a database-driven Web site. PHP scripts in the Web site can store data in and retrieve data from any supported database. PHP also can interact with supported databases outside a Web environment. Database use is one of PHP's best features.

Using PHP with your file system

PHP can interact with your file system — the directories and files that are on your local hard disk or on other computers accessible over a network. PHP can write into a file on your file system, creating the file if it doesn't exist, and can read the contents from files. It can also create directories, copy files, rename files, delete files, change file attributes, and perform many other file system tasks. PHP allows you to perform almost any task related to your file system.

Many Web sites need to interact directly with the file system. For example, a Web application may save information temporarily in a file rather than in a database, or may need to read information from a file.

System administrative and maintenance scripts frequently need to interact with the file system. For example, you may want to use a PHP script to back up files, to clean out directories, or to process text files by reformatting their contents. PHP can perform these tasks quite well.

Using PHP for system commands

PHP can interact with your operating system to perform any task the operating system can perform. You can execute an operating system command and receive the output. For example, you can execute a `dir` or `ls` command (to list the files in your directory) from PHP and receive the list of filenames that the `dir/ls` command produces.

The ability to execute system commands is often useful for system administrative and maintenance tasks. For example, you may want to clean up a directory by deleting files with a particular extension. You can use a system command to get a list of files in a directory and then identify and delete the files with the unwanted extension.

The ability to execute system commands includes the ability to run any other program on the system. Thus, you can run programs in other languages from PHP and make use of the output. Aren't you relieved that you don't have to rewrite all those programs you're using now? You can run Perl, C, shell scripts, or any other language programs from PHP. New PHP programs can add functionality to your system tools, without requiring you to spend time rewriting existing tools.

Understanding How PHP Works

PHP is a high-level language, which means that it's human-friendly, similar to English. Because your computer doesn't understand English, you use PHP to communicate, and the PHP interpreter converts the language in your PHP script to language the computer can understand. The computer then follows your instructions, passed to it by the interpreter.

The PHP interpreter comes in two flavors, one for use with Web sites and one that you run from the command line, independent of the Web. You can install either or both.

PHP as a general-purpose language

When you use PHP as a general-purpose scripting language, you install PHP CLI, the version of PHP developed for this purpose. You access the PHP interpreter from the command line to run your PHP script. The process is similar to other languages, such as Perl or C. For the lowdown on running scripts using PHP CLI, check out Chapter 3.

How the World Wide Web works

It's helpful to understand a little about how the World Wide Web (WWW) works. The Web is a network of computers that offer Web pages. Millions of Web sites are on the Web. To enable Web surfers to find the Web sites they want to visit, each Web page has an address, called a *URL*. This includes the Web site's domain name and the filename, such as `www.mycompany.com/welcome.html`. When Web surfers want to visit a Web page, they type the URL into their Web browsers. The following process is set in motion:

1. The Web browser sends a message out onto the Web, requesting the Web page.
2. The message is sent to the computer at the address specified in the URL.
3. The Web server software on the addressed computer receives the message.
4. The Web server searches for the requested HTML file.
5. The Web server finds the requested file and sends the file to the Web browser that requested it. (If it can't find the file, it sends a message to the browser saying that it couldn't find the file.)
6. The Web browser displays the Web page based on the HTML code it received.

PHP for the Web

When used on your Web site, PHP works in partnership with your Web server. Every Web site requires a Web server. The Web sever is the software that delivers your Web pages to the world. The PHP software works in conjunction with the Web server.

When used on the Web, PHP is an *embedded scripting language.* This means that PHP code is embedded in HTML code. You use HTML tags to enclose the PHP language that you embed in your HTML file. You create and edit Web pages containing PHP the same way you create and edit regular HTML pages.

When PHP is installed, the Web server is configured to look for PHP code embedded in files with specified extensions. It's common to specify the extensions `.php` or `.phtml`, but you can configure the Web server to look for any extension. When the Web server gets a request for a file with the designated extension, it sends the HTML statements as is, but PHP statements are processed by the PHP software before they're sent to the requester.

When PHP language statements are processed, the output consists of HTML statements. The PHP language statements are not included in the HTML sent to the browser, so the PHP code is secure and transparent to the user. For example, consider this simple PHP statement:

```
<?php echo "<p>Hello World"; ?>
```

In this statement, `<?php` is the PHP opening tag, `?>` is the closing tag, and `echo` is a PHP instruction that tells PHP to output the text that follows it as plain HTML code. The PHP software processes the PHP statement and outputs the following:

```
<p>Hello World
```

This is a regular HTML statement that is delivered to the user's browser. The PHP statement itself is not delivered to the browser, so the user never sees any PHP statements.

PHP and the Web server must work closely together. PHP is not integrated with all Web servers but works with many of the most popular ones. PHP is developed as a project under the Apache Software Foundation and, consequently, works best with Apache. PHP also works with Microsoft IIS/PWS, iPlanet (formerly Netscape Enterprise Server), and others.

Serving up Web servers

The software that delivers Web pages to the world is called a *Web server.* Several Web servers are available, but the most popular one is Apache. Approximately 60 percent of Web sites on the World Wide Web use Apache, according to surveys at `www.netcraft.com` and `www.securityspace.com/s_survey/data/`. Apache is open source software, which means it's free. It's available for all major operating systems. It's automatically installed with most Linux distributions and is preinstalled on Mac OS X. You can find information about Apache at `httpd.apache.org`. PHP is a project of the Apache Software Foundation, so PHP runs best with Apache.

Other Web servers are available. Internet Information Server (IIS) is the second most popular Web server with about 30 percent of the Web sites. IIS is developed by Microsoft and runs only on Windows. IIS is installed by default with Windows server software. Other Web servers include Zeus, NCSA, and Sun ONE. No other Web server is used on more than 2.5 percent of the Web sites.

Keeping Up with Changes in PHP

PHP is open source software. If you have only used software from major software publishers — such as Microsoft, Macromedia, or Adobe — you will find that open source software is an entirely different species. It's developed by a group of programmers who write the code in their spare time, for fun and for free. There's no corporate office to call with questions. There's no salesperson to convince you of the wonders of the software. There's no technical support phone number where you can be put on hold.

Sounds like there's no support for PHP, doesn't it? Actually, quite the opposite is true: An incredible amount of support is available. PHP is supported by the developers and by the many PHP users. But you need to look for the support. It's part of your job as a PHP user and developer to search out the information you need.

Open source software changes frequently, rather than once every year or two as commercial software does. It changes when the developers feel it's ready. It also changes quickly in response to problems. When a serious problem, such as a security hole, is found, a new version that fixes the problem may be released in days. You don't receive glossy brochures or see splashy magazine ads for a year before a new version is released. If you don't make the effort to stay informed, you may miss the release of a new version or be unaware of a serious problem with your current version.

Visit the PHP Web site often. You need to know the information that's published there. Join the mailing lists, which often are very high in traffic. When you first start using PHP, the large number of mail messages on the discussion lists brings valuable information into your e-mail box; you can pick up a lot by reading those messages. And soon, you may be able to help others based on your own experience. At the very least, subscribe to the announcement mailing list, which only delivers e-mail occasionally. Any important problems or new versions are announced here. The e-mail you receive from the announcement list contains information you need to know.

So, right now, before you forget, hop over to the PHP Web site and sign up for a list or two at `www.php.net/mailing-lists.php`.

PHP 5

Most of the important changes in PHP version 5 don't affect the coding or the use of PHP. They affect the performance of PHP. The Zend engine (the magic, invisible engine that powers PHP) has been significantly improved, and as a result, scripts run faster and more efficiently.

The object-oriented programming features of PHP are a major focus of PHP 5. Object-oriented programming is greatly improved over PHP 4. The creation and use of objects runs much faster, many object-oriented features have been added, and exceptions are introduced. Programmers who prefer object-oriented programming will be much happier with PHP 5. (Object-oriented programming is described in Chapter 9.)

With PHP 5, the names of the PHP programs changed. PHP for the Web is called `php-cgi`; PHP CLI is called just `php`, as in `php.exe` on Windows. Both are stored in the directory where PHP is installed. Prior to PHP 5, both programs were named `php.exe`, but stored in different subdirectories.

PHP 5 adds support for MySQL 4.1 and later. However, support for MySQL is not included with PHP 5 by default. Support for MySQL 4.0 or MySQL 4.1 must be specified when PHP is installed. Prior to PHP 5, support for MySQL 4.0 and earlier was included automatically.

PHP 5 includes support for SQLite by default. SQLite provides quick and easy methods for storing and retrieving data in flat files.

Previous versions of PHP

You should be aware of some significant changes in previous PHP versions because existing scripts that work fine on earlier versions may have problems when they're run on a later version, and vice versa. The following are some changes you should be aware of:

- **Version 4.3.1:** Fixed a security problem in 4.3.0. It's not wise to continue to run a Web site using versions 4.3.0 or earlier.
- **Version 4.3.0:** Included significant improvements to the CLI version of PHP, which is now built by default when you compile PHP from source code (described in Appendix A). You must disable its build with installation options if you don't want it to be built.
- **Version 4.2.0:** Changed the default setting for `register_globals` to `Off`. Scripts running under previous versions may depend on `register_globals` being set to `On` and may stop running with the new setting. It's best to change the coding of the script so that it runs with `register_globals` set to `Off`.
- **Version 4.1.0:** Introduced the superglobal arrays. Scripts written using the superglobals (described in Chapter 6) won't run in earlier versions. Prior to 4.1.0, you must use the old style arrays, such as `$HTTP_POST_VARS`.

By the time you read this, it's possible that everyone has updated to PHP 5. However, some IT departments and Web hosting companies may not update immediately. Keep the previous changes in mind when using older versions.

Chapter 2

Setting Up the Environment

In This Chapter

- Getting access to PHP through Web hosting companies
- Building your own Web site from scratch
- Testing PHP

Now that you've decided to use PHP, your first task is to set up an environment for PHP development. As I discuss in Chapter 1, PHP is used most often to develop dynamic Web sites, so the majority of this chapter discusses setting up PHP for use with a Web site. If you plan to use PHP only as a general-purpose scripting language, independent of the Web, setting up your environment is much simpler. You can skip the sections about setting up a Web environment and go directly to the section, "Setting Up PHP for General-Purpose Scripting."

Establishing Your Web Environment

PHP for Web development runs in partnership with a Web server, as described in Chapter 1. Thus, a Web site requires a Web server. To use PHP in your Web site, the Web server must be able to exchange information with the PHP software, and, thus, PHP must be installed where the Web server can access it. The Web site environment involves more than just a Web server and PHP on a computer. Here are a few other requirements:

- The computer must be connected to the Internet.
- The computer must have enough resources, such as disk space and memory, to handle the expected Web traffic.
- Other software, such as a database, may be required in the environment.

You may or may not be interested in setting up your own Web environment. You may think that installing software is fun, or you may think it's similar to having the flu. If you want to install your own Web environment from scratch, you can. You may even already have a Web site running on your own computer and are just looking to add to its functionality by using PHP. If you don't want to install your own Web environment, you can use a Web environment installed and maintained by someone else, such as the IT department at work or a commercial Web hosting company. Perhaps you have an existing Web site at a hosting company that you want to make more dynamic. You can use PHP in either a Web environment of your own or one provided by someone else.

Another common development environment includes both your own Web environment and one maintained by someone else. That is, it's common for developers to set up testing Web environments on their own computers where they write and debug Web pages. Then, when everything is working correctly, the Web pages are transferred to their Web site at work, maintained by the IT department, or to a Web hosting company.

The following are some advantages of using someone else's Web environment:

- **It's easier than setting up your own:** You just copy your Web pages onto the other party's computer, and that's it. You don't need to install any software or hardware or resolve any computer problems. Someone else handles that for you.
- **Less technical skill is required:** You need to understand only Web languages, such as HTML and PHP. You don't need to know about Internet connections, Web servers, computer administration, and other technical things. Some people are very interested in these things, but some are not.

The advantages of running your own Web environment are as follows:

- **Control:** You get to make all the decisions. You can set up the Web environment the way that works best for you.
- **Access:** You can access the computer whenever you want to work on your Web site.
- **Stability:** You know the Web site will be there as long as you need it. You won't wake up one morning to discover that your Web hosting company has gone out of business and you have two days to move your site.
- **Security:** Because you control the Web environment, you are the only person who needs to access the computer. You can keep it under lock and key. When you use a Web hosting company, other people have access to the computer, and one of them may be a bad guy who's after your secrets.

Using an existing Web environment

When you use a Web environment set up by someone else, you don't need to understand the installation and administration of the Web site software. Someone else — your company's IT department, a commercial Web hosting company, your next-door neighbor — is responsible for the operation of the Web site. It's their job to provide you with a working Web site, including PHP if it's required. Your job is only to write and install the Web site files.

To use an existing Web environment, you need the following information from the Web site administrator:

- **The location of Web pages:** For the world to see your Web site, the files containing the Web pages must be in a specific location on the computer. The Web server that delivers the Web pages to the world expects to find the files in a specific directory. You need to know where that directory is and have access to the directory.
- **The Web page installation process:** You need to know how to install the files. In most cases, you send the files via FTP to the proper location. FTP (File Transfer Protocol) is a method of copying a file from one computer to another on a network. In some cases, you may copy the files directly or use other methods to install the Web pages. You may need a user ID and password to install the files.
- **The name of the default file:** When users point their browsers at a URL, a file is sent to them. The Web server is set up to send a specific default file when the URL points to a directory. Very often the default file is named `index.htm` or `index.html`, but sometimes other names are used, such as `default.htm`. You need to know what you should name your default file.
- **The PHP file extension:** When PHP is installed, the Web server is instructed to expect PHP statements in files with specific extensions. Frequently, the extensions used are `.php` or `.phtml`, but other extensions can be used. PHP statements in files that do not have the correct extensions won't be processed. You need to know what extension to use for your PHP scripts.

One of the disadvantages of hosting your site in an existing Web environment is that you have no control over your development environment. The administrators of the Web environment provide the environment that works best for them. For instance, PHP has a myriad of options that can be set, unset, or given various values. The administrators decide the option settings based on their needs, which may or may not be ideal for your purposes. They probably set up the environment for ease of maintenance, low cost, and minimal customer defections. You can't change certain parts of your environment; you can only beg the administrators to change it. They will be reluctant to change a working setup because a change may cause problems for their system or for other customers.

Choosing a Web hosting company

A *Web hosting company* provides everything you need to put up a Web site, including the computer space and all the Web site software. You just create the files for your Web pages and move them to a location specified by the Web hosting company.

About a gazillion companies offer Web hosting services. Most charge a monthly fee, which is often quite small, and some are even free. Most of the free ones require you to display advertising. Usually, the monthly fee varies, depending on the resources provided for your Web site. For instance, a Web site with 2MB (megabytes) of disk space for your Web page files costs less than a Web site with 10MB of disk space.

When looking for a place to host your Web site, make sure that the Web hosting company offers PHP. Some do not. Also, make sure the company offers a recent version of PHP. Web hosting companies may not offer a version that has just been released, but they should upgrade their PHP fairly soon after a new version is released.

Don't consider a Web hosting company that offers only PHP 3. PHP 4.3.1 was released in February 2003, so no Web hosting company should still be providing PHP older than 4.3.1, especially because a security issue was discovered in earlier versions and was fixed in PHP 4.3.1. Ideally, by the time you read this, most Web hosting companies will be offering PHP 5.

Other considerations when choosing a Web hosting company include the following:

- **Reliability:** You need a Web hosting company that you can depend on — one that won't go broke and disappear tomorrow. And you want one that has enough computer power and other resources to keep your Web site up. A Web site with more down time than up time is pretty useless. Hopefully, some research on the Web or among colleagues will identify Web hosting companies whose reliability is not up to snuff.
- **Speed:** Web pages that download slowly are a problem because users will get impatient and go elsewhere. Slow pages may be a result of a Web hosting company that started its business on a shoestring and has a shortage of good equipment, or the problem may be a Web hosting company that is so successful that its equipment is overwhelmed by new customers. Either way, Web hosting companies that deliver Web pages too slowly are unacceptable. In some cases, you can find sites that are hosted at the Web hosting company and see the download speed for these sites. Sometimes the Web hosting company's Web site provides some customer links, or the company's salespeople may provide you with this information.
- **Technical support:** Some Web hosting companies have no one available to answer questions or troubleshoot problems. Technical support is

often provided through e-mail only, which can be acceptable if the response time is short. Sometimes you can test the quality of the company's support by calling the tech support number, or test the e-mail response time by sending an e-mail.

- **Domain name:** Each Web site has a *domain name* that Web browsers use to find the site on the Web. Each domain name is registered, for a small yearly fee, so that only one Web site can use it. Some Web hosting companies allow you to use a domain name that you have registered independently of the Web hosting company, some assist you in registering and using a new domain name, and some require you to use their domain name. For instance, suppose your company's name is Good Stuff and you want your Web site to be named JanetsGoodStuff. Some companies allow your Web site to be `JanetsGoodStuff.com`, but some require that your Web site be named `JanetsGoodStuff.webhostingcompanyname.com`, or `webhostingcompanyname.com/~GoodStuff`, or something similar. In general, your Web site will look more professional if you can use your own domain name.
- **Features:** You should select features based on the purpose of your Web site. Usually a hosting company bundles its features into plans — more features generally means higher cost. Some features to consider include the following:
  - **Disk space:** How many MB/GB (gigabytes) of disk space will your Web site require? Media files, such as graphics or music files, can be quite large.
  - **Data transfer:** Some hosting companies charge you for sending Web pages to users. If you expect to have a lot of traffic on your Web site, this cost should be a consideration.
  - **E-mail addresses:** Many hosting companies provide you with a number of e-mail addresses for your Web site. For instance, if your Web site is `JanetsGoodStuff.com`, you could allow users to send you e-mail at `me@JanetsGoodStuff.com`.
  - **Software:** Hosting companies offer access to a variety of software for Web development. In addition to the PHP required for this book, some hosting companies offer databases, such as MySQL or PostgreSQL, and other development tools such as FrontPage extensions, shopping cart software, credit card validation, and other tools.
  - **Statistics:** Often hosting companies can help you gather statistics regarding your Web traffic, such as the number of users, time of access, access by Web page, and so on.
- **Backups:** *Backups* are copies of your Web page files and your database that are stored in case your files or database are lost or damaged. You want to be sure that the company makes regular, frequent backup copies of your application. You also want to know how long it would take for backups to be put in place to restore your Web site to working order after a problem.

It's difficult to research Web hosting companies from a standing start — a search at Google for Web hosting results in over 4 million hits. The best way to research Web hosting companies is to ask for recommendations from people who have experience with those companies. People who have used a hosting company can warn you that the service is slow or that the computers are frequently down. After you have gathered a few names of Web hosting companies from satisfied customers, you can narrow the list to the one that is best suited and most cost-effective for your purposes.

The domain name game

Every Web site needs a unique address on the Web. The unique address used by computers to locate a Web site is the *IP address.* It is a series of four numbers between 0 and 255, separated by dots — for example, `172.17.204.2` or `192.163.2.33`.

Because IP addresses are made up of numbers and dots, they're not easy to remember. Fortunately, most IP addresses have associated names that are much easier to remember. Some examples include `amazon.com`, `www.irs.gov`, or `mycompany.com`. A name that is an address for a Web site is called a *domain name.* A domain can be one computer or many connected computers. When a domain refers to several computers, each computer in the domain may have its own name. A name that includes an individual computer name, such as `thor.mycompany.com`, names a *subdomain* of `mycompany.com`.

The domain or subdomain name is a required component of the URL — the address that a Web surfer types into the browser window to identify the Web site he wants to visit. The URL can contain more elements than just the domain name, but often, the domain name (`amazon.com`, for example) is all that is required. Or the subdomain name (`janet.valade.com`, for example) may be sufficient. When only the domain name is used in the URL, the Web server sends the file with the default filename, such as `index.htm` or `index.html`. Or you can include a filename in the URL, in addition to the domain name, such as `janet.valade.com/links.html`.

Each domain name must be unique to serve as an address. Consequently, a system for registering domain names ensures that no two locations use the same domain name. Anyone can register any domain name, as long as the name is not already taken. You can register a domain name on the Web. First, you test your potential domain name to find out whether it is available. If it's available, you register it in your name or a company name and pay the fee. The name is then yours to use, and no one else can use it. The standard fee for domain name registration is $35.00 per year. You should never pay more, but bargains are often available.

Many Web sites, including those of many Web hosting companies, enable you to register a domain name. A search at Google (`google.com`) for "domain name register" results in over 2 million hits. Shop around to be sure you find the lowest price. Also, many Web sites allow you to enter a domain name and see who it is registered to. These Web sites do a domain name database search by using a tool called *whois.* A search at Google for "domain name whois" results in over half a million hits. A couple places where you can do a whois search are Allwhois (`Allwhois.com`) and Better-Whois (`betterwhois.com`).

You can ask for names from colleagues and friends. Also, people often ask for recommendations for hosting companies on the PHP discussion lists. Many people on the lists have experience using PHP with Web hosting companies and are glad to provide recommendations or warnings. Because people often ask this question, you may get all the information you need from the list archives, which you can search at `marc.theaimsgroup.com/`.

Setting up your own Web environment

If you're starting a Web site from scratch, you need to understand the Web site software fairly well. You have to make several decisions regarding hardware and software. You also need to install a Web server and PHP, as well as maintain, administer, and update the system yourself. Taking this route requires more work and more knowledge. The advantage is that you have total control over the Web development environment.

The following are the general steps for setting up the Web environment needed for the activities described in this book:

1. **Set up the computer.**
2. **Install the Web server.**
3. **Install PHP.**

The first step is outside the scope of this book. You probably have a computer but may be planning to install a new one for your Web site. For more information on buying and setting up computers, pick up a copy of *Buying a Computer For Dummies* or *PCs For Dummies,* 9th Edition, both by Dan Gookin and published by Wiley Publishing, Inc. Web servers and PHP exist for almost all hardware and operating systems, including many flavors of Unix and Linux, Windows, and Mac OS X.

Installing the Web server

When your computer is set up and ready, you need to decide which Web server to install. Apache is generally your best bet because it offers the following advantages:

- **It's free:** What else do I need to say?
- **It runs on a wide variety of operating systems:** Apache runs on Windows, Linux, Mac OS, FreeBSD, and most varieties of Unix.
- **It's popular:** Approximately 60 percent of Web sites on the Internet use Apache, according to surveys at `www.netcraft.com/survey` and at `www.securityspace.com/s_survey/data/`. This wouldn't be true if it didn't work well. Also, this means that a large group of users can provide help.
- **It's reliable:** After Apache is up and running, it should run as long as your computer runs. Emergency problems with Apache are extremely rare.

- **It's customizable:** The open source license allows programmers to modify the Apache software, adding or modifying modules as needed to fit their own environments.
- **It's secure:** Free software is available that runs with Apache to make it into a secure SSL server. SSL is used to provide extra security for Web sites that need to protect important information. It means that the information passed between the Web server and the browser is encrypted so that no one can intercept and read it. Security is an essential issue if you're using the site for e-commerce.

Apache is automatically installed when you install most Linux distributions. Apache is also usually preinstalled on Mac. For most Unix flavors, you want to download the Apache source and compile it yourself, although some *binaries* (programs that are already compiled for specific operating systems) are available. For Windows, you need to install a binary file, preferably on Windows NT/2000/XP, although Apache also runs on Windows 98/Me.

As of this writing, Apache 1.3.27 is the current stable release. Apache 2 is also a stable release, but it is still considered experimental to use PHP and Apache 2. Check the PHP Web site (`www.php.net`) to find out the current status of PHP and Apache 2 together. Apache information, software downloads, documentation, and installation instructions for various operating systems are available at the Apache Web site (`httpd.apache.org`). The Web site provides extensive documentation.

Other Web servers are available. Microsoft offers Internet Information Server (IIS), which is the second most-popular Web server on the Internet with approximately 27 percent of Web sites. Sun offers iPlanet (formerly Netscape Enterprise Server), which serves less than 5 percent of the Internet. Other Web servers are available, but they have even smaller user bases.

Installing PHP

Many computer systems come with PHP already installed. Most Linux distributions include PHP. Some newer versions of Mac OS X also come with PHP installed. Before you install PHP, check whether it's already installed by searching your disk for any PHP files in the following manner:

- **Linux/Unix/Mac:** At the command line, type the following:

  ```
  find / -name "php*"
  ```

- **Windows:** Use the Find feature (choose Start⇨Find) to search for *php**.

If you don't find any PHP files, PHP is not installed. To install PHP, you need access to the Web server for your site. For instance, when you install PHP with Apache, you need to edit the Apache configuration file. All the information and software you need is provided on the PHP Web site (`www.php.net`). Detailed installation instructions are provided in Appendix A.

If you do find PHP files, PHP is already installed, and you may not need to reinstall it. Use the following considerations to decide whether to reinstall PHP:

- **Installation options:** PHP may not have been installed with the options you require. For instance, PHP may not have been installed with support for the database that you're planning to use. Support for ODBC is always included, but support for MySQL, Oracle, MS SQL, and other databases must be specified when PHP is installed. Support is also always included for SQLite, XML, COM, FTP, and others, but other support is not automatically included. If you're planning to use another database or other software or features, you may need to reinstall PHP with added support.

  You can check which options were used when PHP was installed. Follow the directions for testing PHP in the following section. If the test script runs correctly, the table displayed by the `phpinfo()` statement shows all the support that is included in your PHP installation. Check whether the support you need is included. If it's not, you need to reinstall. Detailed instructions for installing PHP are provided in Appendix A.

- **Version:** The installed version may not be the most recent. You need to check the version of PHP that's installed. You can check the version with the following command:

  ```
  php-cgi -v
  ```

  For versions prior to PHP 5, the command to check the version is:

  ```
  php -v
  ```

  You may need to be in the same directory with the file `php-cgi.exe` (or `php.exe`)to execute the preceding command. You see output similar to the following that shows the version of PHP that is installed:

  ```
  PHP 5.0.0 (cgi-fcgi), Copyright (c) 1997-2003 The PHP
          Group
  Zend Engine v2.0.0, Copyright (c) 1998-2003 Zend
          Technologies
  ```

  If the version is not the most recent, you should reinstall it. To see what the latest stable version is, check `www.php.net/downloads.php`.

Testing PHP

After you have the information you need to use PHP on your Web site at the Web hosting company or you have PHP installed on your own computer, you need to test to make sure PHP is working correctly. To test whether PHP is installed and working, follow these steps:

1. **Locate the directory in which your PHP scripts need to be located.**

This directory and the subdirectories under it are called your *Web space*. The default Web space for Apache is `htdocs` in the directory where Apache is installed. For IIS, it is `Inetpub\wwwroot`. In Linux, it may be `/var/www/html`. Different directories may be configured for your Web space when the Web server is installed, so if someone other than you installed the Web server, you may need to ask what the directory is. If you're using a Web hosting company, it will supply the directory name.

2. **Create a file somewhere in your Web space with the name `test.php` that contains the following code:**

```
<html>
<head>
<title>PHP Test</title>
</head>
<body>
<p>This is an HTML line
<?php
   echo "<p>This is a PHP line</p>";
   phpinfo();
?>
</body>
</html>
```

3. **Point your browser at the file `test.php` created in Step 2 by typing the URL to the file.**

The URL will be in the format `http://www.mycompany.com/test.php`. If your Web server, PHP, and the `test.php` file are on the same computer you are testing from, you can type `localhost/test.php`.

In order for the file to be processed by PHP, you need to access the file through the Web server, not by choosing File➪Open in your Web browser.

If your Web server, PHP, and `test.php` file are on the same machine you are testing from, you can type `localhost/test.php`.

You should see the following in the Web browser:

```
This is an HTML line
This is a PHP line
```

Below these lines, you should see a large table, which shows all the information associated with PHP on your system. It shows PHP information, path names and filenames, variable values, what software is supported, and the status of various options. For instance, if you scroll down the table, you see a block of options for FTP that says: `FTP support enabled`.

The table is produced by the line `phpinfo()` in the test script. Any time you have a question about the settings for PHP, you can use the statement `phpinfo()` to display this table and check settings. The `phpinfo()` statement is used often throughout this book.

If there are problems with the PHP installation, you might get one of the following results from the test file:

- You see only `This is an HTML line`. The PHP lines and the table of information are not displayed.
- You see a blank page.
- The browser displays a download window rather than the Web page.

If you get a problem result from the test file and you are not the system administrator, you need to talk to the person who installs and maintains the software, such as an IT staff member at work or a technical support person at your Web hosting company. It's their responsibility to diagnose your problem.

If you get a problem result from the test file and you installed the software yourself, first check to see that PHP is installed. At the command line, change to the directory where PHP is installed and type the following:

```
php-cgi -v
```

or

```
php -v
```

If PHP returns information about its version, PHP is installed. Be sure that you accessed the test file as instructed in Step 3 in the preceding list. Notice the warning for that step.

Be sure that the file test is in a directory in your Web space, as described in Step 1 of the preceding steps. In Apache, you can check the `httpd.conf` file for a line similar to the following line:

```
DocumentRoot "C:/Program Files/Apache Group/Apache/htdocs"
```

This line tells Apache where to look for Web page files.

Double-check the script to make sure you typed it correctly. The script is also available for download from my Web site: `janet.valade.com`.

If you are accessing the test file correctly and it seems to be entered correctly, the problem is probably in your configuration. Reread the instructions for configuring PHP at the end of Appendix A and make sure that you followed all the instructions. In particular, check the following:

- The Web server is configured to know which file extensions to check for PHP code. In Apache, check that the following line is included in the `httpd.conf` file:

  ```
  AddType application/x-httpd-php .php
  ```

This line tells Apache to look for PHP code in files with the extension `.php`. For IIS, access the console, as described in Appendix A, and check the extension tab to be sure the correct extension is set.

- Check to be sure the other lines were correctly added to the `httpd` file for Apache, as described in the configuration sections for the appropriate operating system in Appendix A. Check for any possible misspellings. Also check that the lines were added in the correct location.
- If you're using IIS, check for the following line in `php.ini`:

```
cgi.force_redirect = 0
```

If your `php.ini` doesn't contain this line, add it. If you have the line with a semicolon at its beginning, remove the semicolon. If you find a line with a setting of 1 rather than 0 (zero), change it to 0.

If you check everything carefully and are still having problems, it's possible that you have something unusual in your computer setup or your Web server that is causing the problem. Read all the online documentation related to installation at the PHP Web site. Search the Web site for information on installation problems. You can find a wealth of information there.

If you still can't find the answer, take your question to the PHP discussion lists. First, search the archives at `marc.theaimsgroup.com/`. It's possible that someone has previously asked the same question and you can find the answer quickly in the archives. If not, post your question to the discussion list. Include the following information in your question:

- Indicate the name and version of the operating system you're using.
- Identify the PHP version you're trying to install.
- Copy the content of the test file into your message.
- Describe the exact output that you see in your Web page.

People on the list are very knowledgeable and will help you solve your problem.

Setting Up PHP for General-Purpose Scripting

PHP runs by itself when used as a general-purpose programming language. You don't need to have a Web server installed if you're not using PHP with a Web site. The command line version of PHP — PHP CLI — is a separate program, different than the PHP program you use for Web sites. It needs to be installed separately.

Even if your machine came with PHP installed, PHP CLI may not be there. You can check to see if PHP is on your computer and which version is there. By default, you should find the file in the directory where PHP is installed. The PHP CLI file is named `php.exe` and the PHP CGI file is named `php-cgi.exe`. (Prior to PHP 5, the files were both named `php.exe`, but stored in different subdirectories. PHP CLI was stored in a subdirectory named `/cli`.)Or PHP CLI may have been installed in another location. You can search your disk for all PHP files as follows:

- **Linux/Unix/Mac:** Type the following at the command line:

  ```
  find / -name "php*"
  ```

- **Windows:** Use the Find feature (choose Start⇨Find) to search for *php**.

If you find any PHP files that you think might be PHP CLI, you can check by changing to the directory where the PHP program file is and typing the following:

```
php -v
```

The output will include either `cgi` or `cli`, similar to the following:

```
PHP 5.0.0 (cli) (built: Jun 15, 2003 23:07:34)
```

Notice that the output includes `(cli)`. If it's not the CLI version, it shows `(cgi)`. The previous command also serves to test whether PHP CLI is working. If it responds with the version number rather than an error message, it's working.

If you don't find PHP CLI, you need to install it before you can use PHP for tasks that are unrelated to the Web. Appendix A provides detailed PHP installation instructions, including instructions for PHP CLI.

If you're going to use PHP for both Web sites and general-purpose programming, you need to install two different PHP programs, the version for the Web and PHP CLI. Both need to be the same version of PHP. That is, if you install PHP 5.0.0 for the Web, be sure that you're using PHP CLI 5.0.0 as well. In Windows, PHP requires a file called `php5ts.dll`, which is in your main PHP directory. You need to use the same version of PHP so that both PHP programs use the same version of `php5ts.dll`. (See Appendix A for details.)

Configuring PHP

PHP is very flexible. Configuration settings determine some of PHP's behavior, such as whether it displays error messages, A file called `php.ini` stores the configuration settings. You can change the setting by editing `php.ini`.

When PHP is installed, `php.ini` is created, as described in Appendix A. If you install PHP yourself, remember where you put `php.ini`. You may need to change it. If you're using PHP, but someone else is the PHP administrator (for instance, if you're using a Web hosting company), you are unlikely to have access to `php.ini`. If you need to make a change to the PHP settings, you will have to ask the administrator. For some settings, you can add statements to your script to change the settings temporarily, for that script only. Specific statements that change settings temporarily are discussed in context throughout this book.

Using Tools to Build PHP Scripts

PHP scripts are just text files. You can use your favorite tool for writing text files to write PHP scripts. Many scripts have been written with vi, Notepad, or WordPad. However, you can find tools that make script writing much easier.

It's worthwhile to check out programming editors and Integrated Development Environments (IDEs) before creating your PHP scripts. These tools offer features that can save you enormous amounts of time during development. So download some demos, try out the software, and select the one that suits you best. You can take a vacation on the time you save later.

Programming editors

Programming editors offer many features specifically for writing programs. The following features are offered by most programming editors:

- **Color highlighting:** Highlight parts of the script — such as HTML tags, text strings, keywords, and comments — in different colors so they're easy to identify.
- **Indentation:** Automatically indent inside parentheses and curly braces to make scripts easier to read.
- **Line numbers:** Add temporary line numbers. This is important because PHP error messages specify the line where the error was encountered. It would be cumbersome to have to count 872 lines from the top of the file to the line that PHP says is a problem.

- **Multiple files:** Can have more than one file open at once.
- **Easy code inserting:** Buttons for inserting code, such as HTML tags or PHP statements or functions.
- **Code library:** Save snippets of your own code that can be inserted by clicking a button.

Many programming editors are available on the Internet for free or for a low price. Some of the more popular editors include the following:

- **Arachnophilia:** (`www.arachnoid.com/arachnophilia/`) This multi-platform editor is written in Java. It's CareWare, which means it doesn't cost any money.
- **BBEdit:** (`www.barebones.com/products/bbedit/index.shtml`) This editor is designed for use on a Mac. BBEdit sells for $179.00. Development and support have been discontinued for BBEdit Lite, which is free, but it can still be found and legally used. TextWrangler is offered for $49 as a replacement for BBEdit Lite.
- **EditPlus:** (`www.editplus.com`) This editor is designed for use on a Windows machine. EditPlus is shareware, and the license is $30.
- **Emacs:** (`www.gnu.org/software/emacs/emacs.html`) Emacs works with Windows, Linux, and Unix, and it's free.
- **HomeSite:** (`www.macromedia.com/software/homesite/`) HomeSite is designed for use with Windows and will run you $99.00.
- **HTML-Kit:** (`www.chami.com/html-kit/`) This is another Windows editor that you can pick up for free.
- **vim and gvim:** (`www.vim.org/`) These free, enhanced versions of vi can be used with Windows, Linux, Unix, and Mac OS. The gvim editor has a GUI that makes Windows users feel more at home.

Integrated Development Environment (IDE)

An *Integrated Development Environment (IDE)* is an entire workspace for developing applications. It includes a programming editor as well as other features. Some features included by most IDEs are the following:

- **Debugging:** Has built-in debugging features.
- **Previewing:** Displays the Web page output by the script.
- **Testing:** Has built-in testing features for your scripts.

- **FTP:** Has built-in ability to connect and upload/download via FTP. Keeps track of which files belong in which Web site and keeps the Web site up-to-date.
- **Project management:** Organizes scripts into projects; manages the files in the project; includes file checkout and check-in features.
- **Backups:** Makes automatic backups of your Web site at periodic intervals.

IDEs are more difficult to learn than programming editors. Some are fairly expensive, but their wealth of features can be worth it. IDEs are particularly useful when several people will be writing scripts for the same application. An IDE can make project coordination much simpler and make the code more compatible.

The following are popular IDEs:

- **Dreamweaver MX:** (`www.macromedia.com/dreamweaver`) This IDE is available for the Windows and Mac platforms. It provides visual layout tools so you can create a Web page by dragging elements around and clicking buttons to insert elements. Dreamweaver can write the HTML code for you. It includes the HomeSite editor so you can write your own code. It also supports PHP. Dreamweaver will set you back $399.00.
- **Komodo:** (`www.activestate.com/Products/Komodo/`) Komodo is offered for the Linux and Windows platforms. It's an IDE for open source languages, including Perl and Python, as well as PHP. It's offered for $29.95 for personal or educational use, and $295.00 for commercial use.
- **Maguma:** (`www.maguma.com`) Maguma is available for Windows only. It's an IDE for Apache, PHP, and MySQL on Windows and comes in two versions at different costs: Maguma Studio Desktop and Maguma Studio Enterprise, which offers features for huge sites with multiple servers. Maguma Studio for PHP is a free version with support for PHP only.
- **PHPEdit:** (`www.phpedit.net/products/PHPEdit/`) This free IDE is available only for Windows.
- **Zend Studio:** (`www.zend.com/store/products/zend-studio.php`) Zend Studio is offered for the Linux and Windows platforms. This IDE was developed by the people who developed the Zend engine, which is the engine under the hood of PHP. These people know PHP extremely well. Zend Studio will run you $195.00.

A Web page describing editors and IDEs useful with PHP is available at `phpeditors.linuxbackup.co.uk`. Currently 111 editors are listed.

Chapter 3

Creating Your First PHP Script

In This Chapter

- Writing PHP statements
- Adding PHP sections to HTML files
- Writing PHP output statements
- Documenting your scripts

A *PHP statement* is an instruction that tells PHP to perform an action. A *PHP script* is a series of PHP statements. Theoretically, a script can contain as few as one statement, but it's unlikely that any practical script would consist of a single statement. In most cases, you write scripts that contain several statements in a row. PHP executes the statements one at a time until it reaches the end of the script.

As discussed in Chapter 1, PHP can do many things, and scripts are the method you use to tell PHP what you want it to do. You can tell it to display some text on a Web page or to store data that a user entered into a form on your Web page. PHP can also do things that are unrelated to Web sites, such as back up all the files in a directory on your hard disk. You can write simple scripts that just display `hello` in a Web browser. Or you can write complicated scripts that display different things in the Web browser for different people, or request passwords from Web site visitors and refuse access to visitors who don't enter valid passwords. Applications often consist of two or more scripts that work together to accomplish the job required. A large, complicated application, such as an e-commerce application, can consist of many scripts.

In this chapter, I explain how to write your first script. I also discuss output statements, which are the most common PHP statements. Finally, I illustrate the importance of documenting your script.

Writing PHP Statements

A PHP statement tells PHP to perform an action. One of the most common PHP statements is the `echo` statement. Its purpose is to display output. For instance, take a look at the following `echo` statement:

```
echo "Hi";
```

An `echo` statement says to output everything that is between the double quotes ("). So, this statement tells PHP to output the word `Hi`.

The `echo` statement is a *simple statement.* PHP simple statements end with a semicolon (`;`). PHP reads a simple statement until it encounters a semicolon (or the PHP closing tag, discussed later in this chapter). PHP ignores white space. It doesn't care how many lines it reads. It doesn't consider the content or the syntax of the statement. It just reads until it finds a semicolon and then interprets the entire content as a single statement.

Leaving out the semicolon is a common error, resulting in an error message that looks something like this:

```
Parse error: expecting `','' or `';'' in file.php on line 6
```

Notice that the error message gives you the line number where it encountered problems. Usually, the error is that the semicolon was left off in the line before the indicated line. In this case, the semicolon is probably missing on line 5.

You may prefer to use an editor that displays line numbers. Debugging your PHP scripts is much easier this way. Otherwise, you need to count the lines from the top of the script to find the line containing the error. If your script contains six lines, counting them is no big deal. If your script contains 553 lines, however, this is less than fun. Some editors allow you to indicate a line number, and the editor takes you directly there.

As far as PHP is concerned, an entire script full of simple statements can be written in one long line, as long as the statements are separated by semicolons. However, a human would have a tough time reading such a script. Therefore, you should put simple statements on separate lines.

Sometimes several statements are combined into a block, which is enclosed by curly braces ({ }). Statements in a block execute together. A common use of a block is in a conditional statement where statements are executed only if certain conditions are met. For instance, you may want to include the following instructions:

```
if (time = midnight)
{
   put on pajamas;
   brush teeth;
   go to bed;
}
```

The statements are enclosed in curly braces to ensure they execute as a block. If it's midnight, then all three actions within the block are performed. If the time is not midnight, none of the statements execute (no pajamas, no clean teeth; no going to bed).

PHP statements that use blocks, such as `if` statements, are called *complex statements.* PHP reads the entire complex statement, not stopping at the first semicolon it encounters. PHP knows to expect one or more blocks and looks for the ending curly brace of the last block in complex statements. Notice that there is a semicolon before the ending brace. This semicolon is required, but no semicolon is required after the ending curly brace.

Notice that the statements inside the block are indented. Indenting is not necessary for PHP. Indenting is strictly for readability. You should indent the statements in a block so that people reading the script can tell more easily where a block begins and ends. One of the more common mistakes when writing scripts is to leave out a closing curly brace, particularly when writing blocks inside blocks inside blocks. Tracking down a missing brace is much easier when the blocks are indented.

Building Scripts

To build a script, you add PHP statements one after another to a file that you name with a `.php` extension. Actually, if you are wise, you write the script on paper first, unless the script is very simple or you are quite experienced. Planning makes programming much less prone to errors.

If you're writing a PHP script for your Web site, you insert the PHP statements into the file that contains the HTML for your Web page. If you're writing a script that will run independent of the Web, you type the PHP statements into a file and then you run the script by calling PHP directly. The following sections describe how to do this.

How the server processes PHP files

When a browser is pointed to a regular HTML file (a file with an `.html` or `.htm` extension), the Web server sends the file, as is, to the browser. The browser processes the file and displays the Web page that is described by the HTML tags in the file. When a browser is pointed to a PHP file (a file with a `.php` extension), the Web server looks for PHP sections in the file and processes them, rather than just sending them as is to the browser. The steps the Web server uses to process a PHP file are as follows:

1. The Web server starts scanning the file in HTML mode.

   It assumes that the statements are HTML and sends them to the browser without any processing.

2. The Web server continues in HTML mode until it encounters a PHP opening tag (`<?php`).

3. When the Web server encounters a PHP opening tag, it switches into PHP mode.

   This is sometimes called *escaping from HTML*. The Web server assumes all subsequent statements are PHP statements and executes the PHP statements. If there is output, the server sends the output to the browser.

4. The Web server continues in PHP mode until it encounters a PHP closing tag (`?>`).

5. When the Web server encounters a PHP closing tag, it returns to HTML mode.

   The scanning is then resumed, and the cycle continues from Step 1.

Adding PHP statements to HTML pages

If you're using PHP for your Web site, you do so by adding PHP code to your HTML Web pages. HTML files that have PHP code in them should be named with a `.php` extension so that the Web server knows to check the file for PHP code. (Actually, the Web server administrator may have specified other extensions, such as `.php4` or `.phtml`, to indicate files that can contain PHP code, but `.php` is the most common extension. In this book, I assume that the appropriate extension is `.php`.)

You add PHP code to your Web page by using tags, similar, but not identical, to other tags in the HTML file. The PHP code section is enclosed in PHP tags with the following form:

```
<?php
. . .
PHP statements
. . .
?>
```

Sometimes you can use a shorter version of the PHP tags. You can try using <? and ?>, without including the php. If short tags are enabled, you can save a little typing. You enable or disable short tags in the php.ini file.

Using short tags is sometimes not a good idea. If you move your site to a server where short tags are not enabled, all your PHP tags will quit working. So if you think you might ever move your Web site, using the regular tags is safer.

All statements between the two PHP tags are passed to PHP by the Web server and are processed by the PHP preprocessor. After processing, the PHP section is discarded. If the PHP statements produce output, the output is sent back to the Web server, which then sends the HTML and the output from the PHP sections to the browser. The browser does not see the PHP section, only its output (if there is any output).

For example, you can add the following PHP section to your HTML file. Don't forget to give the HTML file a .php extension:

```
<?php
   echo "This line brought to you by PHP";
?>
```

When the Web server gets the file and sees the .php extension, it checks for PHP tags. When it finds the PHP tag, it executes the PHP echo statement instead of sending it to the browser. Only the output from the PHP section, which is This line brought to you by PHP, is sent on to the browser. In your browser window, you see the output at the location in the page where you added the PHP section. Even if you view the source in your browser, you only see the output, not the PHP code.

Don't look at the PHP file directly with your browser. That is, don't choose File⇨Open⇨Browse in your browser to navigate to the file and click it. You must point at the file using its URL, as discussed in Chapter 2. If you see the PHP code (and not the output) displayed in the browser window, you may not have pointed to the file by using its URL.

You can add several PHP sections to a Web page. For instance, you could have the following code in your file:

```
HTML statements
<?php
   echo "This line brought to you by PHP";
?>
HTML statements
<?php
   echo "This line also brought to you by PHP";
?>
```

Both lines echoed by PHP appear in your Web page at the locations where you inserted the PHP sections.

Using PHP independent of the Web

To use PHP as a general scripting language, independent of the Web, you use the version of PHP called CLI, which stands for Command Line Interface. PHP CLI is a different version of PHP than the version used with a Web server (usually called PHP CGI). PHP CLI is created separately when PHP is installed. Instructions for installing the CLI version are provided in Appendix A.

If you want to use the CLI version, you're probably running PHP on Linux or Unix. Windows programmers are much less likely to need to write general-purpose PHP scripts, but they can if they need to. In this section, I provide the information for the Linux/Unix version, but most of the information is also true when working on Windows. (In some places, I point out the differences.)

The following is a PHP script:

```
<?php
   echo "This line brought to you by PHP";
?>
```

Running PHP scripts on Linux/Unix

If you're used to running shell scripts or Perl scripts on Linux/Unix, you can run PHP scripts in the same way. You can add a line to the top of your script that directs the script to run with PHP CLI, as follows, so that you can just run the script directly without manually calling PHP:

```
#! /usr/bin/php
<?php
   echo "This line brought to
   you by PHP";
?>
```

The first line tells the script to execute by using the program found at `/usr/bin/php`. This line does not work for Windows, but it doesn't do any damage when run on Windows. You can include the first line when you write the script so that it is more convenient on Unix/Linux and not worry about having a broken script if you move the script to Windows.

You execute the program by typing its name. You may need to be in the same directory where the program is located, unless it is in a directory on your system path, or you can type the entire path name to the PHP script. For instance, if the preceding script is called `test.php`, you can execute it by typing the following:

```
test.php
```

Or you may need to type the entire path:

```
/mystuff/test.php
```

You need to give the file execute permission, as you do for any other script that you want to execute directly.

If you have a file named `testcli.php` containing this PHP code, you can run it from the command line by having the file in the same directory where PHP is installed and by typing the following:

```
php testcli.php
```

Or you can type the entire path name to PHP, as in the following example:

```
/usr/local/php/cli/php testcli.php
```

For Windows, use the command prompt. You enter command prompt mode by choosing the appropriate entry on your menu. Usually, you choose Start➪Programs➪Accessories➪Command Prompt.

The CLI version of PHP differs from the CGI version in the following ways:

- **Outputting HTTP headers:** Because the CGI version sends its output to the Web server and then to the browser, it outputs the HTTP *headers* (statements the Web server and browser use to communicate with each other). Thus, the following is the output when the CGI version runs the script in the previous example:

  ```
  Content-type: text/html
  X-Powered-By: PHP/5.0

  This line brought to you by PHP
  ```

  You don't see the two headers on your Web page, but PHP for the Web sends these headers because the Web server needs them. The CLI version, on the other hand, does not automatically send the HTTP headers because it is not sending its output to a Web server. The CLI output is limited to the following:

  ```
  This line brought to you by PHP
  ```

- **Formatting error messages:** The CGI version formats error messages with HTML tags, because the errors are expected to be received by a browser. The CLI version does not use HTML formatting for error messages; it outputs error messages in plain text.
- **Providing `argc` and `argv` by default:** The `argc` and `argv` variables allow you to supply data to the script from the command line (similar to `argc` and `argv` in C and other languages). You aren't likely to want to pass data to the CGI version, but you are likely to want to pass data to the CLI version. Therefore, `argv` and `argc` are available by default in the CLI version and not in the CGI version. (The `argv` and `argc` built-in variables are explained in Chapter 5.)

When you run PHP CLI from the command line, you can use several options that affect the way PHP behaves. For instance, -v is an option that displays the version of PHP being accessed. To use this option, you would type the following:

```
php -v
```

Table 3-1 shows the most useful PHP command-line options.

Table 3-1 PHP Command-Line Options

Option	*What It Does*
-c	Defines the path to the php.ini file to be used. This can be a different php.ini file than the one used by the CGI version. For example, -c /usr/local/php/cli/php.ini. (See Appendix A for more on php.ini.)
-f	Identifies the script to be run. For example, php -f /myfiles/testcgi.php.
-h	Displays a help file.
-i	Displays PHP information in text output. Gives the same information as phpinfo() (described in Chapter 2).
-l	Checks the script file for errors, but doesn't actually execute the code.
-m	Lists the modules that are compiled into PHP. (See Chapter 14 for more on modules.)
-r	Runs PHP code entered at the command line. For example, php -r 'print('Hi');'.
-v	Displays the version number of PHP.

Writing Your First Script

It's sort of a tradition that the first program you write in any language is the Hello World program. You may have written a Hello World program in HTML when you first learned it. If you did, it probably looked similar to the following HTML file:

```
<html>
<head><title>Hello World HTML Program</title></head>
<body>
<p>Hello World!</p>
</body>
</html>
```

If you point your browser at this HTML program, you see a Web page that displays the following output in the browser window:

```
Hello World!
```

Your first PHP script is a script that does exactly the same thing. The following code is a PHP script that includes both HTML and PHP code and displays `Hello World!` in a browser window:

```
<html>
<head><title>Hello World Script</title></head>
<body>
<?php
  echo "<p>Hello World!</p>"
?>
</body>
</html>
```

If you point your browser at this script, it displays the same Web page as the HTML script.

Don't look at the file directly with your browser. That is, don't choose File➪Open➪Browse from your browser menu to navigate to the file and click it. You must point at the file by typing its URL, as discussed in Chapter 2. If you see the PHP code displayed in the browser window, instead of the output you expect, you may not have pointed to the file by using its URL.

In this PHP script, the PHP section consists of the following code:

```
<?php
  echo _<p>Hello World!</p>_
?>
```

The PHP tags enclose only one statement — an `echo` statement — that simply outputs the text between the double quotes.

When the PHP section is processed, it is replaced with the output. In this case, the output is as follows:

```
<p>Hello World!</p>
```

If you replace the PHP section in the HTML version of `Hello World` with the preceding output, the script now looks exactly like the HTML program. If you point your browser at either program, you see the same Web page. If you look at the source code that the browser sees (in the browser, choose View➪Source), you see the same source code listing for both programs.

Discovering More about Output Statements

In your `Hello World` script, created in the preceding section, you used an `echo` statement, which is a good example of an output statement. *Output statements* are used in almost every PHP script. It's rare that you would write a script that would do something and not output anything. True, a script can do things that are invisible, like checking your entire hard disk to see if a certain file exists. You would not see it checking. However, the search is pretty pointless if the script doesn't tell you what it found. You'd want to know where it looked, when it finished, and whether or not it found the file. Because of this, almost all scripts use output statements.

The general format of the `echo` statement is as follows:

```
echo outputitem1,outputitem2,outputitem3, . . .
```

Keep the following points in mind when working with `echo` statements:

- An *`outputitem`* is a number or a string of characters. Numbers are things like 1 or 250. A string is a string of characters, which can include numbers. See Chapter 5 for a discussion of data types.
- Enclose a string of characters with single or double quotes. (Chapter 5 explains when to use which type of quotes.)
- List as many *`outputitem`*s as you need.
- Separate each *`outputitem`* with a comma. No space is added between *`outputitem`*s.
- If you want a space in your output, add it as a character in a character string.

Table 3-2 shows some echo statements and their output.

Table 3-2 echo Statements

Echo Statement	*Output*
`echo 123;`	`123`
`echo "Hello World!";`	`Hello World!`
`echo "Hello","World!";`	`HelloWorld!`
`echo "Hello"," ","World!";`	`Hello World!`
`echo Hello World!;`	Not valid because the string is not enclosed in quotes; results in an error message
`echo 'Hello World!';`	`Hello World!`

Processing PHP output statements

The Hello World script, like most PHP scripts for the Web, is written mainly to output HTML code that the browser then processes and displays in your Web page. When writing PHP code to deliver output to a Web browser, you need to keep in mind that there are two stages, as follows:

1. PHP processes the PHP statement and sends the output to the Web server, which sends the output to the browser.

   PHP does not know anything about HTML code and just sends the output according to the instructions you write in the PHP output statement.

2. The Web browser receives the output from PHP, interprets it as HTML statements, and displays a Web page accordingly.

   The Web browser only understands HTML, not PHP code, so make sure your PHP output is understandable to your browser.

Consider the echo statement from the Hello World script:

```
echo _<p>Hello World!</p>_
```

The `echo` statement says to output everything that is between the double quotes ("). So, for this statement, the two stages are as follows:

1. When PHP processes the `echo` statement, it outputs the following:

   ```
   <p>Hello World!</p>
   ```

   PHP does not understand HTML, so it does not know that `<p>` is an HTML tag and does not see `<p>` as any sort of instruction. It just outputs the statement as text.

2. The Web browser receives the output, recognizes that `<p>` is an HTML tag, and displays the output on the Web page according to the HTML tags. You see the following on the Web page:

   ```
   Hello World!
   ```

   The HTML tags `<p>` and `</p>` indicate the beginning and end of a paragraph and are interpreted by the Web browser, but not displayed on the screen. To see what PHP sent to the browser, view the source by using the selections on your Web browser menu. For instance, in Internet Explorer 5.5, choose View⇨Source. For this Web page, the source would show the following:

   ```
   <p>Hello World!</p>
   ```

Using special characters in output statements

The `echo` statement interprets some special characters that affect the output. One common special-character combination is `\n`, which starts a new line in the output of an `echo` statement. For example, write the following line:

```
echo _<p>Hello\n World!</p>_
```

The `\n` tells PHP that the output should start a new line. However, this does not result in a new line on the Web page. To get a new line in the Web page, you need to send the HTML code for a new line, which is `<br>`. Therefore, to see the output on two lines in the Web page, you use the following statement:

```
echo _<p>Hello<br> World!</p>_
```

A comparison of echo statements in Table 3-3 shows the differences in output at Stage 1 (the PHP output stage) and Stage 2 (the Web browser display stage). The first column contains the echo statement used in a PHP script. The second column shows the output sent by PHP to the browser. The third column is the output displayed on the Web page after the PHP output is interpreted by the browser as HTML code.

Table 3-3 Stages of Web Page Delivery

Echo Statement	*PHP Output*	*Web Page Display*
echo "Hello World!";	Hello World!	Hello World!
echo "Hello"; echo "World!";	HelloWorld!	HelloWorld!
echo "Hello\nWorld!";	Hello World!	Hello World!
echo "Hello World!";	Hello World	Hello World!
echo "Hello \nWorld!";	Hello World!	Hello World!

Notice where spaces are included in the output. The first echo statement includes a space so the space is output. The second row has two echo statements, but neither includes a space, so no space appears in the Web page. The third row shows a space on the Web page, even though no space is included in the echo statement. The space is added by the browser when it reads the PHP output as HTML. In HTML, a new line is not displayed as a new line; it is just interpreted as a single space.

Use \n liberally. Otherwise, your HTML source code will have some really long lines. For instance, if you echo a long form, the whole thing may be one long line in the source code, even though it looks fine in the Web page because you used <br> in all the right places. If your Web page doesn't display correctly, you may need to troubleshoot the problem in the Web page source code, a difficult process if your source code is one mile-long line. Use \n to break the HTML source code into reasonable lines. Taking the extra time to add these line breaks will pay off if you have to troubleshoot a Web page. In addition, some browsers don't handle mile-long lines very well.

PHP executes output statements as instructed. PHP doesn't care whether the output is going to the Web or displayed on the screen. It's your job to know what kind of output you need. If you're writing PHP scripts for use on the Web, the output needs to be in HTML statements. If you're writing code for independent scripts, executed outside the Web environment, the output needs to be in plain text format for display on the screen.

Documenting the Script

Adding comments to your script is essential. Comments describe your script — what it does and how it does it. The larger, more complicated, or more unusual your code is, the more you need comments. After working 20 hours a day on a script, you may believe its code is permanently burned into your brain. From experience, however, I know that two years from now, when you need to revise this script, you will swear it was written by a stranger. And there's also the possibility that your scripts may need to be revised by an actual stranger. You may be long gone, retired in luxury in the Bahamas, when your scripts need to be revised.

Comments are notes that are embedded in the script itself. PHP ignores comments; comments are for humans. You can embed comments in your script anywhere as long as you tell PHP that they are comments. The format for comments is as follows:

```
/*  comment text
more comment text  */
```

Your comments can be as long or as short as you need. When PHP sees code that indicates the start of a comment (/*), it ignores everything until it sees the code that indicates the end of a comment (*/).

It is customary and useful to put a block of comments at the top of your script giving information about the script and an overview of what it does. For example, here's one possible format for a comment block at the top of your script:

```
/*  name:         hello.php
    description:  Displays "Hello World!" on a Web page.
    written by:   Joe Programmer
    created:      2/1/03
    modified:     3/15/03
*/
```

PHP also has a short comment format. You can specify that a single line is a comment by using the # or two slashes (//) in the following manner:

```
# This is comment line 1
// This is comment line 2
```

You can also use # or // in the middle of a line to signal the beginning of a comment. PHP will ignore everything from the # or // to the end of the line. This is useful for commenting a particular statement, as follows:

```
echo "Hello";  // this is my first output statement
```

PHP comments are not included in the HTML code that is sent to the user's browser, so the user does not see these comments.

It's helpful to use descriptive comments as titles for sections of code, such as the following:

```
/* Check whether the customer is over 18 years old */
/* Store the information in the database */
/* Search for the selected file name */
```

Sometimes you really want to emphasize a comment. The following format makes a comment very noticeable:

```
######################################
##  Double-Check This Section       ##
######################################
```

Use comments as often as necessary in the script to make it clear. However, using too many comments is a mistake. Don't comment every line or everything you do in the script. If your script is too full of comments, the really important comments can get lost in the maze. Only use comments to label sections and to explain code that is unusual or complicated, not code that is obvious. For instance, the previous comment, documenting the echo statement, is not a useful comment in most cases. It's obvious what the code is doing; a comment isn't needed.

Be careful that you don't get your comments mixed together. For instance, if you nest one comment section inside another, PHP can't handle it. For instance, a comment such as the following won't work:

```
/* This is the first comment.
   /* This is the comment nested inside */
*/
```

PHP looks at the opening /* of the first comment and ignores everything until it comes to the first */. It ignores the second /* because it considers it part of a comment. PHP considers the comment ended after the first */ and outputs an error message when it comes to the second */. PHP doesn't recognize the second */ as closing a comment because it isn't in comment mode.

Part II
Variables and Data

"I'm sorry, but 'Arf', 'Bark', and 'Woof' are already registered domain names. How about 'Oink', 'Quack', or 'Moo'?"

In this part . . .

In this part, I describe the use of variables in PHP. I explain how to create and use them. I describe the types of data that can be stored in variables and how to store these different types. I also show you how to store related data in complex variables called *arrays*.

Chapter 4

Using Variables in PHP Scripts

In This Chapter

- Naming variables
- Assigning values to variables
- Removing variables
- Using constants
- Handling errors

Variables are containers that hold information. First, you give a variable a name, and then you can store information in it. For example, you could name a variable `$age` and store the number 21 in it. After you store information in a variable, you can use that variable later in the script.

When using PHP on the Web, variables are often used to store the information that users type into an HTML form, such as their names. You can then use the variable later in the script, perhaps to personalize a Web page by displaying the user's name, as in, for example, `Welcome Sam Smith`.

In this chapter, you find out how to create variables, name them, and store information in them. You also discover how to handle errors.

Naming Variables

Variable names or *identifiers* should be very descriptive. I have seen scripts where all the variables were named `$var1`, `$var1`, `$var2`, and so on. It may seem straightforward to name variables like this, but two years from now when you come back to the script, it will take forever to figure out what information is in each variable. PHP won't care or get confused, but humans trying to follow the script will have a hard time. Make your scripts much easier to understand by using descriptive variable names like `$firstName`, `$directory_name`, or `$DateOfBirth`.

The rules for variable names are as follows:

- **All variable names start with a dollar sign ($).** This tells PHP that it is a variable name.
- **Variable names can be any length.**
- **Variable names can include letters, numbers, and underscores only.**
- **Variable names must begin with a letter or an underscore.** They cannot begin with a number.
- **Uppercase and lowercase letters are not the same.** `$favoritecity` and `$Favoritecity` are not the same variable. If you store information in `$FavoriteCity`, you can't retrieve that information later in the script by using the variable name `$favoriteCity`.

The following are valid variable names:

```
$_name
$first_name
$name3
$name_3
```

The following variable names cause error messages:

```
$3name
$name?
$first+name
$first.name
```

The first name is invalid because it doesn't begin with a letter or an underscore, as required. The three remaining names are invalid because they contain characters other than numbers, letters, and underscores.

Assigning variable names is a matter of personal style. Creating descriptive variable names by connecting words with an underscore or by using uppercase letters to denote the beginning of new words (often called *camel caps*) are the two most common variable naming styles, as shown here:

```
$first_name
$firstName
```

Naming your variables by using one of these two common styles makes it easier for other programmers to read your scripts. It's also common to start the name with a lowercase letter. The most important factor in naming variables, however, is to be consistent. Pick a style and use it throughout the entire script.

Assigning and Displaying Variable Values

Variables can hold either numbers or strings of characters. A variable can exist or not exist and can hold information or not hold information; these are two separate ideas. Even if a variable doesn't currently contain any information, it still can exist, just as a drawer exists even when it is empty. Of course, if a variable contains information, it has to exist.

The following sections discuss how to create variables, and how to assign and display their values.

Creating variables

Storing information in a variable creates it.

To store information in a variable, you use a single equal sign (=). For example, the following four PHP statements assign information to variables:

```
$age = 21;
$price = 20.52;
$temperature = -5;
$name = "Clark Kent";
```

In these examples, notice that the numbers are not enclosed in quotes, but the name, which is a string of characters, is. The quotes tell PHP that the characters are a string, handled by PHP as a unit. Without the quotes, PHP doesn't know the characters are a string and won't handle them correctly. The different types of data and their uses are discussed in detail in Chapter 5.

Whenever you put information into a variable that did not previously exist, you create that variable. For example, suppose you use the following PHP statements at the top of your script:

```
$color = "blue";
$color = "red";
```

If the first statement is the first time you mention the variable `$color`, this statement creates the variable and sets it to `"blue"`. The next statement changes the value of `$color` to `"red"`.

You can store the value of one variable in another variable, as shown in the following statements:

```
$name1 = "Sally";
$name2 = "Susan";
$favorite_name = $name2;
```

After these statements are executed, the variable `$favorite_name` contains the value `"Susan"`.

You can create a variable without storing any information in it. For example, the following statement creates a variable:

```
$city = "";
```

The variable now exists but does not contain any value. Chapter 5 contains a discussion of the types of data that can be stored in a variable and their uses.

Displaying variable values

The quickest way to display the value stored in a variable is with the `print_r` statement. You can output the value of a variable as in the following statements:

```
$today = "Sunday";
print_r($today);
```

The output from the preceding statements is `Sunday`.

You can also display the value by using an `echo` statement. If you used the following PHP statements

```
$age = 21;
echo $age;
```

in a PHP section, the output would be `21`.

Using an `echo` statement of the preceding form, with one variable only, provides the same basic output as the `print_r` statement. However, you can do a lot more with the `echo` statement. You can output several items and include numbers and strings together. For example, suppose the variable `$name` has the value `Clark Kent`. You can include the following line in an HTML file:

```
<p>Welcome <?php echo $name ?></p>
```

The output on the Web page is as follows:

```
Welcome Clark Kent
```

If you use a variable that does not exist, you get a warning message. For example, suppose you intend to display `$age`, but type the following statement by mistake:

```
echo $aeg;
```

You get a notice that looks like the following:

```
Notice: Undefined variable: aeg in c:\testvar.php on line 5
```

The notice points out that you're using a variable that has not yet been given a value. The notice is helpful in this case because it pinpoints your typo. However, in some cases, writing a statement using a variable that does not exist may not be a typo; you may be using the variable deliberately. For example, you may be using it for a conditional statement (conditional statements are described in Chapter 7.) The script may be running exactly the way you want it to, and your only problem is the notice. You can prevent the notice from being displayed by using @ before the variable name. If you don't want the notice to display, use the following statement:

```
echo @$aeg;
```

Because the @ turns off the error message and the variable doesn't exist, the `echo` statement displays nothing.

Don't turn off any error message that you don't understand. Be sure you understand the error and are confident that it doesn't affect your program before you shut it off. The message may mean that your script has a problem that needs to be fixed, such as the typo in the variable name shown in the previous example.

Many languages require you to create a variable before you can use it. In these languages, using a variable without creating it first is a fatal error, and the script stops running. PHP, however, doesn't require this, which may be confusing if you have C or Java experience.

Writing Your First Script That Uses Variables

In Chapter 3, the `Hello World` script displays `Hello World!` on a Web page by using a simple `echo` statement. In this section, you write a script that also displays `Hello World!`, but uses a variable in the script. In the script in Chapter 3, the following PHP section is used to display the output:

```
<?php
   echo "<p>Hello World!</p>";
?>
```

The following script is a complete script that contains a PHP section that uses a variable to display `Hello World!`:

```
<html>
<head><title>Hello World Script using Variable</title></head>
<body>
<?php
  $salutation = "Hello World!";
  echo "<p>$salutation</p>";
?>
</body>
</html>
```

If you point your browser at this script by typing the URL into the browser, the following output is displayed on the Web page:

```
Hello World!
```

A variable keeps its information for the whole script, not just for a single PHP section. If a variable is set to 5 at the beginning of a script, it will still hold 5 at the end of the script (unless, of course, you assign it another value). For example, the following script has two separate PHP sections:

```
<html>
<head><title>Hello World Script</title></head>
<body>
<?php
  $salutation = "Hello World!";
  echo "<p>$salutation</p>";
?>
<p>This is an HTML section</p>
<?php
  echo "<p>$salutation again</p>";
?>
</body>
</html>
```

If you point your browser at this script by typing the URL into your browser, the following output displays on the Web page:

```
Hello World!

This is an HTML section

Hello World! again
```

Discovering More about Output Statements with Variables

In Chapter 3, echo statements are shown to have the following format:

```
echo outputitem1,outputitem2,outputitem3,...
```

You can use a variable for any output item. For example, you could write the following PHP section:

```
<?php
   $first_name = "Clark";
   $last_name = "Kent";
   echo "My name is ",$first_name," ",$last_name;
?>
```

And the output of this section is the following:

```
My name is Clark Kent
```

Notice the space included between $first_name and $last_name. If this space isn't added, the output of the two variables runs together like this:

```
My name is ClarkKent.
```

Statements containing more than one variable must follow certain formatting rules to produce the desired output. Table 4-1 shows some echo statements containing variables and their output. The following variables are set for use in the echo statements in the table:

```
$number = 123;
$word1 = "Hello";
$word2 = "World!";
```

Table 4-1 echo Statements with Variables

echo ***Statement***	***Output***
`echo $number;`	`123`
`echo $word1,$word2;`	`HelloWorld!`
`echo $word1," ",$word2;`	`Hello World!`
`echo $word1 $word2;`	Not valid because no commas separate the variables; results in an error message
`echo "$word1 $word2 now";`	`Hello World! now`

Notice that in line 2 of the table, there is no space between the two variable names, so there is no space in the output. In line 3, a space is echoed between the two variables.

In some `echo` statements, PHP can't tell the variable name from the other information around it. In cases where this could be confusing, you need to enclose the variable name in curly braces. For example, suppose you use the following statements:

```
$type = "bird";
echo "Keep the $typecage clean";
```

Rather than the desired output, you get the following message:

```
Notice: Undefined variable: typecage in testvar.php on line 6
```

After notifying you of the problem, the following output is displayed:

```
Keep the clean
```

To make this code work correctly, you need to use the following `echo` statement:

```
echo "Keep the {$type}cage clean";
```

With this statement, the output is the following:

```
Keep the birdcage clean
```

Using Variable Variables

PHP allows you to use dynamic variable names, called *variable variables.* You can name a variable by using the value stored in another variable. That is, one variable contains the name of another variable. For example, suppose you want to construct a variable named `$city` with the value `Los Angeles`. You can use the following statement:

```
$name_of_the_variable = "city";
```

This statement creates a variable that contains the name that you want to give to a variable. Then you use the following statements:

```
$$name_of_the_variable = "Los Angeles";
```

Note the extra dollar sign (`$`) character at the beginning of the variable name. This indicates a variable variable. This statement creates a new variable with the name that is the value in `$name_of_the_variable`, resulting inthe following:

```
$city = "Los Angeles";
```

The value of `$name_of_the_variable` does not change.

The following example shows how this feature works. In its present form, the script statements may not seem that useful; you may see better ways to program this task. The true value of variable variables becomes clear when they are used with arrays and loops, as discussed in Chapters 6 and 7.

Suppose you want to name a series of variables with the names of cities that have values that are the populations of the cities. You can use this code:

```
$Reno= 360000;
$Pasadena = 138000;
$cityname = "Reno";
echo "The size of $cityname is ${$cityname}";
$cityname = "Pasadena";
echo "The size of $cityname is ${$cityname}";
```

The output from this code is:

```
The size of Reno is 360000
The size of Pasadena is 138000
```

Notice that you need to use curly braces around the variable name in the `echo` statement so that PHP knows where the variable name is. If you use the statement without the curly braces, the output is as follows:

```
The size of Reno is $Reno
```

Without the curly braces in `$$cityname`, PHP converts `$cityname` to its value and puts the extra `$` in front of it, as part of the preceding string.

Removing Variables

You can also remove information from a variable. You can use the following statement:

```
$age = "";
```

This takes the information out of the variable `$age`. It now has no value. This does not mean that `$age` is set to 0. It means that `$age` is not storing any information. Technically, it means that `$age` is storing a string of zero characters. If you echo it, you get no error message or notice; it just echoes nothing, a blank.

You can go even further and uncreate the variable by using this statement:

```
unset($age);
```

After this statement, the variable `$age` no longer exists. If you try to echo it, you get an "undefined variable" notice. You can unset more than one variable at once, as follows:

```
unset($age,$name,$address);
```

Working with Constants

Constants are similar to variables. Constants are given names, and values are stored in them. However, constants are constant; they can't be changed by the script. After you set the value for a constant, it stays the same. If you use a constant for weather and set it to `sunny`, it can't be changed. Wouldn't that be grand — only sunny days from now on?

Creating constants

Constants are set by using the `define` statement. The general format is as follows:

```
define("constantname","constantvalue");
```

For example, to set a constant with the weather, use the following statement:

```
define("WEATHER","Sunny");
```

This statement creates a constant called `WEATHER` and sets its value to `"Sunny"`.

When naming constants, use descriptive names, as you do for variables. However, unlike variables, constant names do not begin with a dollar sign ($). By convention, constants are given names that are all uppercase so you can see easily that they're constants. However, PHP accepts lowercase letters without complaint.

You can store either a string or a number in a constant. The following statement, which defines a constant named `INTEREST` and assigns to it the value `.01`, is perfectly okay with PHP:

```
define ("INTEREST",.01);
```

Constants should not be given names that are keywords for PHP. *Keywords* are words that have meaning for PHP, such as `echo`, and they can't be used as constants because PHP treats them as the PHP feature of the same name. PHP will let you define a constant `ECHO` without giving an error message, but it will have a problem when you try to use the constant. For example, if you use the following statement:

```
echo ECHO;
```

PHP gets confused and displays an error message. It sees the constant as the beginning of another `echo` statement, but it can't find all the things it needs to complete the first `echo` statement.

Some PHP keywords include the following:

```
and         echo        list
as          else        new
break       empty       or
case        eval        print
class       exit        require
const       for         return
continue    foreach     switch
declare     function    use
default     global      var
die         if          while
do          include
```

If you're baffled by some code that looks perfectly okay but refuses to work correctly, even after numerous changes, try changing the name of a constant. It's possible that you are using an obscure keyword for your constant, and that's causing your problem. This doesn't happen often, but it's possible.

Although you can use keywords for variable names, because the beginning $ tells PHP the keyword is a variable name, you probably shouldn't. It causes too much confusion for the humans involved.

Understanding when to use constants

If you know the value of something won't change during the script, use a constant. Using a constant allows you to use a descriptive name, making the script clearer. For example, `PRODUCT_COST` is much clearer than `20.50`.

Using a constant allows you set the value once at the beginning of the script. If this value ever needs to be changed, using constants allows you to change it in only one place, instead of finding and changing the value in 20 different places throughout the script. One change is better than 20. It's less work and lessens the likelihood of missing a place that needed to be changed, leading to unknown and unseen havoc.

Using a constant ensures that the value won't be changed accidentally somewhere in the script, leading to the wrong value being used in statements later in the script.

Suppose you have a script that must change money from one currency to another by multiplying the dollar amount by the exchange rate. For example, if the exchange rate from U.S. to Canadian dollars is 1.52, you can write the following code:

```
<?php
    $US_dollars = 20.00;
    $CA_dollars = $US_dollars * 1.52;
?>
```

Now, suppose your script contains 40,000 lines of code and you need to convert U.S. dollars to Canadian dollars in 50 different places in the script. So you use the preceding code in 50 different places. Then you realize that the exchange rate is likely to change every week, so you would need to go through this script every week and change 1.52 to something else, manually, in 50 different places. That's a lot of work.

A better way to handle this is to put the exchange rate in a variable so you could change it only in one place. You change your script to the following:

```
<?php
    $rate = 1.52;

    $US_dollars = 20.00;
    $CA_dollars = $US_dollars * $rate;
?>
```

You set `$rate` at the beginning of the script. Then you can use the two lines that convert the currency in all 50 parts of the script. This is clearly a better option. When the rate changes, you need to change the rate in only one place. For example, if the exchange rate changes to 1.53 next week, you just change the first line of the script to the following:

```
$rate = 1.53;
```

This would work. However, `$rate` is not a very descriptive name. Remember that your script is 40,000 lines of code and the 2 lines of code that convert currency are used in 50 different places. Suppose somewhere in the middle of your script you need to add some code to compute interest. Suppose you accidentally use the following code somewhere in the middle of your script:

```
$interest_rate = 20;
$rate = $interest_rate-1;
$amount = $principal * $rate;
```

All the places after this code will have a different value for `rate`; the 1.52 that you set at the beginning of your script will be replaced by the 19 set by this code. You can guard against this by using more descriptive variable names. Or an even better option is to use a constant, as in the following script:

```
<?php
   define("RATE",1.52);

   $US_dollars = 20;
   $CA_dollars = $US_dollars * RATE;
?>
```

Now you are using a constant, `RATE`, that can't be changed in the script. If you try to add the line

```
RATE = 20;
```

in the middle of your script, PHP won't allow it. So, you won't make the mistake that you made with the variable.

Next week when the exchange rate changes to 1.53, you just edit your script as follows:

```
<?php
define("RATE",1.53);
$US_dollars = 20;
$CA_dollars = $US_dollars * RATE;
?>
```

Of course, this would be even better if you used a more descriptive name, such as the following:

```
define("US_TO_CA",1.52);
```

Keep in mind that mistakes that seem impossible to make when you're looking at a ten-line script, become entirely possible when you think in terms of scripts with thousands of lines of code, especially scripts with more than one programmer involved.

If you know the value of something won't change during the script, use a constant. If you need to manipulate the value somewhere in the script, use a variable.

Displaying constants

You can determine the value of a constant by using `print_r` as follows:

```
print_r(US_TO_CA);
```

You can also use a constant in an `echo` statement:

```
echo US_TO_CA;
```

When you echo a constant, you can't enclose it in quotes. If you do, it echoes the constant name rather than the value. You can echo the constant as shown in the preceding example, or you can enclose it with parentheses. You can build more complicated output statements by using commas, as in the following example:

```
echo "The Canadian exchange rate is $",US_TO_CA;
```

The output from this statement is the following:

```
The Canadian exchange rate is $1.52.
```

Notice that the dollar sign is inside the quoted string in the first output string, not in the second output item as part of the constant name.

Utilizing built-in PHP constants

PHP has many built-in constants that you can use in your scripts. For example, the constant `__LINE__` has a value that is the line number where it is used, and `__FILE__` contains the name of the file in which it is used. (These constants begin with two underscores and end with two underscores.) For example, you can use the following statement:

```
echo __FILE__;
```

The output looks similar to the following:

```
c:\program files\apache group\apache\htdocs\testvar2.php
```

PHP has many other built-in constants. For example, `E_ALL` and `E_ERROR` are constants you can use to affect how PHP handles errors. These constants are explained in the next section.

Handling Error Messages

PHP tries to be helpful when problems arise by providing error messages. It provides the following types of messages:

- **Error message:** You receive this message when the script has a problem that prevents it from running. The script displays an error message and stops running. The message contains as much information as possible to help you identify the problem. The following is a common error message:

  ```
  Parse error: parse error in c:\test.php on line 6
  ```

  Often, you receive this error message because you've forgotten a semicolon, a parenthesis, or a curly brace.

- **Warning message:** You receive a warning message when the script sees a problem but the problem does not prevent the script from running. Warning messages do not mean the script can't run; they indicate that PHP believes something is probably wrong. You should identify the source of the warning and then decide whether it needs to be fixed. It usually does. For example, you see the following message if you don't include a variable name in the `print_r` statement — `print_r()` rather than `print_r($varname)`.

  ```
  Warning: print_r() expects at least 1 parameter, 0 given
          in d: test1.php on line 9
  ```

  Because this is a warning, not an error, the script continues to execute the statements after the `print_r` statement. However, a warning usually indicates a more serious problem than a notice. In this case, you need to fix the problem.

- **Notice:** You receive a notice when PHP sees a condition that may be an error or may be perfectly okay. One common condition that produces a notice is echoing variables that don't exist. Here's an example of what you might see in that instance:

  ```
  Notice: Undefined variable: age in testing.php on line 9
  ```

Error messages, warning messages, and notices all indicate the filename causing the problem and the line number where the problem was encountered.

The types of error messages that are displayed depend on the error level that PHP is set to. You need to see all the error messages, but you may not want to see all the warnings and notices. (Often the only problem with a notice is the unsightly notice; the code is working correctly.) Or, you may want warning messages and notices displayed during development but not after customers are using the application. Or, you may want to send all the error messages to a log file, rather than have them output for users to see.

The next few sections tackle the subject of setting PHP to give you the type of error messages that you want.

Changing the error level for your Web site

The error level for your Web site is defined in the `php.ini` file. You can change the error level if you are the PHP administrator and have access to the `php.ini` file. If you are not the administrator (which will be the case if, for example, you are using a Web hosting company), you can change the error level for each script, as described in the next section. (See Appendix A for more on the `php.ini` file.)

To see what the current error level is, open `php.ini` in an editor and look for a line similar to the following:

```
error_reporting  = E_ALL; display all errors, warnings and
          notices
```

This statement causes all errors, warnings, and notices to be displayed. This setting is useful when you're developing the script. However, when you release the script for users, you probably don't want notices displayed.

In the preceding example, notice that there is a semicolon (;) after `E_ALL` but not at the beginning of the line. The semicolon is the character that indicates a comment in the `php.ini` file. Therefore, the text on the line after the semicolon is just a comment, not part of the statement. If there were a semicolon at the beginning of the line, the entire line would be a comment, and the statement would not be in effect.

When you look in your `php.ini` file, you will probably find several statements like the preceding line, except with semicolons at the beginning of the lines. These statements are included as examples, not as statements that execute. Look for the statement without a semicolon in front of it to see which statement is currently active.

`E_ALL` is a built-in PHP constant that refers to all errors, warnings, and notices. `E_NOTICE` is a built-in constant representing notices. You can use these two constants in the following statement:

```
error_reporting = E_ALL & ~E_NOTICE
```

`E_ALL` tells PHP to display all errors, warnings, and notices. However, the second term `~E_NOTICE` tells PHP not to display notices. The result is that only errors and warnings are displayed. This method of specifying the errors to be displayed is shorter than listing all the types of errors that you want to display.

The two statements shown in this section are used most often. You can use other constants to specify error levels, but `E_ALL` and `E_NOTICE` are usually sufficient for most scripts. You can find a listing of all the constants in the `php.ini` file. For a complete discussion of error levels, check out the PHP online manual.

You can stop error reporting all together. You may not want users to see any of the PHP-generated error or warning messages because they may contain compromising information. Usually if you do this, you want to save error messages in a log instead, as described later in this chapter in the section, "Sending messages to a log."

To turn off error reporting, find the line that says `display_errors = On` in `php.ini` and change `On` to `Off`.

You need to restart your Web server before any changes you make in `php.ini` will go into effect.

Changing the error level for a script

If you want to set the error level for a particular script, add a statement with the following format to the beginning of the script:

```
error_reporting(OPTIONS);
```

The *OPTIONS* in the statement are the built-in constants discussed in the preceding section. For example, you can have all errors, warnings, and notices displayed in the script by adding the following statement:

```
error_reporting(E_ALL);
```

Suppose the setting in `php.ini` is set to `E_ALL`. You may be satisfied with that level while developing your scripts, but then want to stop displaying notices when users start running your scripts. To override the `php.ini` setting, you can add the following statement to the scripts after they are fine-tuned and ready to go:

```
error_reporting(E_ALL & ~E_NOTICE);
```

You can set error reporting so that no messages are displayed by using the following statement:

```
error_reporting(0);
```

Sometimes you want to turn error and warning messages off when your scripts are complete and being used by the world. You may not want users to see the error messages that PHP sends because the information in the PHP messages can represent a security issue, but you may want to see any error messages from PHP yourself. You can turn error reporting off by using a setting of zero, but log the error messages to a file at the same time. Users don't see the messages, but you can look at them. Sending messages to a log is described in the next section.

Sending messages to a log

You can send the errors and warnings from PHP to a log file. You may want to have a permanent record of errors as well as display them, or you may want to send the errors to a file rather than display them for the world to see.

You can set up an error message log for the whole site by using settings in the `php.ini` file, if you have access to it. Open `php.ini` and find the following line:

```
log_errors = Off
```

You need to change `Off` to `On`. You also need to tell PHP where to send the error messages. To do this, find the following line:

```
;error_log = filename
```

Now remove the semicolon from the beginning of the line. This changes the line from a comment to a statement. Change `filename` to the path to the file into which you want the messages saved. For example, you could use the following statement:

```
error_log = c:\temp\php_error_log
```

The directory (often called folder in Windows) must exist. For this statement, you must create the directory `c:\temp` before the error messages can be logged there. You don't need to create the file; PHP can create the file as long as it can find the directory.

You need to restart your Web server before any changes you make in `php.ini` will go into effect.

Advanced error handling

This section describes advanced error handling. Newbies do not need to read this section. Come back and read this section after you have some experience with the programming techniques described in the rest of the book.

The standard PHP errors and error messages may not be sufficient for your needs. For example, you may know something is an error in your script, although PHP sees nothing wrong with the problem. For example, you may be writing a script to design a house. In such a case, if `$height_of_door` is larger than `$height_of_house`, you know that something is wrong. You know this, but PHP doesn't. PHP would not recognize this as an error condition. To get PHP to check for this error in the script, you could write the following statement:

```
If ($height_of_door > $height_of_house)
{
    trigger_error("Impossible condition",E_USER_ERROR);
}
```

Using `if` statements is explained in detail in Chapter 7.

The `E_USER_ERROR` in the statement tells PHP that the condition is an error. The string `"Impossible condition"` is the message to be displayed when the error is encountered. If the condition is true, the following message is displayed:

```
Fatal error: Impossible condition in d:\testerr.php on line 9
```

The script stops at this point because you told PHP that it was an error, rather than a warning or a notice. You can use `E_USER_WARNING` or `E_USER_NOTICE`, rather than `E_USER_ERROR`, to have PHP treat the condition as a warning or notice.

If you want to handle the error in your own way, instead of using PHP standard error procedures, you can write your own statements to perform actions, such as send a message, log a message, send an e-mail, or stop the script. For example, you could simply echo an error message to the user and stop the script, as follows:

```
If ($height_of_door > $height_of_house)
{
    echo "This is impossible<br>";
    exit();
}
```

If `$height_of_door` is larger than `$height_of_house`, the message is echoed, and `exit()` stops the script. No more statements are executed.

You could also send a message to a PHP error log when this condition occurs by using the following type of statement:

```
error_log(message,3,logfilename);
```

For example, you could use the following `if` block:

```
If ($height_of_door > $height_of_house)
{
   error_log("The door is taller than the
            house",3,"/temp/err_log");
   exit();
}
```

After this statement, if `$height_of_door` is larger than `$height_of_house`, the message `"The door is taller than the house"` is stored in the log file `/temp/err_log`. The `3` in the statement tells PHP to store the message in the specified log file. The directory `/temp` must exist, but PHP will create the file if it doesn't already exist.

Alternatively, you might want to send yourself an e-mail message when the error occurs. The `error_log` statement can be used for this purpose as well as for logging an error message. The `1` in the following `error_log` statement tells PHP to send the message as e-mail to the specified e-mail address:

```
error_log("The door is taller than the
            house",1,"me@mymail.com");
```

This statement assumes that e-mail can be accessed from PHP. See the discussion of PHP and e-mail in Chapter 13.

On the other hand, you may be willing to accept PHP's definition of an error, but want it to behave differently when it encounters an error. You could have procedures you want performed in the event of an error. You may want PHP to display a message written by you or to execute statements written by you. For example, you may want to be informed by e-mail of error messages, or you may want certain files opened or closed before the script stops.

You can write your own code to handle errors and instruct PHP to use your code whenever it encounters an error. To do this, you write your own error-handling code and save it as a *function,* which is a piece of code you write and call repeatedly whenever you need it. (Instructions for writing functions are provided in Chapter 8.) You can tell PHP to use your function rather than its own procedure for error handling by using the following statement:

```
set_error_handler(functionname);
```

For example, you could use the following:

```
set_error_handler(my_error_handler);
```

Further instructions for writing `my_error_handler` are provided in Chapter 8 where functions are discussed.

Another method for handling errors recognized by PHP is to use the `die` statement to display a message when a function fails. The `die` statement is discussed in detail in Chapter 8 along with the discussion of functions.

Chapter 5

Working with Data

In This Chapter

- Understanding data types
- Performing arithmetic
- Manipulating character strings
- Using dates and times

Variables can store data of different types, and different types of data can do different things. For example, you can add variables whose values are numbers (1 + 2), but adding variables whose values are characters (a + b) doesn't make much sense. In this chapter, you find out what data types PHP can handle and how you can use them.

Understanding Data Types

You can store the following simple types of data in PHP variables:

- **Integer:** A whole number (no fractions), such as –43, 0, 1, 27, or 5438. The range of integers that is allowed varies, depending on your operating system, but in general, you can usually use any number from –2 billion up to +2 billion.
- **Floating point number:** A number (usually not a whole number) that includes decimal places, such as 5.24 or 123.456789. This is often called a *real number* or a *float.*
- **Character string:** A series of single characters, such as `hello`. There is no practical limit on the length of a string.
- **Boolean:** A TRUE or FALSE value. See the nearby sidebar for more information.

True or false? Boolean values

Boolean data types represent two possible states — TRUE or FALSE. Boolean values are used mainly to compare conditions for use in conditional statements. For example, PHP evaluates an expression, such as `$a > $b`, and the outcome is either TRUE or FALSE.

PHP considers the following values FALSE :

- The string FALSE (can be upper- or lowercase)
- The integer 0
- The float 0.0
- An empty string
- The one-character string 0
- The constant NULL

Any other values in a Boolean variable are considered TRUE. If you echo a Boolean variable, the value FALSE displays as a blank string; the value TRUE echoes as a 1. Functions often return a Boolean variable that you can test to see whether the function succeeded or failed. For more information on using Boolean variables with functions, check out Chapter 8.

Assigning data types

Most other languages require that you initialize the variable before using it, specifying what type of data it can hold, but PHP is more informal. You don't need to tell PHP which data type is in a variable. PHP evaluates the data when you assign it to the variable and then stores it as the appropriate type. Generally, this is helpful. PHP guesses the data type pretty accurately.

PHP also converts data when it needs to be converted. For example, if you have the following statements, PHP converts the data types with no problem:

```
$firstNumber = 1;      # PHP stores it as an integer
$secondNumber = 1.1;    # PHP stores it as a float
$sum = $firstNumber + $secondNumber;
```

Technically, the third statement is not possible because the data to be added are different types. However, PHP converts the integer to a float so that the addition proceeds smoothly. This happens automatically and invisibly and is very helpful.

Type casting

On a rare occasion, PHP guesses badly when it stores the data. You might need to do something with a variable, and PHP won't let you because the data is the wrong type. In such a case, you can specify how you want PHP to store the data, rather than let PHP decide for itself. This is called *type casting*. To specify a particular type, use a statement like one of the following:

```
$newint = (int) $var1;
$newfloat = (float) $var1;
$newstring = (string) $var1;
```

The value in the variable on the right side of the equal sign is stored in the variable on the left side as the specified type. So the value in `$var1` is stored in `$newint` as an integer, as specified by `(int)`.

Be careful when doing type casts. Sometimes you can get unexpected results. For example, when you cast a float into an integer, it loses its decimal places. To do this, PHP rounds the float toward 0. For example, if `$number = 1.8` and you cast it into an integer — `$newnumber = (int) $number` — `$newnumber` will equal 1.

You can find out the data type of a variable by using a statement like the following:

```
var_dump($myvariable);
```

For example, the following statement checks the data type of `$checkvar`:

```
var_dump($checkvar);
```

The output from this statement is `int(27)`, which tells you that `$checkvar` contains the integer 27.

Working with Numbers

The data types `float` and `integer` are both numbers. You store them in variables as follows:

```
$intvar = 3;
$floatvar = 9.3;
```

PHP automatically stores the values as the correct data type.

Performing mathematical operations

PHP allows you to do mathematical operations on numbers. You indicate mathematical operations by using two numbers and a mathematical operator.

For example, one operator is the plus (+) sign, so you can indicate a mathematical operation like this:

```
1 + 2
```

You can also do math with variables:

```
$var1 + $var2;
```

If you plan to use numbers in mathematical operations, don't enclose them in quotes when assigning them to variables. Using quotes sets the numbers as character strings, and you can't perform mathematical operations on character strings. However, PHP, as opposed to most other languages, will automatically convert strings to numbers when it needs to. For example, suppose you have the following statements:

```
$var1 = "1";
$var2 = 2;
$total = $var1 + $var2;
```

Technically, you can't add these two numbers together because `$var1` is a character string. However, PHP automatically converts the string 1 to a number 1 when it gets to the third statement and then adds the numbers.

If you use the following statements, PHP also converts the string so it can add the numbers, but the results are not as obvious:

```
$var1 = "x";
$var2 = 2;
$total = $var1 + $var2;
```

Because x is not a number that PHP can convert, it uses 0 in the addition. The result is that `$total` equals `2`. In most cases, this conversion is not what you want. The automatic conversion feature is useful, and saves some typing, but be careful when depending on it. Sometimes you don't get the results you expect, as shown in the previous example.

PHP can also guess wrong because it doesn't understand certain human notation. For example, the following statements cause PHP to get it wrong:

```
$var1 = "2,000";
$var2 = 2;
$total = $var1 + $var2;
```

Although people understand what commas mean in numbers, PHP does not. PHP thinks 2,000 ends at the comma. After these statements are executed, `$total` equals `4`.

Table 5-1 shows the mathematical operators that you can use.

Table 5-1 Mathematical Operators

Operator	*Description*
+	Adds two numbers together.
-	Subtracts the second number from the first number.
*	Multiplies two numbers together.
/	Divides the first number by the second number.
%	Finds the remainder when the first number is divided by the second number. This is called *modulus*. For example, in `$a = 13 % 4`, `$a` is set to `1`.

Understanding the order of operations

You can do several mathematical operations at once. For example, the following statement performs three operations:

```
$total = 1 + 2 * 3 + 1;
```

The order in which the arithmetic is performed is important. You can get different results depending on which operation is performed first. PHP does multiplication and division first, and then addition and subtraction. If other considerations are equal, PHP goes from left to right. Consequently, the preceding statement sets `$total` to `8`, in the following order:

```
$total = 1 + 2 * 3 + 1 #first, it does the multiplication
$total = 1 + 6 + 1     #next, it does the leftmost addition
$total = 7 + 1         #next, the remaining addition
$total = 8
```

You can change the order in which the arithmetic is performed by using parentheses. The arithmetic inside the parentheses is performed first. For example, you can write the previous statement with parentheses, like this:

```
$total = (1 + 2) * 3 + 1;
```

This statement sets `$total` to `10`, in the following order:

```
$total = (1 + 2) * 3 + 1 #first, the math in the parentheses
$total = 3 * 3 + 1        #next, the multiplication
$result = 9 + 1           #next, the addition
$result = 10
```

The general order of operations is in force inside of parentheses when there is more than one operation, such as `(3 + 2 * 5)`. In this example, the multiplication is performed first. You can use parentheses inside of parentheses to change that order as well.

On the better-safe-than-sorry principle, it's best to use parentheses whenever more than one answer is possible.

Incrementing and decrementing

PHP provides a shortcut for adding 1 to a variable. If you want to add 1 to a variable, you can use a statement like the following:

```
$counter=$counter+1;
```

PHP also lets you write a shorter statement that does the same thing:

```
$counter++;
```

For example, you could use the following statements:

```
$counter=0;
$counter++;
echo $counter;
```

This echo statement outputs `1`, because ++ adds 1 to the current value of `$counter`. You can also subtract 1 by using the following statement:

```
$counter--;
```

Another shortcut for adding a number to an existing variable is `+=1`, which adds 1 to the variable. You can add any number to a variable by using this shortcut. You can also subtract, multiply, or divide by using a similar shortcut. The following are some valid statements using this shorter format:

```
$counter+=2;
$counter-=3;
$counter*=2;
$counter/=3;
```

These statements add 2 to $counter, subtract 3 from $counter, multiply $counter by 2, and divide $counter by 3, respectively.

Using built-in higher-math functions

PHP provides functions to perform more complicated math for you. (Functions are described further in Chapter 8.) For example, if you need to compute a square root, you don't have to write code that does all the math. PHP has already written this code for you. You can just use a statement like one of these:

```
$rootvar = sqrt(91);
$rootvar = sqrt($number);
```

The first statement takes the square root of a number, and the second statement takes the square root of a variable's value.

You can use a statement like the following to round up to the next integer:

```
$upnumber = ceil(27.63);
```

The result is 28. You can also round down by using the following format:

```
$downnumber = floor(27.63);
```

The result of this segment is 27.

PHP offers many math functions, including functions for simple math, such as maximum, minimum, and random numbers; and functions for advanced math, such as sine, tangent, and converting to binary or octal numbers. To find a particular mathematical function, see Appendix B.

Formatting numbers for output

Often you want to display a number in a familiar format, such as with commas dividing the thousands or formatted as dollar amounts with two decimal places. But PHP stores and displays numbers in the most efficient format. If the number is 10.00, it is displayed as 10. Therefore, you need to tell PHP how you want the number displayed.

One PHP statement that formats numbers is the number_format statement, which has the following general form:

```
number_format(number,decimals,"decimalsep","thousandsep")
```

In this format, each piece of input has a meaning:

- `number` is the number to be formatted. This must always be included.
- `decimals` is the number of decimal places. If `decimals` is not included, the number of decimal places is 0 by default, and `number` is rounded to the closest integer. If you are going to include `thousandsep` and `decimalsep`, you must include `decimals`.
- `decimalsep` is the character used to separate the decimal places. The default is a decimal point. If you include this, you must also include `thousandsep`.
- `thousandsep` is the character used to separate the number into thousands. The default is a comma. If you include this parameter, you must also include `decimalsep`.

Table 5-2 shows some `number_format` statements and their output.

Table 5-2 `number_format` Statements

`$number`	*Format*	*Output*
12321	`number_format($number)`	12,321
12321.66	`number_format($number,2)`	12,321.66
12321.66	`number_format($number)`	12,322
12321.6	`number_format($number,3)`	12,321.600
12321	`number_format($number,0,".",".")`	12.321
12321.66	`number_format($number,2,".","")`	12321.66

After formatting, the number is converted to a string data type, so perform any arithmetic on the number before you format it.

For more complicated formatting, PHP provides the statements `printf` and `sprintf`:

- `printf` outputs the formatted number directly.
- `sprintf` is used to store the formatted number into a variable.

The formatting statements `printf` and `sprintf` can be used to format character strings as well as numbers, and to output strings and numbers in the same output statement. For a more complete description of these statements, check out the section "Formatting output strings," later in this chapter.

Working with Character Strings

Characters are letters, numbers, and punctuation, and a *character string* is a series of characters. When a number is used as a character, it is just a stored character, the same as a letter. It can't be used in arithmetic. For example, a phone number usually is stored as a character string and not a number because it only needs to be stored, not added or multiplied.

When you store a character string in a variable, you use double quotes or single quotes to tell PHP where the string begins and ends. For example, the following two statements are the same:

```
$string = _Hello World!_;
$string = _Hello World!_;
```

Storing really long strings

PHP provides a feature called a *heredoc* that is useful for assigning values to really long strings that span several lines. A heredoc enables you to tell PHP where to start and end reading a string. A heredoc statement has the following format:

```
$varname = <<<ENDSTRING
text
ENDSTRING;
```

ENDSTRING is any string you want to use. You enclose the text you want stored in the variable `$varname` by typing *ENDSTRING* at the beginning and again at the end. When PHP processes the heredoc, it reads the first *ENDSTRING* and knows to start reading text into `$varname`. It continues reading text into `$varname` until it encounters the same ENDSTRING again. At that point, it ends the string.

The string created by a heredoc statement evaluates variables and special characters in the same manner as a double-quoted string. (For details on double-quoted strings, see the section, "Comparing single-quoted strings and double-quoted strings," later in this chapter.)

The following statements create a string by using the heredoc method:

```
$distance = 10;
$herevariable = <<<ENDOFTEXT
The distance between
Los Angeles and Pasadena
is $distance miles.
ENDOFTEXT;
echo $herevariable;
```

The output of the echo statement is as follows:

```
The distance between Los
   Angeles and Pasadena is 10
   miles.
```

But be careful. PHP is picky about its *ENDSTRING*s. When it first appears, the *ENDSTRING* (*ENDOFTEXT* in this example) must occur at the end of the first line, with nothing following it, not even a space. And the *ENDSTRING* on the last line must occur at the start of the line, with nothing before it, not even a space, and nothing following it other than the semicolon. If these rules are broken, PHP won't recognize the ending string and will continue looking for it throughout the rest of the script. It will eventually display a parse error showing a line number that is the last line in the script.

Using special characters in strings

PHP provides some special characters you can use in strings: \n and \t. You can use \n to start a new line in a string, as in the following statements:

```
$string = "Hello \nWorld";
echo $string;
```

The output is broken into two lines:

```
Hello
World
```

You can use \t to insert a tab, as in the following statements:

```
$string = "Line 1 \n\tLine 2";
echo $string;
```

The second line of the output is indented:

```
Line 1
     Line 2
```

Special characters can be used only in strings enclosed with double quotes. In single-quoted strings, special characters have no special meaning; they are output the same way as any other character. The difference between single and double quotes is explained in the next section.

Comparing single-quoted strings and double-quoted strings

Single-quoted and double-quoted strings are handled differently:

- Single-quoted strings are stored literally, with the exception of \', which is stored as an apostrophe. (For more information about \', see the next section, "Escaping characters.")
- In double-quoted strings, variables and special characters are evaluated before the string is stored.

The following examples show the difference in output produced by single and double quotes.

If you enclose a variable in double quotes, PHP uses the value of the variable. However, if you enclose a variable in single quotes, PHP uses the literal variable name. For example, the following statements use both the single and double quote methods with a variable:

```
$name = "Sam";
$output1 = _$name_;
$output2 = _$name_;
echo $output1;
echo $output2;
```

The output of these `echo` statements is as follows:

```
Sam
$name
```

If you use special characters in a string enclosed by double quotes, PHP outputs the string after evaluating the special characters. However, if you enclose the string in single quotes, PHP outputs the special characters as literals. For example, the following statements use both single and double quotes with the new line character `\n` and the tab character `\t`:

```
$string1 = "String in \n\tdouble quotes";
$string2 = 'String in \n\tsingle quotes';
```

When `$string1` is displayed, you get the following:

```
String in
     double quotes
```

When `$string2` is displayed, you get the following:

```
String in \n\tsingle quotes
```

The quotes that enclose the entire string determine the treatment of variables and special characters, even if there are other sets of quotes inside the string. For example, look at the following statements:

```
$number = 10;
$string1 = "There are '$number' people in line.";
$string2 = 'There are "$number" people waiting.';
echo $string1,"\n";
echo $string2;
```

The output is as follows:

```
There are '10' people in line.
There are "$number" people waiting.
```

You can see that even though `$number` is enclosed in single quotes in `$string1`, the double quotes around the entire string cause the output to contain the value of the variable rather than the name of the variable. Similarly, even though `$number` is enclosed in double quotes in `$string2`, the single quotes around the entire string cause the output to contain the name of the variable rather than the value of the variable

Escaping characters

Sometimes you want a character in a double-quoted string to be treated as a literal, not as a special character, even though it has special meaning. For example, you may want to output a dollar sign as a dollar sign, rather than have the dollar sign treated as the first character of a variable name. You can tell PHP to output characters, rather than use their special meaning, by preceding the character with a backslash (\). This is called *escaping* the character. For example, the following two strings produce the same output:

```
$string = 'The variable name is $var1';
$string = "The variable name is \$var1";
```

The output from either string is the following:

```
The variable name is $var1
```

Suppose you want to store a string as follows:

```
$string = _Where is Sally_s house_;
echo $string;
```

These statements won't work because when PHP sees the ' (single quote) after Sally, it thinks this is the end of the string. It displays the following:

```
Where is Sally
```

You need to tell PHP to interpret the single quote (') as an apostrophe, not as the end of the string. You can do this by using a backslash (\) in front of the single quote. The backslash tells PHP that the single quote does not have any special meaning; it's just an apostrophe. To display the string correctly, use the following statement:

```
$string = _Where is Sally\_s house_;
```

When you enclose a string in double quotes, you must also use a backslash in front of any double quotes inside the string.

Joining strings together

You can join strings together, a process called *concatenation,* by using a dot (.). For example, you can join `$string1` and `$string2` with the following statements:

```
$string1 = _Hello_;
$string2 = _World!_;
$stringall = $string1.$string2;
echo $stringall;
```

The `echo` statement outputs one string:

```
HelloWorld!
```

Notice that no space appears between `Hello` and `World!`. That's because no spaces are included in the two strings that are joined. You can add a space between the words by joining three strings together — the two variables and a string that contains a single space — with the following statement rather than the earlier statement:

```
$stringall = $string1._ _.$string2;
```

You can use `.=` to add characters to an existing string. For example, you can use the following statements, in place of the preceding statements:

```
$stringall = "Hello";
$stringall .= " World!";
echo $stringall;
```

The `echo` statement outputs this:

```
Hello World!
```

Manipulating strings

PHP provides many built-in functions for manipulating strings. (Functions are discussed in detail in Chapter 8.) Using PHP functions, you can find substrings or characters, replace part of a string with different characters, take a string apart, count the length of a string, and perform many other string manipulations.

Often you want to remove blank spaces before or after a string. You can remove leading or trailing spaces by using the following statements:

```
$string = trim($string)  # removes leading & trailing spaces
$string = ltrim($string) # removes leading spaces
$string = rtrim($string) # removes trailing spaces
```

PHP can help you split a string into words, which is often handy. The general form of this function is as follows:

```
str_word_count("string",format)
```

In this expression, `format` can be 1, meaning return the words as a numeric array; or 2, meaning return the words as an array where the key is the position of the first character of the word. (Arrays are explained in Chapter 6.) If you don't include a format, the function returns the number of words. The following examples use `str_word_count`:

```
$string = "Counting Words";
$numberOfWords = str_word_count($string);
$word1 = str_word_count($string,1);
$word2 = str_word_count($string,2);
```

After the statements are executed, the following variables exist:

```
$numberOfWords = 2
$word1[0] = Counting
$word1[1] = Words
$word2[0] = Counting
$word2[9] = Words
```

Notice that the first word starts at position 0 (not position 1 as you and I might think), and the next word starts at position 9. I explain this more fully in Chapter 6 when I discuss arrays.

Some additional useful string manipulation statements are shown in Table 5-3 with examples. When looking at the examples, remember that the first position in the string is 0, not 1.

Table 5-3 String Manipulation

Function Format	What It Does	Example	Result
`str_repeat("str",n)`	Repeat *str n* times	`$x=str_repeat("x",5);`	`$x=xxxxx`
`str_replace("a","b", "str")`	Replace all *a* with *b* in *str*	`$a="abc abc";` `$s=str_replace("b","i",$a);`	`$s= aic aic`
`strchr("string", "char");`	Returns *string* from *char* to end	`$str="aBc abc";` `$sub=strchr($str,"b");`	`$sub=bc`
`stristr("string", "char");`	Same as `strchr`, except not case sensitive	`$str="aBc abc";` `$sub=stristr($str,"b");`	`$sub= Bc abc`
`strlen("string")`	Returns length of *string*	`$n=strlen("hello");`	`$n=5`
`strpos("string", "substr")`	Returns position of first *substr* beginning	`$str="hello";` `$n=strpos($str,"ll");`	`$n=2`
`strrchr("string", "char");`	Same as `strchr`, except finds only the last instance of *char*	`$str="abc abc";` `$sub=strrchr($str,"b");`	`$sub=bc`
`strrev("string")`	Reverses *string*	`$n=strrev("abcde");`	`$n=edcba`
`strrpos("string", "substr")`	Returns position of last instance of *substr*	`$str="abc abc";` `$n=strrpos($str,"bc");`	`$n=5`
`strtolower("string")`	Returns a lowercase version of *string*	`$str=strtolower("YES");`	`$str=yes`

(continued)

Table 5-3 (continued)

Function Format	What It Does	Example	Result
strtoupper("*string*")	Returns an uppercase version of *string*	$str=strtoupper("yes");	$str=YES
"*str1*","*str2*")	Replaces all *str1* with *str2* in *string*	$str="aa bb cc"; $new=strtr($str,"bb","xx");	$new= aa xx cc
substr("*string*",*n1*,*n2*)	Returns *string* between *n1* and *n2*	$sstr=substr("hello",2,4);	$sstr=llo
substr_count("*str*", "*sub*")	Returns the number of occurrences of *sub* in *str*	$str="abc ab abc"; $s="bc"; $n=substr_count($str,$s);	$n=2
substr_replace("*s*", "*r*",*n*,*l*)	Replace *r* into *s*, beginning with *n* for *l* characters	$s="abc abc"; $t= substr_replace($s,"x",2,3);	$t= abxbc
ucfirst("*string*")	Changes first letter of *string* to uppercase	$str="a B c"; $str2=ucfirst($str);	$str2= A B c
ucwords("*string*")	Changes each word of *string* to uppercase	$str="aa Bb cc"; $str2=ucwords($str);	$str2= Aa Bb Cc

Formatting output strings

The output produced by PHP is always in string format. That is, the output of the echo statement is a string, even if the output statement included a variable containing a number. The following is an output statement:

```
$number = 4;
echo "Sally has $number children.";
```

The output is as follows:

```
Sally has 4 children.
```

The output is a string, even though 4 was a number when it was in the variable named $number. The echo statement outputs 4 as part of a character string.

Formatting the output is an important part of scripting. The echo statement allows quite a bit of flexibility in formatting output. In the section, "Formatting numbers for output," earlier in this chapter, I describe some possibilities for formatting numbers by using the number_format statement. PHP provides additional statements for formatting output strings. The printf and sprintf statements allow you to format strings, numbers, and a mix of both strings and numbers.

The general format is as follows:

```
printf("format",$varname1,$varname2,. . .);
$newvar = sprintf("format",$varname1,$varname2,. . .);
```

The printf statement outputs formatted strings; sprintf stores the formatted output in a variable. You can format strings or numbers or both together, including variable values. The information in *format* gives instructions for the format, and *$varname* contains the value(s) to be formatted. The following statement is valid:

```
$newvar = sprintf("Hello World!");
```

This statement outputs the literal string, as given, because no format is included. The string "Hello World!" is now assigned to the variable $newvar. However, you can mix variables with literals by using the following statements:

```
$nboys = 3;
$ngirls = 2;
printf("%s boys and %s girls",$nboys,$ngirls);
```

The `%s` is a formatting instruction that tells `printf` to insert the variable value as a string. Thus, the output is: `3 boys and 2 girls`. The `%` character signals `printf` that a formatting instruction starts here. The formatting instruction has the following format:

```
%pad-width.dectype
```

These are the components of the formatting instructions:

- *%:* Signals the start of the formatting instruction.
- *pad*: A padding character that is used to fill out the string when the value to be formatted is smaller than the width assigned. (See *width*, later in this list.) If you don't specify a character, a space is used. `pad` can be a space, a 0, or any character preceded by a single quote ('). For example, it is common to pad numbers with 0 — for example, 01 or 0001.
- *-:* A symbol meaning to left-justify the characters. If this is not included, the characters are right-justified.
- *width:* The number of characters to use for the value. If the value doesn't fill the width, the padding character is used to pad the value. For example, if the width is 5, the padding character is 0, and the value is 1, the output is `00001`.
- *.dec:* The number of decimal places to use for a number. This value is preceded by a decimal point.
- *type:* The type of value. Use `s` (string) for most values. Use `f` (float) for numbers that you want to format with decimal places.

The following are some possible `sprintf` statements:

```
$money = 30;
$pet = "Kitten";
$new = sprintf("It costs $%03.2f for a %s.\n",$money,$pet);
$new2 = sprintf("%'.-20s%3.2f",$pet,$money);
echo $new;
echo $new2;
```

The output of these statements is

```
It costs $030.00 for a Kitten.
Kitten.............. 30.00
```

Notice that the format for `$money` is `3.2f` (3 digits wide with 2 decimal places) for both `$new` and `$new2`, but in `$new`, it's padded with a 0. In `$new2`, the number format is not padded, so there is a space before 30.

For `$new2`, the format for `$pet` is `'.-20`. The `20` makes the space for `$pet` 20 characters wide. The value Kitten takes up 6 characters. The format characters `'.` tell `sprintf` to pad the space with dots, so that produces 14 dots.

The - format character says to left justify Kitten, so Kitten is on the left side of the space, and the padding comes after Kitten. If the - is left out, Kitten is right justified by default, which means that Kitten is on the right side of the space, with the dots coming before it.

Often scripts need to display columns of numbers. For example, you might have three numbers: 12.3, 1, and 234.55. If you just echo them, they display as follows:

```
12.3
1
234.55
```

Even if you use `number_format` to specify two decimal places, they display as follows:

```
12.30
1.00
234.55
```

You can display them in an orderly column, however, by using `printf` as follows:

```
printf("%5.2f\n",$number1);
printf("%5.2f\n",$number2);
printf("%5.2f\n",$number3);
```

Your output is as follows:

```
 12.30
  1.00
234.55
```

In the preceding statements, `%5.2f\n` is the format that tells PHP how to format the number in the output. Here's a closer look:

- `%`: Tells PHP that the following digits are a formatting instruction.
- `5`: The width — how long the number should be. If the number is less than 5 digits wide, it is *right-justified,* which means it's moved as far right as it can go. Right-justified is the default, so no symbol is needed in the format to right-justify the numbers.
- `.2`: Means that the number should be displayed with 2 decimal places.
- `f`: Tells PHP to display the number as a float.
- `\n`: Tells PHP to start a new line.

To put numbers into the proper format for dollars, you can use `sprintf`. The following statement formats a number into a dollar amount:

```
$newvariablename = sprintf("$%.2f", $oldvariablename);
```

This statement reformats the number in `$oldvariablename` and stores it in the new format in `$newvariablename`. For example, the following statements display money in the correct format:

```
$price = 25;
printf("$%.2f",$price);
```

You see the following output:

```
$25.00
```

Working with Dates and Times

Dates and times can be important elements in a script. PHP has the ability to recognize dates and times and handle them differently than plain character strings. The computer stores dates and times in a format called a *timestamp,* which is expressed entirely in seconds. However, because this is an impractical format for humans to read, PHP converts dates from your notation into a timestamp the computer understands and from a timestamp into a format that is familiar to people. PHP handles dates and times by using built-in functions.

The timestamp format is a UNIX Timestamp, an integer that is the number of seconds from January 1, 1970 00:00:00 GMT to the time represented by the timestamp. This format makes it easy to calculate the time between two dates — just subtract one timestamp from the other.

Formatting dates

The function you will use most often is `date`. The `date` function converts a date or time from the timestamp format into a format you specify. The general format is as follows:

```
$mydate = date("format",$timestamp);
```

`$timestamp` is a variable with a timestamp stored in it. You previously stored the timestamp in the variable by using a `time` or `mktime`, as described in the next section. If *`$timestamp`* is not included, PHP obtains the current time from the operating system. Thus, you can get today's date with the following statement:

```
$today = date("Y/m/d");
```

If today is March 10, 2004, this statement returns:

```
2004/03/10
```

The *format* is a string that specifies the date format you want stored in the variable. For example, the format "y-m-d" returns 04-3-10, and "M.d.Y" returns Mar.10.2004. Table 5-4 lists some of the symbols that you can use in the format string. (For a complete list of symbols, see the documentation at www.php.net.) The parts of the date can be separated by hyphens (-), dots (.), slashes (/), or spaces.

Table 5-4 Date Format Symbols

Symbol	*Meaning*	*Example*
M	Month in text, abbreviated	Jan
F	Month in text not abbreviated	January
m	Month in numbers with leading zeros	02 or 12
n	Month in numbers without leading zeros	1 or 12
d	Day of the month; two digits with leading zeros	01 or 14
j	Day of the month without leading zeros	3 or 30
l	Day of the week in text not abbreviated	Friday
D	Day of the week in text as an abbreviation	Fri
w	Day of the week in numbers from 0 (Sunday) to 6 (Saturday)	5
Y	Year in four digits	2004
y	Year in two digits	04
g	Hour between 0 and 12 without leading zeros	2 or 10
G	Hour between 0 and 24 without leading zeros	2 or 15
h	Hour between 0 and 12 with leading zeros	01 or 10
H	Hour between 0 and 12 with leading zeros	00 or 23
i	Minutes	00 or 59
s	Seconds	00 or 59
a	am or pm in lowercase	am
A	AM or PM in uppercase	AM
U	Unix seconds	1056244941

Storing a timestamp in a variable

You can assign a timestamp with the current date and time to a variable with the following statement:

```
$today = time();
```

Another way to store a current timestamp is with the following statement:

```
$today = strtotime("today");
```

You can store a specific date and time as a timestamp by using the function `mktime`. The format is

```
$importantDate = mktime(h,m,s,mo,d,y);
```

where *h* is hours, *m* is minutes, *s* is seconds, *mo* is month, *d* is day, and *y* is year. For example, you would store the date January 15, 2003, by using the following statement:

```
$importantDate = mktime(0,0,0,1,15,2003);
```

You can also store specific timestamps by using `strtotime` with various keywords and abbreviations that are very much like English. For instance, you can create a timestamp for January 15, 2003, as follows:

```
$importantDate = strtotime("January 15 2003");
```

`strtotime` recognizes the following words and abbreviations:

- **Month names:** Twelve month names and abbreviations
- **Days of the week:** Seven days and some abbreviations
- **Time units:** Year, month, fortnight, week, day, hour, minute, second; am, pm
- **Some useful English words:** Ago, now, last, next; this, tomorrow, yesterday
- **Plus and minus:** + or -
- **All numbers**
- **Time zones:** For example, gmt (Greenwich Mean Time), pdt (Pacific Daylight Time), and akst (Alaska Standard Time)

You can combine the words and abbreviations in a variety of ways. The following statements are all valid:

```
$importantDate = strtotime("tomorrow");    #24 hours from now
$importantDate = strtotime("now + 24 hours");
$importantDate = strtotime("last saturday");
$importantDate = strtotime("8pm + 3 days");
$importantDate = strtotime("2 weeks ago"); # at current time
$importantDate = strtotime("next year gmt"); #1 year from now
$importantDate = strtotime("tomorrow 4am");
```

You can find differences between timestamps by using subtraction. For example, if `$importantDate` is in the past and you want to know how long ago `$importantDate` was, you can subtract it from the variable `$today` you defined earlier. For example:

```
$timeSpan = $today - $importantDate;
```

This gives you the number of seconds between the important date and today.

You can also use the following statement to find out how many hours have transpired since the important date:

```
$timeSpan =(($today - $importantDate)/60)/60;
```

Chapter 6

Storing Data in Groups by Using Arrays

In This Chapter

- Building arrays
- Assigning values to arrays
- Sorting arrays
- Using values in arrays
- Building multidimensional arrays

Arrays are complex variables that store a group of values under a single variable name. An array is useful for storing a group of related values. For example, you can store information about a car, such as model, color, and cost, in a single array named `$FordInfo`. Information in an array can be handled, accessed, and modified easily. For example, PHP has several methods for sorting the information inside an array.

In this chapter, you find out how to create, modify, copy, and use arrays.

Creating and Working with Arrays

Arrays are an important feature in PHP programming. This section describes how to create, modify, and remove arrays.

Creating arrays

To create a variable, you assign a value to it. Similarly, the simplest way to create an array is to assign a value to it. For instance, assuming that you have not referenced `$customers` at any earlier point in the script, the following statement creates an array called `$customers`:

```
$customers[1] = "Sam Smith";
```

At this point, the array named `$customers` has been created and holds only one value — Sam Smith. Next, you use the following statements:

```
$customers[2] = "Sue Jones";
$customers[3] = "Mary Huang";
```

Now, the array `$customers` contains three values: Sam Smith, Sue Jones, and Mary Huang.

An array can be viewed as a list of *key/value* pairs, stored as follows:

```
$arrayname['key1'] = value1;
$arrayname['key2'] = value2;
$arrayname['key3'] = value3;
```

and so on up to any number of elements in the array.

The key is also referred to as the *index*.

Arrays can use either numbers or strings for keys. In the `$customers` array, the keys are numbers — 1, 2, and 3. However, you can also use strings for keys. For example, the following statements create an array of state capitals:

```
$capitals['CA'] = "Sacramento";
$capitals['TX'] = "Austin";
$capitals['OR'] = "Salem";
```

Or you can use shortcuts to create arrays, rather than write separate assignment statements for each number. One shortcut uses the following statements:

```
$streets[] = "Elm St.";
$streets[] = "Oak Dr.";
$streets[] = "7th Ave.";
```

When you create an array by using this shortcut, the values are automatically assigned keys that are serial numbers, starting with the number 0. For example, consider the following statement:

```
echo "$streets[0]";
```

It sends the following output:

```
Elm St.
```

The first value in an array with a numbered index is 0, unless you deliberately set it to a different number. One common mistake when working with arrays is to think of the first number as 1, rather than 0.

An even shorter shortcut is to use the following statement:

```
$streets = array ( "Elm St.","Oak Dr.","7th Ave.");
```

This statement creates the same array as the preceding shortcut. It assigns numbers as keys, starting with 0. If you want the array to start with the number 12, instead of 0, you can use the following statement:

```
$streets = array ( 12 => "Elm St.","Oak Dr.","7th Ave.");
```

This statement creates an array as follows:

```
$streets[12] = Elm St.
$streets[13] = Oak Dr.
$streets[14] = 7th Ave.
```

You can use a similar statement to create arrays with words as keys. For example, the following statement creates the array of state capitals with an array statement, instead of using separate statements for each element of the array:

```
$capitals = array ( "CA" => "Sacramento",
                    "TX" => "Austin",
                    "OR" => "Salem" );
```

Notice the structure of this statement. PHP doesn't pay attention to the white spaces or new lines. The statement could be written as one long line. The organization of this statement is solely to make it easier for people to read. You should make your statements as clear and legible as possible. When you are troubleshooting your scripts, you will be glad you took the time to make them more people-friendly.

You can also create an array with a range of values by using the following statement:

```
$years = range(2001, 2010);
```

The resulting array looks like the following:

```
$years[0] = 2001
$years[1] = 2002
. . .
$years[8] = 2009
$years[9] = 2010
```

Similarly, you can use a statement, as follows:

```
$reverse_letters = range("z", "a");
```

This statement creates an array with 26 elements:

```
$reverse_letters[0]=z
$reverse_letters[1]=y
. . .
$reverse_letters[24]=b
$reverse_letters[25]=a
```

Viewing arrays

You can see the structure and values of any array by using one of two statements — `var_dump` or `print_r`. The `print_r()` statement, however, gives somewhat less information. To display the `$customers` array, use the following statement:

```
print_r($customers);
```

This `print_r` statement provides the following output:

```
Array
(
    [1] => Sam Smith
    [2] => Sue Jones
    [3] => Mary Huang
)
```

This output shows the key and the value for each element in the array. To get more information, use the following statement:

```
var_dump($customers);
```

This statement gives the following output:

```
array(3) {
  [1]=>
  string(9) "Sam Smith"
  [2]=>
  string(9) "Sue Jones"
  [3]=>
  string(10) "Mary Huang"
}
```

This output shows the data type of each element, such as a string of 9 characters, in addition to the key and value. An array containing the customer name and age would display as follows:

```
array(2) {
  ["name"]=>
  string(9) "Sam Smith"
  ["age"]=>
  int(12)
}
```

The integer value is identified as an integer with `int`, and the value of `age` is shown. This customer is 12 years old.

Remember, this output is sent by PHP. If you're using PHP for the Web, the output displays on the Web page with HTML, which means that it displays in one long line. To see the output on the Web in the useful format that I describe here, send HTML tags that tell the browser to display the text as received, without changing it, by using the following statements:

```
echo "<pre>";
var_dump($customers);
echo "</pre>";
```

Modifying arrays

Arrays can be changed at any time in the script, just as variables can. The individual values can be changed, elements can be added or removed, and elements can be rearranged. For example, if you have an existing array named `$capitals`, you can use the following statement to change the value of an element:

```
$capitals['TX'] = "Big Springs";
```

This statement changes the value of this element of the `$capitals` array, although the people in Austin might object to the change. Or you could use the following statement:

```
$capitals['RI'] = "Providence";
```

The statement adds a new element to the array, leaving the existing elements intact.

Suppose that your array has numbers for keys, as is the case with the following array, which is created at the beginning of a script:

```
$customers[1] = Sam Smith
$customers[2] = Sue Jones
$customers[3] = Mary Huang
```

You can use the following statement later in the script:

```
$customers[] = "Juan Lopez";
```

`$customers` now becomes an array with four elements, as follows:

```
$customers[1] = Sam Smith
$customers[2] = Sue Jones
$customers[3] = Mary Huang
$customers[4] = Juan Lopez
```

You can also copy an entire existing array into a new array with this statement:

```
$customerCopy = $customers;
```

Removing values from arrays

Sometimes you need to completely remove a value from an array. For example, suppose you have the following array:

```
$colors = array ( "red", "green", "blue", "pink", "yellow" );
```

This array has five values. Now you decide that you no longer like the color pink, so you use the following statement to try to remove pink from the array:

```
$colors[3] = "";
```

Although this statement sets `$colors[3]` to blank, it does not remove it from the array. You still have an array with five values, one of the values being an empty string. To totally remove the item from the array, you need to unset it with the following statement:

```
unset($colors[3]);
```

Now your array has only four values in it and looks as follows:

```
$colors[0] = red
$colors[1] = green
$colors[2] = blue
$colors[4] = yellow
```

Notice that the other keys did not change when element 3 was removed.

After an array has been created, it does not cease to exist unless it is deliberately removed. Removing all the values doesn't remove the array itself, just like removing all the drawers from a dresser doesn't make the dresser disappear. To remove the array itself, you can use the following statement:

```
unset($colors);
```

Sorting Arrays

One of the most useful features of arrays is that PHP can sort them for you. PHP originally stores array elements in the order in which you create them. If you display the entire array without changing the order, the elements are displayed in the order in which they were created. Often, you want to change this order. For example, you may want to display the array in alphabetical order by value or by key.

PHP can sort arrays in a variety of ways. To sort an array that has numbers as keys, use a `sort` statement as follows:

```
sort($arrayname);
```

This statement sorts arrays by the values and assigns new keys that are the appropriate numbers. The values are sorted with numbers first, uppercase letters next, and lowercase letters last. For example, consider the `$streets` array:

```
$streets[0] = "Elm St.";
$streets[1] = "Oak Dr.";
$streets[2] = "7th Ave.";
```

You enter the following `sort` statement:

```
sort($streets);
```

Now the array becomes as follows:

```
$streets[0] = "7th Ave.";
$streets[1] = "Elm St.";
$streets[2] = "Oak Dr.";
```

If you use `sort()` to sort an array with words as keys, the keys are changed to numbers, and the word keys are thrown away.

To sort arrays that have words for keys, use the `asort` statement as follows:

```
asort($capitals);
```

This statement sorts the capitals by value, but it keeps the original key for each value instead of assigning a number key. For example, consider the state capitals array created in the preceding section:

```
$capitals['CA'] = "Sacramento";
$capitals['TX'] = "Austin";
$capitals['OR'] = "Salem";
```

You use the following `asort` statement,

```
asort($capitals);
```

The array becomes as follows:

```
$capitals['TX'] = Austin
$capitals['CA'] = Sacramento
$capitals['OR'] = Salem
```

Notice that the keys stayed with the value when the elements were reordered. Now the elements are in alphabetical order, and the correct state key is still with the appropriate state capital. If the keys has been numbers, the numbers would now be in a different order. For example, suppose the original array was as follows:

```
$capitals[1] = "Sacramento";
$capitals[2] = "Austin";
$capitals[3] = "Salem";
```

After an `asort` statement, the new array would be as follows:

```
$capitals[2] = Austin
$capitals[1] = Sacramento
$capitals[3] = Salem
```

It's unlikely that you want to use `asort` on an array with numbers as a key.

You can use several other `sort` statements to sort in other ways. Table 6-1 lists all the available `sort` statements.

Table 6-1 Ways You Can Sort Arrays

Sort Statement	*What It Does*
`sort($arrayname)`	Sorts by value; assigns new numbers as the keys.
`asort($arrayname)`	Sorts by value; keeps the same key.
`rsort($arrayname)`	Sorts by value in reverse order; assigns new numbers as the keys.

Sort Statement	*What It Does*
`arsort($arrayname)`	Sorts by value in reverse order; keeps the same key.
`ksort($arrayname)`	Sorts by key.
`krsort($arrayname)`	Sorts by key in reverse order.
`usort($arrayname, functionname)`	Sorts by a function (see Chapter 8 for information on functions).
`natsort($arrayname)`	Sorts mixed string/number values in natural order. For example, given an array with values day1, day5, day11, day2, it sorts into the following order: day1, day2, day5, day11. The previous sort functions sort the array into this order: day1, day11, day2, day5.

Using Arrays in Statements

Arrays can be used in statements in the same way that variables are used in statements. This section shows the use of arrays in PHP statements.

You can retrieve any individual value in an array by accessing it directly, as in the following example:

```
$CAcapital = $capitals['CA'];
echo $CAcapital ;
```

You get the following output from these statements:

```
Sacramento
```

If you use an array element that doesn't exist in a statement, a notice is displayed. For example, suppose you use the following statement:

```
$CAcapital = $capitals['CAx'];
```

If the array `$capitals` exists, but no element has the key `CAx`, you see the following notice:

```
Notice: Undefined index: CAx in d:\testarray.php on line 9
```

A notice does not cause the script to stop. Statements after the notice will continue to execute. But because no value has been put into `$CAcapital`, any subsequent `echo` statements will echo a blank space. You can prevent the notice from being displayed by using the @ symbol:

```
@$CAcapital = $capitals['CAx'];
```

Using arrays in echo statements

You can echo an array value like this:

```
echo $capitals['TX'];
```

It displays the following:

```
Austin
```

If you include the array value in a longer `echo` statement that's enclosed by double quotes, you may need to enclose the array value name in curly braces like this:

```
echo "The capital of Texas is {$capitals['TX']}";
```

The output is as follows:

```
The capital of Texas is Austin
```

Using arrays in list statements

You can retrieve several values at once from an array with the `list` statement. The `list` statement copies values from an array into variables. Suppose you create the following array:

```
$shoeInfo = array("loafer", "black", 22.00);
```

You can display the array with the following statement:

```
print_r($shoeInfo);
```

The output is as follows:

```
Array
(
    [0] => loafer
    [1] => black
    [2] => 22
)
```

The following statements show the use of the `list` statement on the `$shoeInfo` array:

```
list($first,$second) = $shoeInfo;
echo $second," ",$first;
```

This `list` statement creates two variables named `$first` and `$second` and copies the first two values from `$shoeInfo` into the two new variables, as if you had used the following two statements:

```
$first=$shoeInfo[0];
$second=$shoeInfo[1];
```

The third value in `$shoeInfo` is not copied into a variable because the `list` statement contains only two variables. The output from the `echo` statement is as follows:

```
black loafer
```

In some cases, you may want to retrieve the key from an array element rather than the value. Suppose the following element is the first element in an array:

```
$shoeInfo['style'] = loafer;
```

The following statements retrieve the key, along with the value, and echo them:

```
$value = $shoeInfo['style'];
$key = key($shoeInfo);
echo "$key: $value";
```

The output from these statements is as follows:

```
style: loafer
```

The first statement puts `loafer` into `$value`. The second statement puts `style` into `$key`. The `key` statement gets the key of an array element. In this case, it retrieves the key from the first element because that was the current element where the pointer is located. You can get any key in the array by walking through the array. The next section explains what the pointer is and how to walk through arrays.

Walking through an Array

You will often want to do something to every value in an array. You may want to echo each value, store each value in a database, or add six to each value in the array. In technical talk, walking through each and every element in an array, in order, is called *iteration.* It is also sometimes called *traversing.* This section describes two ways to walk through an array:

- **Traversing an array manually:** Uses a pointer to move from one array value to another
- **Using `foreach`:** Automatically walks through the array, from beginning to end, one value at a time

Traversing an array manually

You can walk through an array manually by using a pointer. To do this, think of your array as a list. Imagine a pointer pointing to a value in the list. The pointer stays on a value until you move it. After you move it, it stays there until you move it again. You can move the pointer with the following instructions:

- `current($arrayname)`: Refers to the value currently under the pointer; does not move the pointer
- `next($arrayname)`: Moves the pointer to the value after the current value
- `previous($arrayname)`: Moves the pointer to the value before the current pointer location
- `end($arrayname)`: Moves the pointer to the last value in the array
- `reset($arrayname)`: Moves the pointer to the first value in the array

The following statements manually walk through an array containing state capitals:

```
$value = current ($capitals);
echo "$value<br>";
$value = next ($capitals);
echo "$value<br>";
$value = next ($capitals);
echo "$value<br>";
```

Unless you have moved the pointer previously, the pointer is located at the first element when you start walking through the array. If you think the array pointer may have been moved earlier in the script or if your output from the array seems to start somewhere in the middle, use the `reset` statement before you start walking, as follows:

```
reset($capitals);
```

Using this method to walk through an array, you need an assignment statement and an `echo` statement for every value in the array — for each of the 50 states. The output is a list of all the state capitals.

This method gives you flexibility. You can move through the array in any manner, not just one value at a time. You can move backwards, go directly to the end, skip every other value by using two consecutive `next` statements, or employ whatever method is useful. However, if you want to go through the array from beginning to end, one value at a time, PHP provides an easier method: the `foreach` statement, which does exactly what you need more efficiently. The `foreach` statement is described in the next section.

Using foreach to walk through an array

You can use `foreach` to walk through an array one value at a time and execute a block of statements by using each value in the array. The general format is as follows:

```
foreach ( $arrayname as $keyname => $valuename  )
{
   block of statements;
}
```

In this format, you need to fill in the following information:

- *arrayname:* The name of the array you are walking through.
- *keyname:* The name of the variable where you want to store the key. The *keyname* variable is optional. If you leave out `$keyname =>`, only the value is stored into `$valuename`.
- *valuename:* The name of the variable where you want to store the value.

For example, the following `foreach` statement walks through a sample array of state populations and echoes a list:

```
$state_population = array ( "CA" => 34501130,
                            "WY" => 494423,
                            "OR" => 3472867);
ksort($state_population);
foreach($state_population as $state => $population )
{
   $population = number_format($population);
   echo "$state: $population.<br>";
}
```

The preceding statements give the following Web page output:

```
CA: 34,501,130
OR: 3,472,867
WY: 494,423
```

You can use the following line in place of the foreach line in the previous statements:

```
foreach ( $state_population as $population )
```

With this statement, the key (state) is not stored in a variable. Only the populations are available for the output.

When foreach starts walking through an array, it moves the pointer to the beginning of the array. You don't need to reset an array before walking through it with foreach.

Finding Array Size

To see the structure and values of your array, you can use var_dump and print_r (described earlier in this chapter in "Viewing arrays"), but sometimes you just want to know the size of your array, rather than see everything that's in it.

You can find out the size of your array by using either the count statement or a sizeof statement. The format for these statements is as follows:

```
$n = count($arrayname);
$n = sizeof($arrayname);
```

After either of these statements, $n will contain the number of elements in the array.

Converting Arrays into Strings (And Vice Versa)

Sometimes you want to perform an operation on information, but the operation requires the information to be in a different format. For instance, you may want to display every word in a sentence on a separate line. One way to do this is to add a \n on the end of each word before you display it. You could use a foreach statement to do that easily if the sentence is in an array, rather than in a string. PHP allows you to create an array that contains one word of the sentence in each element.

You can create an array that contains the contents of a string by using a statement in the following format:

```
$arrayname = explode("s",string);
```

The first item in the parentheses (*s*) is the character to use to divide the string. The second item is the string itself. For example, the following statement creates an array that contains the characters in a string:

```
$string1 = "This:is a: new:house";
$testarray = explode(":",$string1);
print_r($testarray);
```

The `explode` statement tells PHP to split the string at each colon (`:`) and create an array containing the substrings. The output is the following:

```
Array
(
    [0] => This
    [1] => is a
    [2] =>  new
    [3] => house
)
```

`$string1` is not affected.

Conversely, you can convert an array into a string by using the following statement:

```
$resString = implode("s",$array);
```

The statement tells PHP to create a string containing all the elements in `$array`, with *s* separating the text from each array element, and store the string in `$resString`. For example, you could use the following statements:

```
$arrayIn = array( "red", "blue", "green");
$stringOut = implode(";",$arrayIn);
echo $stringOut;
```

The output string from `implode` is stored in `$stringOut`. The `implode` statement, as you might guess, doesn't affect `$arrayIn`. In general, these statements do not affect the input to the statement; they just read it. If any statement changes the input, I will point it out to you.

The following is the output of this `echo` statement:

```
red;blue;green
```

There is no space between the elements in the string because no space was specified in the `implode` statement. Using a space in *s*, as in the following `implode` statement, puts spaces into the resulting string:

```
$stringOut = implode("; ",$arrayIn);
```

With this statement, the output is as follows:

```
red; blue; green
```

Converting Variables into Arrays (And Vice Versa)

Sometimes you want the information in an array stored in variables that you can use in PHP statements. Or you need variables converted to array elements. For example, you might want to perform the same operation on a bunch of variables, such as add 1 to each variable value. If you convert the variables into elements of an array, you can use one `foreach` statement to access the variable values one at a time, rather than write a bunch of statements to access each variable separately.

Using the `extract` statement, you can retrieve all the values from an array, and insert each value into a variable, by using the key for the variable name. In other words, each array value is copied into a variable named for the key. For example, the following statements get all the information from an array and echo it:

```
$testarray = array( "pink"=>"carnation", "red"=>"rose");
extract($testarray);
echo "My favorite red flower is a $red.\n";
echo "My favorite pink flower is a $pink.";
```

The output for these statements is the following:

```
My favorite red flower is a rose.
My favorite pink flower is a carnation.
```

Conversely, you can also convert a group of simple variables into an array by using a `compact` statement that copies the value from each specified variable name into an array element. The use of the `compact` statement is, shown in the following statements:

```
$color1 = "red";
$color2 = "blue";
$a = "purple";
$b = "orange";
$arrayIn = array("a","b");
$arrayOut = compact("color1","color2",$arrayIn);
```

The result is the following array:

```
$arrayOut[color1] = red
$arrayOut[color2] = blue
$arrayOut[a] = purple
$arrayOut[b] = orange
```

As you can see, the names of the variables are used as the keys.

Notice that two different methods are used in the compact statement to specify the variables that make up the array:

- **First method:** You can use the variable names directly, as strings. The two variables color1 and color2 in the example show this method.
- **Second method:** You use an array that contains the names of the variables. In the previous code, $arrayIn contains the variable names: a and b. Then in the compact statement, the array name is used to add the variables to the array.

You can use either method. If you have only a few variables to compact into an array, the first method of just using the variable names is probably fine. However, if you have a lot of variables to include, you may prefer putting the names into an array first, and then using the array in the compact statement.

Splitting and Merging Arrays

You often need to put arrays together or take them apart. For example, suppose you have two classes of students and you have two arrays, each of which stores the names of the students in one class. If the two classes were to merge, you would want to merge the two arrays containing the student names.

You can split an array by creating a new array that contains a subset of an existing array. You can do this by using a statement of the following general format:

```
$subArray = array_slice($arrayname,n1,n2);
```

The *n1* in the statement is the sequence number of the element where the new array should start, such as 0 for the first element in the array or 1 for the second element. The *n2* is the length of the new array. For example, consider the following statements:

```
$testarray = array( "red", "green", "blue","pink");
$subArray = array_slice($testarray,1,2);
```

The new array, $subArray, will contain the following:

```
[0] => green
[1] => blue
```

It starts with element 1 of $testarray and takes 2 elements.

Unless you specify otherwise, arrays begin with 0, not 1. Therefore, element 1 of $testarray is green. Red is element 0.

Conversely, you can merge two or more arrays together by using the following statement:

```
$bigArray = array_merge($array1,$array2,...);
```

For example, you might use the following statements to merge arrays:

```
$array1 = array("red","blue");
$array2 = array("green","yellow");
$bigArray = array_merge($array1,$array2);
```

After the statement, $bigArray is the following array:

```
$bigArray[0] = red
$bigArray[1] = blue
$bigArray[2] = green
$bigArray[3] = yellow
```

You can merge arrays with keys that are words, rather than numbers, as well. However, if the keys are the same for any of the elements, the later element with the same key word will overwrite the first element of the same key. For example, suppose you merge the following arrays:

```
$array1 = array("color1"=>"red","color2"=>"blue");
$array2 = array("color1"=>"green","color3"=>"yellow");
$bigArray = array_merge($array1,$array2);
```

The output array is as follows:

```
$bigArray[color1] = green
$bigArray[color2] = blue
$bigArray[color3] = yellow
```

If you need to merge arrays that have identical keys, you can use the statement array_merge_recursive rather than array_merge. The array_merge_recursive statement creates a multidimensional array when keys are identical, instead of overwriting the value as array_merge does. Multidimensional arrays are explained in the section, "Multidimensional Arrays," later in this chapter.

Comparing Arrays

You may need to know whether two arrays are the same. You can identify the elements that are different or the elements that are the same. To find out which elements are different, use the following statement:

```
$diffArray = array_diff($array1,$array2,...);
```

After this statement, `$diffArray` contains the elements from `$array1` that are not present in any of the other listed arrays. The elements in the result array will have the same keys. For example, you can use the following statements:

```
$array1 = array( "a"=>"apple", "b"=>"orange", "c"=>"banana");
$array2 = array( "prune", "orange", "banana" );
$diffArray = array_diff($array1,$array2);
```

After this code, `$diffArray` looks like this:

```
$diffArray[a] = apple;
```

The element `apple` is in the array because `apple` is in `$array1` but not in `$array2`.

The order in which you list the arrays to be compared makes a difference. For example, if you used the following statement, instead of the preceding one, you'd get a different output:

```
$diffArray = array_diff($array2,$array1);
```

After this statement, `$diffArray` looks like the following:

```
$diffArray[0] = prune;
```

Because `$array2` is listed first in this statement, the resulting difference array contains only `prune` because `prune` is in `$array2`, listed first, but not in `$array1`, listed second.

If you want to find array elements that differ in either the value or the key, you can use the following statement:

```
$diffArray = array_diff_assoc($array1,$array2);
```

Using the same `$array1` and `$array2` as the previous examples, the resulting array would look like this:

```
$diffArray[a] = apple
$diffArray[b] = orange
$diffArray[c] = banana
```

In this case, none of the elements in `$array1` appear in `$array2` because the keys are all different.

You can create an array that contains the elements that are the same, rather than different, in two or more arrays by using the following statement:

```
$simArray = array_intersect($array1,$array2,. . .);
```

For example, using the same arrays, you could use the following statement:

```
$simArray = array_intersect($array1,$array2);
```

The results array would look like this:

```
$simArray[b] = orange
$simArray[c] = banana
```

This `array_intersect` statement adds an element to the new array for any values that are in both the arrays. If you want both the value and the key to be the same, use the following statement:

```
$simArray = array_intersect_assoc($array1,$array2);
```

This statement requires both the value and the key to be identical before adding an element to the array. Using the same arrays, `$simArray` is empty after the statement, because even though two of the values are the same, none of the keys are the same.

Working with Other Array Operations

The following sections describe these miscellaneous operations on arrays:

- Adding the values of an array
- Removing duplicate items from an array
- Exchanging keys and values in an array

Summing arrays

To add all the values in an array, use the following statement:

```
$sum = array_sum($array);
```

For example, you can use the following statements;

```
$arrayAdd = array(3,3,3);
$sum = array_sum($arrayAdd);
echo $sum;
```

The output is 9.

Of course, you are only going to add elements in an array of numbers. As mentioned in Chapter 5, PHP converts strings to 0 if you try to add them.

Removing duplicate items

You sometimes need to remove duplicate elements from an array. For example, if you want to print a list of customer names from the elements of an array, you probably want each name listed only once. You can do so with the following statements:

```
$names = array( "Mary", "Sally", "Sally","Sam");
$names2 = array_unique($names);
```

The array `$names2` looks like this:

```
$names2[0] => Mary
$names2[1] => Sally
$names2[3] => Sam
```

As you can see, the duplicate element and its key are not in the resulting array.

Exchanging keys and values

You can exchange values and keys in an array. For example, suppose you have the following array:

```
$testarray['rose'] = red
$testarray['iris'] = purple
```

To exchange the values, use the following statement:

```
$arrayFlipped = array_flip($testarray);
```

The array `$arrayFlipped` looks like this:

```
$testarray['red'] = rose
$testarray['purple'] = iris
```

Multidimensional Arrays

In the earlier sections of this chapter, I describe arrays that are a single list of key/value pairs. However, on some occasions, you may want to store values with more than one key. For example, suppose you want to store the following food prices together in one variable:

- onion, 0.50
- apple, 2.50
- orange, 2.00
- bacon, 3.50
- potato, 1.00
- ham, 5.00

You can store these products in an array as follows:

```
$foodPrices['onion'] = 0.50;
$foodPrices['apple'] = 2.50;
$foodPrices['orange'] = 2.00;
$foodPrices['bacon'] = 3.50;
$foodPrices['potato'] = 1.00;
$foodPrices['ham'] = 5.00;
```

Your script can easily look through this array whenever it needs to know the price of an item. But suppose you have 3,000 products. Your script would need to look through 3,000 products to find the one with *onion* or *ham* as the key.

Notice that the list of foods and prices includes a variety of food that can be classified into three groups: vegetable, fruit, and meat. If you classify the products, then the script needs to look through only one classification to find the correct price. Classifying the products is much more efficient. You can classify the products by putting the costs in a multidimensional array as follows:

```
$foodPrices['vegetable']['onion'] = 0.50;
$foodPrices['vegetable']['potato'] = 1.00;
$foodPrices['fruit']['apple'] = 2.50;
$foodPrices['fruit']['orange'] = 2.00;
$foodPrices['meat']['bacon'] = 3.50;
$foodPrices['meat']['ham'] = 5.00;
```

This kind of array is called a *multidimensional* array because it's like an array of arrays. Figure 6-1 shows the structure of `$foodPrices` as an array of arrays. The figure shows that `$foodPrices` has three key/value pairs. The value for each key — vegetable, fruit, and meat — is an array with two key/value pairs. For example, the value for the key `meat` is an array with the two key/value pairs: *bacon/3.50* and *ham/5.00*.

$foodPrices	key	value	
		key	*value*
	vegetable	onion	0.50
		potato	1.00
	fruit	orange	2.00
		apple	2.50
	meat	bacon	3.50
		ham	5.00

Figure 6-1: The structure of `$foodPrices`, an array of arrays.

`$foodPrices` is a two-dimensional array. PHP can also understand multidimensional arrays that are four, five, six, or more levels deep. However, my head starts to hurt if I try to comprehend an array that is more than three levels deep. The possibility of confusion increases as the number of dimensions increases.

Creating multidimensional arrays

You can create multidimensional arrays in the same ways you create one-dimensional arrays. You can create them with a series of direct statements, as follows:

```
$foodPrices['vegetable']['potato'] = 1.00;
$foodPrices['fruit']['apple'] = 2.50;
```

You can also use a shortcut and allow PHP to choose the keys, as follows:

```
transportation['car'][] = "Ford";
transportation['car'][] = "Jeep";
```

PHP will assign numbers as keys so that the array looks like the following:

```
transportation[car][0] = Ford;
transportation[car][1] = Jeep;
```

You can also create a multidimensional array by using the array statement, as follows:

```
$foodPrices = array(
          "vegetable"=>array("potato"=>1.00,"onion"=>.50),
          "fruit"=>array("apple"=>2.50,"orange"=>2.00));
```

Notice that `foodPrices` is an array, created by the first array statement. The first array statement sets two elements — vegetable and fruit. The values for the two elements are themselves set by array statements, resulting in an array of arrays. This statement creates the following multidimensional array:

```
$foodPrices[vegetable][potato] = 1.00
$foodPrices[vegetable][onion] = .50
$foodPrices[fruit][apple] = 2.50
$foodPrices[fruit][orange] = 2.00
```

Viewing multidimensional arrays

You can view a multidimensional array in the same ways you can view any array — by using the `print_r` or the `var_dump` statements. The output of the `var_dump` statement is shown here:

```
array(2) {
  ["vegetable"]=>
  array(2) {
    ["potato"]=>
    float(1)
    ["onion"]=>
    float(0.5)
  }
  ["fruit"]=>
  array(2) {
    ["apple"]=>
    float(2.5)
    ["orange"]=>
    float(2)
  }
}
```

The first line identifies the first array and says it has two elements. The first element, with the key `vegetable`, contains an array of two elements with the keys `potato` with a value of 1 of type float, and the second element with the key `onion` and a value of 0.5 of type float. The second element of the main array, with the key `fruit`, also contains an array with two elements.

Using multidimensional arrays in statements

You can get values from a multidimensional array by using the same procedures that you use with a one-dimensional array. For example, you can access a value directly with this statement:

```
$hamPrice = $foodPrices['meat']['ham'];
```

You can also echo the value:

```
echo $foodPrices['meat']['ham'];
```

However, if you combine the value within double quotes, you need to use curly braces to enclose the variable name. The $ that begins the variable name must follow the { immediately, without a space, as follows:

```
echo "The price of ham is \${$foodPrices['meat']['ham']}";
```

Notice the backslash (\) in front of the first dollar sign ($). The backslash tells PHP that $ is a literal dollar sign, not the beginning of a variable name. The output is

```
The price of ham is $5
```

Earlier in this chapter, I describe several statements that convert strings to arrays (and vice versa) and convert arrays to variables (and vice versa) and statements for other operations on arrays. Most of the statements don't make sense with multidimensional arrays and won't work correctly. However, remember that a multidimensional array is an array of arrays. Therefore, you can use one of the elements of the multidimensional array (which is an array itself) in these statements. For instance, the `implode` statement described earlier in this chapter converts an array into a string. You can't use the `implode` statement with a multidimensional array because its values are arrays, not strings. However, you can use any one of the elements in the `implode` statements, as follows:

```
$resString = implode(": ",$foodPrices['vegetable']);
```

This statement puts the value for each element of the `vegetable` array into the string, separating them by :. When you echo `$resString`, you see the following output:

```
1: 0.5
```

The output is the value of potato (1) and the value of onion (0.5). The two values are separated by a semicolon and a space, as specified in the `implode` statement.

Walking through a multidimensional array

You can walk through a multidimensional array by using `foreach` statements (described in the section "Walking through an Array," earlier in this chapter). Because a two-dimensional array, such as `$foodPrices`, contains two arrays, it takes two `foreach` statements to walk through it. One `foreach` statement is inside the other `foreach` statement. (Putting statements inside other statements is called *nesting*.)

The following statements echo the values from the multidimensional array:

```
foreach ( $foodPrices as $category )
{
   foreach ( $category as $food => $price )
   {
     $f_price = sprintf("%01.2f", $price);
     echo "$food: \$$f_price \n";
   }
}
```

The output is the following:

```
onion: $0.50
potato: $1.00
apple: $2.50
orange: $2.00
bacon: $3.50
ham: $5.00
```

Here is how PHP interprets these `foreach` statements:

1. The first key/value pair in the `$foodPrices` array is retrieved, and the value is stored in the variable `$category`. (The value is an array.)
2. The first key/value pair in the `$category` array is retrieved. The key is stored in `$food`, and the value is stored in `$price`.
3. The value in `$price` is formatted into the correct format for money.
4. One row for the product and its price is echoed.
5. The next key/value pair in the `$category` array is reached.
6. The price is formatted, and the next row for the food and its price is echoed.
7. Because there are no more key/value pairs in `$category`, the inner `foreach` statement ends.
8. The next key/value pair in the outer `foreach` statement is reached. The next value is put in `$category`, which is an array.
9. The procedure in Steps 1 through 8 is repeated until the last key/value pair in the last `$category` array is reached. The inner `foreach` statement ends. The outer `foreach` statement ends.

In other words, the outer `foreach` starts with the first key/value pair in the array. The key is `vegetable`, and the value of this pair is an array that is put into the variable `$category`. The inner `foreach` then walks through the array in `$category`. When it reaches the last key/value pair in `$category`, it ends. The script is then back in the outer loop, which goes on to the second key/value pair . . . and so on until the outer `foreach` reaches the end of the array.

Built-in PHP Arrays

PHP has several built-in arrays that you can use when writing PHP scripts. Different types of information are stored in different arrays. For example, information about your server (such as headers, paths, and script locations) is stored in an array called `$_SERVER`. When you want to display the name of the current script that is running, it's available in the `$_SERVER` built-in array in `$_SERVER['PHP_SELF']`.

Using superglobal arrays

Currently, two sets of built-in arrays contain the same information. One set of arrays, introduced in PHP 4.1.0, are called *superglobals* or *autoglobals* because they can be used anywhere, even inside a function. (Functions and the use of variables inside functions are explained in Chapter 8.) The older arrays, with long names such as `$HTTP_SERVER_VARS`, must be made global before they can be used in an array, as explained in Chapter 8. Unless you're using an old version of PHP, use the newer arrays, those whose names begin with an underscore (_). The older arrays should be used only when you're forced to use a version of PHP older than PHP 4.1.0.

A new `php.ini` setting introduced in PHP 5 allows you to prevent PHP from automatically creating the older, long arrays. It's very unlikely that you will need to use them, unless you're using some old scripts containing the long variables. The following line in `php.ini` controls this setting:

```
register_long_arrays = On
```

At the current time, this setting is `On` by default. Unless you're running old scripts that need the old arrays, you should change the setting to `Off` so that PHP doesn't do this extra work.

Although the setting is currently `On` by default, that could change. The default setting might change to `Off` in a future version. If you're using some old scripts and getting errors on lines containing the long arrays, such as `$HTTP_GET_VARS`, check your `php.ini` setting for long arrays. It might be `Off`, and the long arrays needed by the older script are not being created at all.

The built-in arrays are listed in Table 6-2, along with a short description. The use of specific arrays is described in detail in this book where the related subjects are described. For example, the built-in arrays that contain form variables are discussed in Chapter 10 when I discuss the use of forms.

Table 6-2 Handy Built-in Arrays

Array	*Description*
`$GLOBALS`	Contains all the global variables. For example, if you use the statement, `$testvar = 1`, you can then access the variable as `$GLOBALS ['testvar']`.
`$ _POST`	Contains all the variables contained in a form if the form uses `method="post"`.
`$HTTP_POST_VARS`	Same as `$ _POST`.
`$ _GET`	Contains all the variables passed from a previous page as part of the URL. This includes variables passed in a form using `method="get"`.
`$HTTP_GET_VARS`	Same as `$ _GET`.
`$ _COOKIE`	Contains all the cookie variables.
`$HTTP_COOKIE_VARS`	Same as `$ _COOKIE`.
`$ _SESSION`	Contains all the session variables.
`$HTTP_SESSION_VARS`	Same as `$ _SESSION`.
`$_REQUEST`	Contains all the variables together that are in `$_POST`, `$_GET`, and `$_SESSION`.
`$_FILES`	Contains the names of files that have been uploaded.
`$HTTP_FILES_VARS`	Same as `$_FILES`.
`$_SERVER`	Contains information about your server. Because your Web server provides the information, the information that's available depends on what server you're using.
`$HTTP_SERVER_VARS`	Same as `$_SERVER`.
`$_ENV`	Contains information provided by your operating system, such as the operating system name, the system drive, and the path to your temp directory. This info varies depending on your operating system.
`$HTTP_ENV_VARS`	Same as `$_ENV`.

Using $_SERVER and $_ENV

The `$_SERVER` and `$_ENV` arrays contain different information, depending on the server and operating system you're using. You can see what information is in the arrays for your particular server and operating system by using the following statements:

```
foreach($_SERVER as $key =>$value)
{
   echo "Key=$key, Value=$value\n";
}
```

The output includes such lines as the following:

```
Key=DOCUMENT_ROOT, Value=c:/program files/apache
          group/apache/htdocs
Key=PHP_SELF, Value=/test.php
```

The `DOCUMENT_ROOT` element shows the path to the directory where Apache expects to find the Web page files.

The `PHP_SELF` element shows the file that contains the script that is currently running.

You can see the information in the `$_ENV` array by using the `phpinfo()` statement with a `16` to specify the environmental variables, as follows:

```
phpinfo(16);
```

Built-in arrays are available only if `track-vars` is enabled. As of PHP 4.0.3, `track-vars` is always enabled, unless the PHP administrator deliberately turns `track-vars` off when installing PHP. It's rare that `track-vars` would be turned off. If the built-in arrays don't seem to be available, check with `phpinfo()` to make sure that `track-vars` is turned on. If it's turned off, PHP has to be reinstalled.

Using $argv and $argc

Sometimes you want to pass information into a script from the outside. One way to do this is to pass the information to the script on the command line when you start the script. You rarely want to do this when using PHP for the Web, but you may want to do this when running PHP CLI from the command line. For example, suppose you write a script that can add any two numbers together and you want to pass the two numbers into the script when you start it. You can give PHP the two numbers you want it to add together when you start the script, on the command line, as follows:

```
php add.php 2 3
```

In this statement, the script is named `add.php`, and `2` and `3` are the numbers you want the script to add together. These numbers are available inside the script in an array called `$argv`. This array contains all the information on the command line, as follows:

```
$argv[0]=add.php
$argv[1]=2
$argv[2]=3
```

So, `$argv` always contains at least one element — the script name.

Then, in your script, you can use the following statements:

```
$sum = $argv[1] + $argv[2];
echo $sum;
```

The output is the following:

```
5
```

Another variable is also available called `$argc`. This variable stores the number of elements in `$argv`. Thus, `$argc` always equals at least 1, which is the name of the script. In the preceding example, `$argc` equals 3.

Part III
Basic PHP Programming

"I can't really explain it, but every time I animate someone swinging a golf club, a little divot of code comes up missing on the home page."

In this part . . .

In this part, you find out how to write complete PHP scripts. You discover how to combine simple statements into a finished script. You find out about complex statements that allow you to write scripts that perform complex tasks. You see the usefulness of reusing code and find out how to write code that can be reused. When you finish this part, you will know everything you need to know to write useful and complex PHP scripts.

Chapter 7

Controlling the Flow of the Script

In This Chapter

- Changing the order in which statements are executed
- Setting up conditions
- Joining simple conditions to make complex conditions
- Using conditions in conditional statements and loops
- Writing if statements
- Building and using loops for repeated statements
- Breaking out of loops

PHP scripts are a series of instructions in a file. PHP begins at the top of the file and executes each instruction, in order, as it comes to it. However, some scripts need to be more complicated. You may want your script to display one page to new customers and a different page to existing customers. Or you may need to display a list of phone numbers by executing a single echo statement repeatedly, once for each phone number. This chapter describes how to change the order in which simple statements are executed by using complex statements such as conditional statements or loops.

Changing the Order of Statement Execution

Simple statements in PHP are executed one after another from the beginning of the script to the end. For example, the following statements in a script are executed in order:

```
$a = "Good Morning";
echo $a;
$a = "Good Afternoon";
echo $a;
```

To change the order of execution of these statements, you have to change the order of the statements themselves, as follows:

```
$a = "Good Afternoon";
echo $a;
$a = "Good Morning";
echo $a;
```

However, suppose you want to display the appropriate greeting for the time of day. You want to echo `Good Morning` if it's before noon, and you want to echo `Good Afternoon` if it's after noon. In other words, you want to do the following:

```
if (time is before noon)
{
    $a = Good Morning;
    echo $a;
}
or else if (time is after noon)
{
    $a = Good Afternoon;
    echo $a;
}
```

To display the appropriate greeting, you need a complex statement that tests the condition of time. PHP provides two types of complex statements that enable you to perform tasks like this — tasks that change the order in which statements are executed:

- **Conditional statements:** Sometimes you need to set up statements that execute only when certain conditions are met. For example, you may want to provide your catalog only to customers who have paid their bills and not to customers who owe you money. This type of statement is called a *conditional statement.* The PHP conditional statements are the `if` statement and the `switch` statement.
- **Looping statements:** Frequently you need to set up a block of statements that is repeated. For example, you may want to send an e-mail message to all your customers. To do that, you can use two statements: one that gets the customer's e-mail address from the database and one that sends the customer an e-mail message. You would need to repeat these two statements for every customer in the database. The feature that enables you to execute statements repeatedly is called a *loop.* Three types of loops are `for` loops, `while` loops, and `do..while` loops.

Both types of complex statements execute a block of statements based on a condition. That is, if a condition is true, the block of statements executes. In conditional statements, the block of statements executes once. For example, if the time is after noon, the script echoes Good Afternoon. In loops, the block of statements executes repeatedly, until the condition is no longer true. For example, if another customer in the database has not yet received an e-mail message, send that person one. The loop repeats this process as long as there is another customer who has not received an e-mail.

Setting Up Conditions

Conditions are expressions that PHP tests or evaluates to see whether they are true or false. Conditions are used in complex statements to determine whether or not a block of simple statements should be executed. To set up conditions, you compare values. Some questions you may ask in comparing values for conditions are as follows:

- **Are two values equal?** Is Sally's last name the same as Bobby's last name? Or, is Nick 15 years old? (Does Nick's age equal 15?)
- **Is one value larger or smaller than another?** Is Nick younger than Bobby? Or, did Sally's house cost more than a million dollars?
- **Does a string match a pattern?** Does Bobby's name begin with an *S?* Does the zip code have five numeric characters?

You can also set up conditions in which you ask two or more questions. For example, you may ask: Is Nick older than Bobby and is Nick younger than Sally? Or you may ask: Is today Sunday and is today sunny? Or you may ask: Is today Sunday or is today Monday?

Using comparison operators

PHP offers several comparison operators that you can use to compare values. Table 7-1 shows these comparison operators.

Table 7-1 Comparison Operators

Operator	*What It Means*
==	Are the two values equal in value?
===	Are the two values equal in both value *and* data type?
>	Is the first value larger than the second value?
>=	Is the first value larger than or equal to the second value?
<	Is the first value smaller than the second value?
<=	Is the first value smaller than or equal to the second value?
!=, <>	Are the two values not equal to each other in value?
!==	Are the two values not equal to each other in either value or data type?

You can compare both numbers and strings. Strings are compared alphabetically, with all uppercase characters coming before any lowercase characters. For example, `SS` comes before `Sa`. Punctuation characters also have an order, and one character can be found to be larger than another character. However, comparing a comma to a period doesn't have much practical value.

Strings are compared based on their ASCII code. In the ASCII character set, each character is assigned an ASCII code that corresponds to a number between 0 and 127. When strings are compared, they are compared based on this code. For example, the number that represents the comma is 44. The period corresponds to 46. Therefore, if a period and a comma are compared, the period is seen as larger.

The following are some valid comparisons that PHP can test to determine whether they are true:

- `$a == $b`
- `$age != 21`
- `$ageNick < $ageBobby`
- `$house_price >= 1000000`

The comparison operator that asks whether two values are equal consists of two equal signs (==). One of the most common mistakes is to use a single equal sign for a comparison. A single equal sign puts the value into the variable. Thus, a statement like `if ($weather = "raining")` would set `$weather` to `raining` rather than check whether it already equaled raining, and would always be true.

PHP tests comparisons by evaluating them and returning a Boolean value, either `TRUE` or `FALSE`. For example, look at the following comparison:

```
$a == $b
```

If `$a=1` and `$b=1`, the comparison returns `TRUE`. If `$a =1` and `$b =2`, the comparison returns `FALSE`.

If you write a negative (by using `!`), the negative condition is true. Look at the following comparison:

```
$age != 21
```

The condition is that `$age` does not equal `21`. That's the condition that is being tested. Therefore, if `$age = 20`, the comparison is `TRUE`.

Checking variable content

Sometimes you just need to know whether a variable exists or what type of data is in the variable. Here are some common ways to test variables:

```
isset($varname)     # True if variable is set, even if
                      nothing is stored in it.
empty($varname)     # True if value is 0 or is a string with
                      no characters in it or is not set.
```

You can also test what type of data is in the variable. For example, to see if the value is an integer, you can use the following:

```
is_int($number)
```

The comparison is `TRUE` if the value in `$number` is an integer. Some other tests provided by PHP are as follows:

- `is_array($var2)`: Checks to see if `$var2` is an array
- `is_float($number)`: Checks to see if `$number` is a floating point number
- `is_null($var1)`: Checks to see if `$var1` is equal to 0
- `is_numeric($string)`: Checks to see if `$string` is a numeric string
- `is_string($string)`: Checks to see if `$string` is a string

You can test for a negative, as well, by using an exclamation point (`!`) in front of the expression. For example, the following statement returns `TRUE` if the variable does not exist at all:

```
!isset($varname)
```

Pattern matching with regular expressions

Sometimes you need to compare character strings to see whether they fit certain characteristics, rather than to see whether they match exact values. For example, you may want to identify strings that begin with *S* or strings that have numbers in them. For this type of comparison, you compare the string to a pattern. These patterns are called *regular expressions.*

You have probably used some form of pattern matching in the past. When you use an asterisk (*) as a wild card when searching for files (`dir ex*.doc` or `ls ex*.txt`, for example), you're pattern matching. For example, `ex*.txt` is a pattern. Any string that begins with `ex` and ends with the string `.txt`, with any characters in between the `ex` and the `.txt`, matches the pattern. The strings `exam.txt`, `ex33.txt`, and `ex3x4.txt` all match the pattern. Using regular expressions is just a more complicated variation of using wild cards.

One common use for pattern matching is to check the input from a Web page form. If the information input doesn't match a specific pattern, it may not be something you want to store in your database. For example, if the user types a zip code into your form, you know the format needs to be five numbers or a zip + 4. So, you can check the input to see if it fits the pattern. If it doesn't, you know it's not a valid zip code, and you can ask the user to type in the correct information.

Using special characters in patterns

Patterns consist of literal characters and special characters. Literal characters are normal characters, with no special meaning. An *e* is an *e,* for example, with no meaning other than that it's one of 26 letters in the alphabet. Special characters, on the other hand, have special meaning in the pattern, such as the asterisk (*) when used as a wild card. Table 7-2 shows the special characters that you can use in patterns.

Table 7-2 Special Characters Used in Patterns

Character	*Meaning*	*Example*	*Matches*	*Does Not Match*
^	Beginning of line	`^e`	`exam`	`math exam`
$	End of line	`m$`	`exam`	`exams`
.	Any single character	`..`	`up, do` Longer words match because they contain a string of two characters.	`A, 2`
?	The preceding character is optional	`ger?m`	`germ, gem`	`geam`
( )	Groups literal characters into a string that must be matched exactly	`g(er)m`	`germ`	`Gem, grem`
[ ]	Encloses a set of optional literal characters	`g[er]m`	`gem, grm`	`germ, gel`

Character	Meaning	Example	Matches	Does Not Match
`[^]`	Encloses a set of nonmatching optional characters	`g[^er]m`	`gym`, `gum`	`gem`, grem, `germ`
-	Represents all the characters between two characters (a range of possible characters)	`g[a-c]m`	`gam`, `gbm`, `gcm gal`	`gdm`, `gxm`,
+	One or more of the preceding items	`bldg [1-3]+`	`bldg111`, `bldg132`	`bldg`, `bldg555`
*	Zero or more of the preceding items	`ge*m`	`gm`, `geeem`	`germ`, `grm`
`{n}`	Repeat *n* times	`ge{5}m`	`geeeeem`	`geeeem`, `geeeeeem`
`{n1,n2}`	Specifies a range of repetitions of the preceding character(s).	`a{2,5}`	`aa`, `aaa`, `aaaa`, `145aaaaa`	`1`, `a3`
\	The following character is literal	`g\*m`	`g*m`	`gem`, `germ`
`( | | )`	A set of alternate strings	`(Sam|Sally)`	`Samuel Go Sally`	`Sarah`, `Salmon`

Considering some example patterns

Literal and special characters are combined to make patterns, sometimes long complicated patterns. A string is compared to the pattern, and if it matches, the comparison is true. Some example patterns follow, with a breakdown of the pattern and some sample matching and non-matching strings:

Example 1

```
^[A-Za-z].*
```

This pattern defines strings that begin with a letter and have two parts:

- `^[A-Za-z]` The first part of the pattern dictates that the beginning of the string must be a letter (either uppercase or lowercase).
- `.*` The second part of the pattern tells PHP the string of characters can be one or more characters long.

The expression ^[A-Za-z].* matches the following strings: play it again, Sam and I.

The expression ^[A-Za-z].* does not match the following strings: 123 and ?.

Example 2

```
Dear (Kim|Rikki)
```

This pattern defines two alternate strings and has two parts:

- Dear The first part of the pattern is just literal characters.
- (Kim|Rikki) The second part defines either Kim or Rikki as matching strings.

The expression Dear (Kim|Rikki) matches the following strings: Dear Kim and My Dear Rikki.

The expression Dear (Kim|Rikki) does not match the following strings: Dear Bobby and Kim.

Example 3

```
^[0-9]{5}(\-[0-9]{4})?$
```

This pattern defines any zip code and has several parts:

- ^[0-9]{5} The first part of the pattern describes any string of five numbers.
- \- The slash indicates that the hyphen is a literal.
- [0-9]{4} This part of the pattern tells PHP that the next characters should be a string of numbers consisting of four characters.
- ( )? These characters group the last two parts of the pattern and make them optional.
- $ The dollar sign dictates that this string should end (no characters are allowed after the pattern).

The expression ^[0-9]{5}(\-[0-9]{4})?$ matches the following strings: 90001 and 90002-4323.

The expression ^[0-9]{5}(\-[0-9]{4})?$ does not match the following strings: 9001 and 12-4321.

Example 4

```
^.+@.+\.com$
```

This pattern defines any string with @ embedded that ends in `.com`. In other words, it defines an e-mail address. This expression has several parts:

- `^.+` The first part of the pattern describes any string of one or more characters that precedes the @.
- @ This is a literal @ (at sign). @ is not a special character and does not need to be preceded by a \.
- `.+` This is any string of one or more characters.
- `\.` The slash indicates that PHP should look for a literal dot.
- `com$` This defines the literal string `com` at the end of the string, and the `$` marks the end of the string.

The expression `^.+@.+\.com$` matches the following strings: `you@yourcompany.com` and `johndoe@somedomain.com`.

The expression `^.+@.+\.com$` does not match the following strings: `you@yourcompany.net`, `you@.com`, and `@you.com`.

Comparing strings to patterns

You can compare a string to a pattern by using `ereg`. The general format is as follows:

```
ereg("pattern",value);
```

For example, to check the name that a user typed in a form, compare the name (stored in the variable `$name`) to a pattern as follows:

```
ereg("^[A-Za-z' -]+$",$name)
```

The pattern in this statement does the following:

- Uses `^` and `$` to signify the beginning and end of the string. That means that all the characters in the string must match the pattern.
- Encloses all the literal characters that are allowed in the string in `[ ]`. No other characters are allowed. The allowed characters are upper and lower case letters, an apostrophe ('), a blank space, and a hyphen (-).

  You can specify a range of characters using a hyphen within the `[ ]`. When you do that, as in A-Z above, the hyphen does not represent a literal character. Since you want the hyphen included as a literal character that is allowed in your string, you need to add a hyphen that is not between any two other characters. In this case, the hyphen is included at the end of the list of literal characters,
- Follows the list of literal characters in the `[ ]` with a +. The plus sign means that the string can contain any number of the characters inside the `[ ]`, but must contain at least one character.

Joining multiple comparisons

Often you need to ask more than one question to determine your condition. For example, suppose your company offers catalogs for different products in different languages. You need to know which type of product catalog the customer wants to see *and* which language he or she needs to see it in. This requires you to join comparisons, which have the following the general format:

```
comparison1 and|or|xor comparison2 and|or|xor comparison3
            and|or|xor ...
```

Comparisons are connected by one of the following three words:

- and: Both comparisons are true.
- or: One of the comparisons or both of the comparisons are true.
- xor: One of the comparisons is true but not both of the comparisons.

Table 7-3 shows some examples of multiple comparisons.

Table 7-3 Multiple Comparisons

Condition	*Is True If . . .*
`$ageBobby == 21 or $ageBobby == 22`	Bobby is 21 or 22 years of age.
`$ageSally > 29 and $state =="OR"`	Sally is older than 29 *and* lives in Oregon.
`$ageSally > 29 or $state == "OR"`	Sally is older than 29 *or* lives in Oregon *or both.*
`$city == "Reno" xor $state == "OR"`	The city is Reno *or* the state is Oregon, but *not both.*
`$name != "Sam" and $age < 13`	The name is anything except Sam *and* age is under 13 years of age.

You can string together as many comparisons as necessary. The comparisons using and are tested first, the comparisons using xor are tested next, and the comparisons using or are tested last. For example, the following condition includes three comparisons:

```
$resCity == "Reno" or $resState == "NV" and $name == "Sally"
```

If the customer's name is Sally and she lives in NV, this statement is true. The statement is also true if she lives in Reno, regardless of what her name is. This condition is not true if she lives in NV but her name is not Sally. You get these results because the script checks the condition in the following order:

1. The `and` is compared.

   The script checks `$resState` to see if it equals `NV` and checks `$name` to see if it equals `Sally`. If both match, the condition is true, and the script does not need to check `or`. If only one or neither of the variables equal the designated value, the testing continues.

2. The `or` is compared.

   The script checks `$resCity` to see if it equals `Reno`. If it does, the condition is true. If it doesn't, the condition is false.

You can change the order in which comparisons are made by using parentheses. The connecting word inside the parentheses is evaluated first. For example, you can rewrite the previous statement with parentheses as follows:

```
($resCity == "Reno or $resState == "NV") and $name == "Sally"
```

The parentheses change the order in which the conditions are checked. Now the `or` is checked first because it is inside the parentheses. This condition statement is true if the customer's name is Sally and she lives in either Reno or NV. You get these results because the script checks the condition as follows:

1. The `or` is compared.

   The script checks to see if `$resCity` equals `Reno` or `$resState` equals `NV`. If it does not, the entire condition is false, and testing stops. If it does, this part of the condition is true. However, the comparison on the other side of the `and` must also be true, so the testing continues.

2. The `and` is compared.

   The script checks `$name` to see if it equals `Sally`. If it does, the condition is true. If it does not, the condition is false.

Use parentheses liberally, even when you believe you know the order of the comparisons. Unnecessary parentheses can't hurt, but comparisons that have unexpected results can.

If you're familiar with other languages, such as C, you may have used `||` (for *or*) and `&&` (for *and*) in place of the words. The `||` and `&&` work in PHP as well. The statement `$a < $b && $c > $b` is just as valid as the statement `$a < $b and $c > $b`. The `||` is checked before the word *`or`*, and the `&&` is checked before the word *`and`*.

Using Conditional Statements

A *conditional statement* executes a block of statements only when certain conditions are true. Here are two useful types of conditional statements:

- **An `if` statement:** Sets up a condition and tests it. If the condition is true, a block of statements is executed.
- **A `switch` statement:** Sets up a list of alternative conditions. It tests for the true condition and executes the appropriate block of statements.

Using if statements

An `if` statement tests conditions, executing a block of statements when a condition is true. The general format of an `if` conditional statement is as follows:

```
if ( condition )
{
   block of statements
}
elseif  ( condition )
{
   block of statements
}
else
{
   block of statements
}
```

The `if` statement consists of three sections:

- `if`: This section is required. It tests a condition:
  - **If the condition is true:** The block of statements is executed. After the statements are executed, the script moves to the next instruction following the conditional statement; If the conditional statement contains any `elseif` or `else` sections, the script skips over them.
  - **If the condition is not true:** The block of statements is not executed. The script skips to the next instruction, which can be an `elseif`, an `else`, or the next instruction after the `if` conditional statement.
- `elseif`: This section is optional. You can use more than one `elseif` section if you want. It also tests a condition:
  - **If the condition is true:** The block of statements is executed. After executing the block of statements, the script goes to the next instruction following the conditional statement; if the `if` statement

contains any additional elseif sections or an else section, the script skips over them.

- **If the condition is not true:** The block of statements is not executed. The script skips to next instruction, which can be an elseif, an else, or the next instruction after the if conditional statement.

- else: This section is also optional. Only one else section is allowed. This section does not test a condition, rather it executes the block of statements. If the script has entered this section, it means that the if section and all the elseif sections are not true.

Here's an example. Pretend you're a teacher. The following if statement, when given a test score, sends your student a grade and a snappy little text message. It uses all three sections of the if statement, as follows:

```
if ($score > 92 )
{
   $grade = "A";
   $message = "Excellent!";
}
elseif ($score <= 92 and $score > 83 )
{
   $grade = "B";
   $message = "Good!";
}
elseif ($score <= 83 and $score > 74 )
{
   $grade = "C";
   $message = "Okay";
}
elseif ($score <= 74 and $score > 62 )
{
   $grade = "D";
   $message = "Uh oh!";
}
else
{
  $grade = "F";
  $message = "Doom is upon you!";
}
echo $message."\n";
echo "Your grade is $grade\n";
```

The if conditional statement proceeds as follows:

1. The value in $score is compared to 92.

   If $score is greater than 92, $grade is set to A, $message is set to Excellent!, and the script skips to the echo statement. If $score is 92 or less, $grade and $message are *not* set, and the script skips to the elseif section.

2. The value in `$score` is compared to `92` and to `83`.

   If `$score` is `92` or less *and* greater than `83`, `$grade` and `$message` are set, and the script skips to the `echo` statement. If `$score` is `83` or less, `$grade` and `$message` are *not* set, and the script skips to the second `elseif` section.

3. The value in `$score` is compared to `83` and to `74`.

   If `$score` is `83` or less *and* greater than `74`, `$grade` and `$message` are set, and the script skips to the `echo` statement. If `$score` is `74` or less, `$grade` and `$message` are *not* set, and the script skips to the next `elseif` section.

4. The value in `$score` is compared to `74` and to `62`.

   If `$score` is `74` or less *and* greater than `62`, `$grade` and `$message` are set, and the script skips to the `echo` statement. If `$score` is `62` or less, `$grade` and `$message` are *not* set, and the script skips to the `else` section.

5. `$grade` is set to `F`, and `$message` is set to `Doom is upon you!`.

   The script continues to the `echo` statement.

When the block to be executed by any section of the `if` conditional statement contains only one statement, the curly braces are not needed. For example, say the preceding example had only one statement in the blocks, as follows:

```
if ($grade > 92 )
{
    $grade = "A";
}
```

You could write it as follows:

```
if ($grade > 92 )
    $grade = "A";
```

This shortcut can save some typing, but when several `if` statements are used, it can lead to confusion.

Negating if statements

You can write an `if` statement so that the statement block is executed when the condition is false by putting an exclamation point (`!`) at the beginning of the condition. For example, you can use the following `if` statement:

```
if (ereg("^S[a-z]*",$string))
{
    $list[]=$string."\n";
}
```

This if statement creates an array of strings that begin with S. More specifically, if $string matches a pattern that specifies one uppercase S at the beginning, followed by a number of lowercase letters, the statement block is executed. However, if you were to place an exclamation point at the beginning of the condition, things would change considerably. For example, say you use the following statements instead:

```
if (!egreg("^S[a-z]*",$string)
{
   $list[]=$string."\n";
}
```

In this case, the array $list contains all the strings *except* those that begin with S. In this case, because a ! appears at the beginning of the condition, the condition is "$string does *not* match a pattern that begins with S." So, when $string does not begin with S, the condition is true.

Nesting if statements

You can have an if conditional statement inside another if conditional statement. Putting one statement inside another is called *nesting*. For example, suppose you need to contact all your customers who live in Idaho. You plan to send e-mail to those who have e-mail addresses and send letters to those who do not have e-mail addresses. You can identify the groups of customers by using the following nested if statements:

```
if ( $custState == "ID" )
{
   if ( $EmailAdd = "" )
   {
     $contactMethod = "letter";
   }
   else
   {
     $contactMethod = "email";
   }
}
else
{
   $contactMethod = "none needed";
}
```

These statements first check to see if the customer lives in Idaho. If the customer does live in Idaho, the script tests for an e-mail address. If the e-mail address is blank, the contact method is set to letter. If the e-mail address is not blank, the contact method is email. If the customer does not live in Idaho, the else section sets the contact method to indicate that the customer will not be contacted at all.

Using switch statements

For most situations, the `if` conditional statement works best. However, sometimes you have a list of conditions and want to execute different statements for each condition. For example, suppose your script computes sales tax. How do you handle the different state sales tax rates? The `switch` statement was designed for such situations.

The `switch` statement tests the value of one variable and executes the block of statements for the matching value of the variable. The general format is as follows:

```
switch ( $variablename )
{
  case value :
     block of statements;
     break;
  case value :
     block of statements;
     break;
  ...
  default:
     block of statements;
     break;
}
```

The `switch` statement tests the value of *`$variablename`*. The script then skips to the `case` section for that value and executes statements until it reaches a `break` statement or the end of the `switch` statement. If there is no `case` section for the value of *`$variablename`*, the script executes the default section. You can use as many `case` sections as you need. The default section is optional. If you use a default section, it's customary to put the default section at the end, but as far as PHP is concerned, it can go anywhere.

The following statements set the sales tax rate for different states:

```
switch ( $custState )
{
  case "OR" :
     $salestaxrate = 0;
     break;
  case "CA" :
     $salestaxrate = 1.0;
     break;
  default:
     $salestaxrate = .5;
     break;
}
$salestax = $orderTotalCost * $salestaxrate;
```

In this case, the tax rate for Oregon is 0, the tax rate for California is 100 percent, and the tax rate for all the other states is 50 percent. The `switch` statement looks at the value of `$custState` and skips to the section that matches the value. For example, if `$custState` is `TX`, the script executes the default section and sets `$salestaxrate` to `.5`. After the `switch` statement, the script computes `$salestax` at `.5` times the cost of the order.

The `break` statements are essential in the `case` section. If a `case` section does not include a `break` statement, the script does *not* stop executing at the end of the `case` section. The script continues executing statements past the end of the `case` section, on to the next `case` section, and continues until it reaches a `break` statement or the end of the `switch` statement. This is a problem for every `case` section except the last one because it will execute sections following the appropriate section.

The last `case` section in a `switch` statement doesn't actually require a `break` statement. You can leave it out. However, it's a good idea to include it for clarity and consistency.

Repeating Actions by Using Loops

Loops are used frequently in scripts to set up a block of statements that repeat. The loop can repeat a specified number of times. For example, a loop that echoes all the state capitals needs to repeat 50 times. Or the loop can repeat until a certain condition is met. For example, a loop that echoes the names of all the files in a directory needs to repeat until it runs out of files, regardless of how many files there are. Here are three types of loops:

- **A `for` loop:** Sets up a counter; repeats a block of statements until the counter reaches a specified number
- **A `while` loop:** Sets up a condition; checks the condition, and if it's true, repeats a block of statements until the condition becomes false
- **A `do..while` loop:** Sets up a condition; executes a block of statements; checks the condition; if the condition is true, repeats the block of statements until the condition becomes false

I describe each of these loops in detail in the following few sections.

Using for loops

The most basic `for` loops are based on a counter. You set the beginning value for the counter, set the ending value, and set how the counter is incremented each time the statement block is executed. The general format is as follows:

```
for (startingvalue;endingcondition;increment)
{
    block of statements;
}
```

Within the `for` statement, you need to fill in the following values:

- *`startingvalue`*: The *`startingvalue`* is a statement that sets up a variable to be your counter and sets it to your starting value. For example, the statement `$i=1;` sets `$i` as the counter variable and sets it equal to `1`. Frequently, the counter variable is started at 0 or 1. The starting value can be a number, a combination of numbers (like `2 + 2`), or a variable.
- *`endingcondition`*: The *`endingcondition`* is a statement that sets your ending value. As long as this statement is true, the block of statements keeps repeating. When this statement is not true, the loop ends. For example, the statement `$i<10;` sets the ending value for the loop to 10. When `$i` is equal to 10, the statement is no longer true (because `$i` is no longer less than 10), and the loop stops repeating. The statement can include variables, such as `$i<$size;`.
- *`increment`*: A statement that increments your counter. For example, the statement `$i++;` adds 1 to your counter at the end of each block of statements. You can use other increment statements, such as `$i=+1;` or `$i–;`.

A basic `for` loop sets up a variable, like `$i`, that is used as a counter. This variable has a value that changes during each loop. The variable `$i` can be used in the block of statements that is repeating. For example, the following simple loop displays `Hello World!` three times:

```
for ($i=1;$i<=3;$i++)
{
  echo "$i. Hello World!<br>";
}
```

The statements in the block do not need to be indented. PHP doesn't care whether they're indented. However, indenting the blocks makes it much easier for you to understand the script.

The following is the output from these statements:

```
1. Hello World!
2. Hello World!
3. Hello World!
```

Nesting for loops

You can nest for loops inside of for loops. Suppose you want to print out the times tables from 1 to 9. You can use the following statements:

```
for($i=1;$i<=9;$i++)
{
   echo "\nMultiply by $i \n";
   for($j=1;$j<=9;$j++)
   {
       $result = $i * $j;
       echo "$i x $j = $result\n";
   }
}
```

The output is as follows:

```
Multiply by 1
1 x 1 = 1
1 x 2 = 2
...
1 x 8 = 8
1 x 9 = 9

Multiply by 2
2 x 1 = 2
2 x 2 = 4
...
2 x 8 = 16
2 x 9 = 18

Multiply by 3
3 x 1 = 3
```

and so on.

Designing advanced for loops

The structure of a for loop is quite flexible and allows you to build loops for almost any purpose. A for loop has this general format:

```
for (beginning statements; conditional statements; ending
            statements)
{
     block of statements;
}
```

The statements within a for loop have the following roles:

- The beginning statements execute once at the start of the loop. They can be statements that set any needed starting values or other statements that you want to execute before your loop starts running.

- The conditional statements are tested for each iteration of your loop.
- The ending statements execute once at the end of the loop. They can be statements that increment your values or any other statements that you want to execute at the end of your loop.

Each statement section is separated by a semicolon (;). Each section can contain as many statements as needed, separated by commas. Any section can be empty.

The following loop has statements in all three sections:

```
$t = 0;
for ($i=0,$j=1;$t<=4;$i++,$j++)
{
  $t = $i + $j;
  echo "$t<br>";
}
```

The two statements in the first section are the beginning statements; the conditional statement in the second section is the conditional statements; and the two statements in the third section are the ending statements.

The output of these statements is as follows:

```
1
3
5
```

The loop is executed in the following order:

1. The beginning section containing two statements is executed.

   `$i` is set to `0`, and `$j` is set to 1.

2. The conditional section containing one statement is evaluated.

   Is `$t` less than or equal to `4`? Yes, so the statement is true. The loop continues to execute.

3. The statements in the statement block are executed.

   `$t` becomes equal to `$i` plus `$j`, which is 0 + 1, which equals 1. Then `$t` is echoed to give the output `1`.

4. The ending section containing two statements (`$i++` and `$j++`) is executed.

   Both `$i` and `$j` are incremented by one, so `$i` now equals 1, and `$j` now equals 2.

5. The conditional section is evaluated.

   Is `$t` less than or equal to `4`? Because `$t` is equal to 1 at this point, the statement is true. The loop continues to execute.

6. The statements in the statement block are executed.

   `$t` becomes equal to `$i` plus `$j`, which is 1 + 2, which equals 3. Then `$t` is echoed to give the output `3`.

7. The ending section containing two statements (`$i++` and `$j++`) is executed.

   Both `$i` and `$j` are incremented by one, so `$i` now equals 2, and `$j` now equals 3.

8. The conditional section is evaluated.

   Is `$t` less than or equal to `4`? Because `$t` now equals 3, the statement is true. The loop continues to execute.

9. The statements in the statement block are executed.

   `$t` becomes equal to `$i` plus `$j`, which is 2 + 3, which equals 5. Then `$t` is echoed to give the output `5`.

10. The ending section containing two statements (`$i++` and `$j++`) is executed.

    Both `$i` and `$j` are incremented by 1, so `$i` now equals 2, and `$j` now equals 3.

11. The conditional section is evaluated.

    Is `$t` less than or equal to `4`? Because `$t` now equals 5, the statement is not true. The loop does not continue to execute. The loop ends, and the script continues to the next statement after the end of the loop.

Using while loops

A `while` loop continues repeating as long as certain conditions are true. The loop works as follows:

1. You set up a condition.
2. The condition is tested at the top of each loop.
3. If the condition is true, the loop repeats. If the condition is not true, the loop stops.

The following is the general format of a `while` loop:

```
while ( condition )
{
   block of statements
}
```

The following statements set up a `while` loop that looks through an array for an apple:

```
$fruit = array ( "orange", "apple", "grape" );
$testvar = "no";
$k = 0;
while ( $testvar != "yes" )
{
  if ($fruit[$k] == "apple" )
  {
    $testvar = "yes";
    echo "apple\n";
  }
  else
  {
    echo "$fruit[$k] is not an apple\n";
  }
  $k++;
}
```

These statements generate the following output:

```
orange is not an apple
apple
```

The script executes the statements as follows:

1. The variables are set before starting the loop.

   `$fruit` is an array with three values, `$testvar` is a test variable set to `"no"`, and `$k` is a counter variable set to 0.

2. The loop starts by testing whether `$testvar != "yes"` is true.

   Because `$testvar` was set to `"no"`, the statement is true, so the loop continues.

3. The condition in the `if` statement is tested.

   Is `$fruit[$k] == "apple"` true? At this point, `$k` is `0`, so the script checks `$fruit[0]`. Because `$fruit[0]` is `"orange"`, the statement is not true. The statements in the `if` block are not executed, so the script skips to the `else` statement.

4. The statement in the `else` block is executed.

   The `else` block outputs the line `"orange is not an apple"`. This is the first line of the output.

5. `$k` is incremented by one.

   Now `$k` becomes equal to 1.

6. The bottom of the loop is reached.

   Flow returns to the top of the loop.

7. The condition `$testvar != "yes"` is tested again.

   Is `$testvar != "yes"` true? Because `$testvar` has not been changed and is still set to `"no"`, it is true, so the loop continues.

8. The condition in the `if` statement is tested again.

   Is `$fruit[$k] == "apple"` true? At this point, `$k` is 1, so the script checks `$fruit[1]`. Because `$fruit[1]` is `"apple"`, the statement is true. So the loop enters the `if` block.

9. The statements in the `if` block are executed.

   These statements set `$testvar` to `"yes"` and output `"apple"`. This is the second line of the output.

10. `$k` is incremented again.

    Now `$k` equals 2.

11. The bottom of the loop is reached again.

    Once again, the flow returns to the top of the loop.

12. The condition `$testvar != "yes"` is tested one last time.

    Is `$testvar != "yes"` true? Because `$testvar` has been changed and is now set to `"yes"`, it is *not* true. The loop stops.

It's possible to write a `while` loop that is infinite — that is, a loop that loops forever. You can easily, without intending to, write a loop in which the condition is always true. If the condition never becomes false, the loop never ends. For a discussion of infinite loops, see the section "Avoiding infinite loops," later in this chapter.

Using do..while loops

A `do..while` loop is very similar to a `while` loop. Like a `while` loop, a `do..while` loop continues repeating as long as certain conditions are true. Unlike `while` loops, however, those conditions are tested at the bottom of each loop. If the condition is true, the loop repeats. When the condition is not true, the loop stops.

The general format for a `do..while` loop is as follows:

```
do
{
   block of statements
} while ( condition );
```

The following statements set up a loop that looks for an apple. This script does the same thing as the script in the preceding section that uses a `while` loop:

```
$fruit = array ( "orange", "apple", "grape" );
$testvar = "no";
$k = 0;
do
{
  if ($fruit[$k] == "apple" )
  {
    $testvar = "yes";
    echo "apple\n";
  }
  else
  {
    echo "$fruit[$k] is not an apple\n";
  }
  $k++;
} while ( $testvar != "yes" );
```

The output of these statements in a browser is as follows:

```
orange is not an apple
apple
```

This is the same output shown for the `while` loop example. The difference between a `while` loop and a `do..while` loop is where the condition is checked. In a `while` loop, the condition is checked at the top of the loop. Therefore, the loop will never execute if the condition is never true. In the `do..while` loop, the condition is checked at the bottom of the loop. Therefore, the loop always executes at least once, even if the condition is never true.

For example, in the preceding loop that checks for an apple, suppose the original condition is set to `yes`, instead of `no`, by using this statement:

```
$testvar = "yes";
```

The condition tests false from the beginning. It is never true. In a `while` loop, there is no output. The statement block never runs. However, in a `do..while` loop, the statement block runs once before the condition is tested. Thus, the `while` loop produces no output, but the `do..while` loop produces the following output:

```
orange is not an apple
```

The `do..while` loop produces one line of output before the condition is tested. It does not produce the second line of output because the condition tests false.

Avoiding infinite loops

You can easily set up loops so that they never stop. These are called *infinite loops.* They repeat forever. However, seldom does anyone create an infinite loop intentionally. It is usually a mistake in the programming. For example, a slight change to the script that sets up a `while` loop can make it into an infinite loop.

Here is the script shown in the section, "Using while loops," earlier in this chapter, with a slight change:

```
$fruit = array ( "orange", "apple", "grape" );
$testvar = "no";
while ( $testvar != "yes" )
{
  $k = 0;
  if ($fruit[$k] == "apple" )
  {
    $testvar = "yes";
    echo "apple\n";
  }
  else
  {
    echo "$fruit[$k] is not an apple\n";
  }
  $k++;
}
```

The small change is moving the statement `$k = 0;` from outside the loop to inside the loop. This small change makes it into an endless loop. This changed script has the following output:

```
orange is not an apple
orange is not an apple
orange is not an apple
orange is not an apple
...
```

This will repeat forever. Every time the loop runs, it resets `$k` to `0`. Then it gets `$fruit[0]` and echoes it. At the end of the loop, `$k` is incremented to `1`. However, when the loop starts again, `$k` is set back to `0`. Consequently, only the first value in the array, `orange`, is ever read. The loop never gets to the `apple`, and `$testvar` is never set to `"yes"`. The loop is endless.

Don't be embarrassed if you write an infinite loop. I guarantee that the best programming guru in the world has written many infinite loops. It's not a big deal. If you are testing a script and get output repeating endlessly, there's no need to panic. Do one of the following:

- **If you're using PHP on a Web page:** Wait. It will stop by itself in a short time. The default time is 30 seconds, but the timeout period may have been changed by the PHP administrator. You can also click the Stop button on your browser to stop the display in your browser.
- **If you're using PHP CLI:** Press Ctrl + C. This stops the script from running. Sometimes the output will continue to display a little longer, but it will stop very shortly.

Then figure out why the loop is repeating endlessly and fix it.

A common mistake that can result in an infinite loop is using a single equal sign (=) when you mean to use double equal signs (==). The single equal sign stores a value in a variable; the double equal signs test whether two values are equal. The following condition using a single equal sign is always true:

```
while ($testvar = "yes")
```

The condition simply sets `$testvar` equal to `"yes"`. This is not a question that can be false. What you probably meant to write is this:

```
while ($testvar == "yes")
```

This is a question asking whether `$testvar` is equal to `"yes"`, which can be answered either true or false.

Another common mistake is to leave out the statement that increments the counter. For example, in the script earlier in this section, if you leave out the statement `$k++;`, `$k` is always `0`, and the result is an infinite loop.

Breaking out of a loop

Sometimes you want your script to break out of a loop. PHP provides two statements for this purpose:

- `break`: Breaks completely out of a loop and continues with the script statements after the loop.
- `continue`: Skips to the end of the loop where the condition is tested. If the condition tests positive, the script continues from the top of the loop.

The `break` and `continue` statements are usually used in conditional statements. In particular, `break` is used most often in `switch` statements, discussed earlier in this chapter.

The following statements show the difference between `continue` and `break`. This first section is an example of the `break` statement:

```
$counter = 0;
while ( $counter < 5 )
{
  $counter++;
  If ( $counter == 3 )
  {
      echo "break\n";
      break;
  }
  echo "Last line in loop: counter=$counter\n";
}
echo "First line after loop\n\n";
```

The output of this statement is the following:

```
Last line in loop: counter=1
Last line in loop: counter=2
break
First line after loop
```

Notice that the first loop ends at the `break` statement. It stops looping and jumps immediately to the statement after the loop. That's not true of the `continue` statement.

The following section is an example of the `continue` statement:

```
$counter = 0;
while ( $counter < 5 )
{
  $counter++;
  If ( $counter == 3 )
  {
      echo "continue\n";
      continue;
  }
  echo "Last line in loop: counter=$counter\n";
}
echo "First line after loop\n";
```

The output of this statement is the following:

```
Last line in loop: counter=1
Last line in loop: counter=2
continue
Last line in loop: counter=4
Last line in loop: counter=5
First line after loop
```

Unlike the `break` statement loop, this loop does not end at the `continue` statement. It just stops the third repeat of the loop and jumps back up to the top of the loop. It then finishes the loop, with the fourth and fifth repeats, before it goes to the statement after the loop.

One use for `break` statements is insurance against infinite loops. The following statements inside a loop can stop it at a reasonable point:

```
$test4infinity++;
if ($test4infinity > 100 )
{
   break;
}
```

If you're sure that your loop should never repeat more than 100 times, these statements will stop the loop if it becomes endless. Use whatever number seems reasonable for the loop you're building.

Chapter 8

Reusing PHP Code

In This Chapter

- Including files in scripts
- Understanding security for included files
- Writing functions
- Using functions

Often scripts need to perform the same actions in several different locations in the script. For example, a script may need to get data from a database several different times. It may even be the case that you use the same code in different scripts. If you find yourself typing the same ten lines of code over and over (or cutting and pasting it repeatedly), you can move that code into a separate file and get it from that file whenever you need it. Here are several reasons to reuse code:

- **Less typing:** Less work is always a good reason for anything.
- **Debug once:** You can write the code once, debug it so you know it works, and then use it whenever you need it. It's rare to write code that doesn't have a typo or two in it, let alone occasional peculiar logic, so code always has to be debugged. It saves time to use proven code when possible, instead of writing new code that will have to be debugged.
- **Easier to understand:** A shorter script that is less cluttered with code is easier for people to read and understand. For example, one line in your script that says `getData()` is easier to understand than the ten lines that actually get the data.
- **Easier to maintain:** If you reuse code and you need to change something in the code, you only need to change it in one external file, instead of having to find and change it in a dozen places in your script. For example, if you change the name of your database, you can change the name in one file, rather than having to change it repeatedly in many scripts.

You can reuse code two ways: by inserting a file containing code into a script or by writing and calling a function. In this chapter, you find out how to use both methods.

Inserting Code in Your Script

You can put as many lines of code as you need into a file, separate from your script, and include that file in the script wherever you need it. PHP provides the `include` statement to insert code where it's needed.

Including files

Suppose you're writing an online product catalog and your application contains many pages that display pictures of your products. You can define the height and width for the pictures in constants and use the constants in your HTML image tags, thereby displaying all your pictures consistently. By using constants, you can change the size of the graphics simply by changing the constant definition; you don't have to change every image tag in your script. You can define these constants by using the following statements in the top of your script:

```
define("HEIGHT",60);
define("WIDTH",60);
```

You can then use the constants in your HTML image tags as follows:

```
<img src="mypic.jpg" height="<?php echo HEIGHT?>"
          width="<?php echo WIDTH?>" />;
```

If you display the product pictures in many different scripts, you don't have to add the `define` statements in the top of every script. Instead, you can put the statements into a separate file and include the file in the top of the scripts. You can create a file called `size.inc` (you can use any extension for include files, but `.inc` is often used by convention) that contains the following:

```
<?php
 define("HEIGHT",60);
 define("WIDTH",60);
?>
```

You can then include the file at the top of each script with the following statement:

```
include("size.inc");
```

When PHP sees the `include` statement, it reads the code from the file so the code is inserted at the location where the `include` statement is used. That means that the constants are defined when `size.inc` is included, and the image tags in your file will be output as follows:

```
<img src="mypic.jpg" height="60" width="60" />
```

This HTML code displays the image on your Web page. If you want to change the height or width at any time, just change the definitions of `HEIGHT` and `WIDTH` in `size.inc`, and all the images will automatically change size. Actually, because the image tag that displays the picture is rather complex, you could put the image statement into a file called `displayPix.inc` and include the file whenever you want to display an image. You could have the image tag alone in `displayPix.inc` and include both `size.inc` and `displayPix.inc` at the beginning of each script, or you could include `size.inc` in `displayPix.inc` and only include `displayPix.inc` in your script.

Forgetting the PHP tags in the include file is a common mistake. It's also a security problem because without the PHP tags, the code in the file is displayed to the user as HTML. If the user sees the size of the graphic files, it's not much of a problem. However, suppose you had the password for your database in the include file — that would be a problem.

Instead of the standard `include` statement, you can use the following similar statement:

```
include_once("filename");
```

This statement prevents included files with similar variables from overwriting each other. For example, you can use `include_once` to include your function definitions (which are discussed later in this chapter) to be sure that they are only defined once.

PHP also provides the `require` and `require_once` statements that work just like `include` statements, differing only in the way errors are handled. This difference arises when you use an `include` or a `require` statement that calls a file that doesn't exist. If you require a file that doesn't exist, it is a fatal error, and your script stops running. If you include a file that doesn't exist, you only receive a warning, and the script continues to run.

You can use a variable name for the filename as follows:

```
include ("$filename");
```

For example, you might want to display different messages on different days: You might store these messages in files that are named for the day on which the message should display. For example, you could have a file named `Sun.inc` with the following contents:

```
echo "Go ahead. Sleep in. No work today.";
```

And similar files for all days of the week. The following statements can be used to display the correct message for the current day:

```
$today = date("D");
include("$today"."inc");
```

After the first statement, `$today` contains the day of the week in abbreviation form. The `date` statement is discussed in Chapter 5. The second statement includes the correct file, using the day stored in `$today`. If `$today` contains `Sun`, the statement includes a file called `Sun.inc`.

Storing include files

Where you store include files can be a security issue, especially for Web sites. Files stored on Web sites can be downloaded by any user, unless the files are protected. Theoretically, a user could connect to your Web site by using the following type of URL:

```
http://yourdomain.com/secretpasswords.inc
```

Suppose you happen to have a file in your Web space named `secretpasswords.inc` that contains the following statements:

```
<?php
  $mysecretaccount="account48756";
  $mypassword="secret";
?>
```

In most cases, the Web server is not configured to process PHP sections in files with any extensions other than PHP. Therefore, the Web server would not process these statements. Instead, it would obligingly display the contents of `secretpasswords.inc` to the user, as if the lines were HTML code. You can protect against this in one of the following ways:

- **Name include files with `.php` extensions.** The Web server will then process the PHP sections, rather than treat them the same as the HTML sections. However, you need to think carefully about the contents of the include files if you name them with a `.php` extension. In some cases, running the PHP sections in an include file independently, without the context provided when they are run by including them in a script, can be a problem. For example, suppose you had code in your include file that deleted a record in the database (highly unlikely). Running the code outside of a script might have negative consequences. Another drawback is that it can be convenient to name files with an `.inc` extension so you can see at a glance that the file is a fragment, not a script intended to run by itself.
- **Configure the Web server to scan for PHP sections in files with the `.inc` extension, as well as the `.php` extension.** This allows you to recognize include files by their name. However, you still have the problem of possible unintended consequences of running the file independently, as discussed in the preceding bullet.

- **Store the file in a location that is not accessible to outside users.** This is the preferred solution, but it may not be possible in some environments, such as when you're using a Web hosting company.

The best place to store include files is in a directory that outside users can't access. For example, for your Web site, you can set up an include directory that is outside your Web space. That is, you can create a directory in a location that outside users can't access with their browsers. For example, the default Web space for Apache — unless it has been changed in the configuration file (usually called `httpd.conf`) — is `apache/htdocs`. If you store your include files in a directory that is not in your Web space, such as `d:\include`, you can protect the files from outside users.

Setting up include directories

You can set up an include directory where PHP looks for any files specified in an `include` statement. If you are the PHP administrator, you can set up an include directory in the `php.ini` file (the PHP configuration file in your system directory, as described in Appendix A). Find the setting for `include_path` and change it to the path to your preferred directory. If there is a semicolon at the beginning of the line, before `include_path`, remove it. The following are examples of `include_path` settings in the `php.ini` file:

```
include_path=".;d:\include";              # for Windows
include_path=".:/user/local/include";  # for Unix/Linux/Mac
```

Both of these statements specify two directories where PHP looks for include files. The first directory is dot (meaning the current directory), followed by the second directory path. You can specify as many include directories as you want, and PHP will search them for the include file in the order in which they are listed. The directory paths are separated by a semicolon for Windows and a colon for Unix/Linux.

If you don't have access to `php.ini`, you can set the path in each individual script by using the following statement:

```
ini_set("include_path","d:\hidden");
```

This statement sets the `include_path` to the specified directory only while the script is running. It doesn't set the directory for your entire Web site.

To access a file from an include directory, just use the file name, as follows. You don't need to use the full path name.

```
include("secretpasswords.inc");
```

If your include file is not in an include directory, you may need to use the entire path name in the include statement. If the file is in the same directory as the script, the file name alone is sufficient. However, if the file is located in another directory, such as a subdirectory of the directory the script is in or a hidden directory outside the Web space, you need to use the full path name to the file, as follows:

```
include("d:/hidden/secretpasswords.inc");
```

Creating Reusable Code (Functions)

Applications often perform the same task at different points in the script or in different scripts. This is when functions come in handy. A *function* is a group of PHP statements that perform a specific task. You can use the function wherever you need to perform the task.

For example, suppose you add a footer to the bottom of every Web page by using the following statements:

```
echo '<img src="greenrule.jpg" width="100%" height="7" />
<address>My Great Company
<br />1234 Wonderful Rd.
<br />San Diego, CA 92126
</address></font>
<p>or send questions to
     <a href="mailto:sales@company.com">sales </a>
<img src="greenrule.jpg" width="100%" height="7" />';
```

It's not uncommon for Web pages to have headers or footers much longer than this. So, rather than type this code into the bottom of every Web page, probably incurring at least a couple of typos in the process, you can create a function that contains the preceding statements and name it `add_footer`. Then at the end of every page, you can just use the function (a process referred to as *calling* the function) that contains the footer statements. The code for this simple function call is as follows:

```
add_footer();
```

Notice the parentheses after the function name. These are required in a function call because they tell PHP that this is a function.

Defining functions

You can create a function by putting the code into a function block. The general format is as follows:

```
function functionname()
{
   block of statements;
   return;
}
```

For example, you create the function `add_footer()` that I discuss in the preceding section with the following statements:

```
function add_footer()
{
   echo '<img src="greenrule.jpg" width="100%" height="7" />
   <address>My Great Company
   <br />1234 Wonderful Rd.
   <br />San Diego, CA 92126
   </address></font>
   <p>or send questions to
       <a href="mailto:sales@company.com">sales </a>
   <img src="greenrule.jpg" width="100%" height="7" />';
   return;
}
```

The `return` statement stops the function and returns to the main script. (The `return` statement at the end of the function is not required, but it makes the function easier to understand. The return statement is discussed in more detail in the section "Returning a value from a function," later in this chapter.)

You can write a function anywhere in the script, but the usual practice is to put all the functions together at the beginning or the end of the script file. Functions that you plan to use in more than one script can be in a separate file, and you can include the file in any scripts that need to use the functions.

At this point, you're probably wondering, "Why can't I just put the footer statements into a separate file called `footer.inc` and include `footer.inc` at the end of each Web page?" Good question! Actually, you can. In fact, you should. In this case, the instructions for creating the footer consist of a simple block of statements that echo static HTML code. You could just put the HTML in the include file and include it at the end of the page. You wouldn't even need to use PHP tags in the include file.

However, suppose the company has three divisions and you want to include the division name in the footer and have the e-mail address send the e-mail to the appropriate division. You could write three different include files and include the correct one. However, a function works better in this situation because functions are more flexible and faster. You can send information to the function (called *passing values*), telling it which division to use in the output. The function looks like this:

```
function add_footer($division)
{
    echo '<img src="greenrule.jpg" width="100%" height="7" />
    <p>'.$division.' Division</p>
    <address>My Great Company
    <br />1234 Wonderful Rd.
    <br />San Diego, CA 92126
    </address></font>
    <p>or send questions to
    <a href="mailto:'.$division.'@company.com">'
            .$division.'</a>
    <img src="greenrule.jpg" width="100%" height="7" />';
    return;
}
```

In this version, the function is expecting a value to be passed to it. It stores the passed value in a variable called `$division` and uses the variable for the text that needs to change. When you use this function, you must pass it a value, as follows:

```
add_footer("Sales");
```

You can change the division by calling the function with a different value:

```
add_footer("Accounting");
```

Notice the format of the `echo` statement. The string is enclosed in single quotes. In the previous function, without variables, the format was simple — just a single quote at the beginning and another single quote at the end. In this function example, using a variable, the quoted string is ended when `$division` is used and reopened after the variable. Remember, variables are not evaluated inside single quotes. If `$division` were used inside single quotes, the output would show `$division Division`, instead of `Sales Division`.

You can pass a value back from a function, called *returning* a value. Values are returned by using the `return` statement. For example, suppose you want the function to put the footer into a variable rather than echo the footer. In that case, the function looks like this:

```
function add_footer($division)
{
   $str='<img src="greenrule.jpg" width="100%" height="7" />
   <p>'.$division.' Division</p>
   <address>My Great Company
   <br />1234 Wonderful Rd.
   <br />San Diego, CA 92126
   </address></font>
   <p>or send questions to
   <a href="mailto:'.$division.'@company.com">'
         .$division.'</a>
   <img src="greenrule.jpg" width="100%" height="7" />';
   return $str;
}
```

In this case, you could use these statements:

```
$footer = add_footer("Sales");
echo $footer;
```

When you echo `$footer`, you output the entire footer string that was created in the function.

The rest of this chapter describes in detail how to create and use functions. A good programmer looks for opportunities to put script code into functions, which improves readability and maintainability, as well as makes the script run faster.

Using variables in functions

You can create and use a variable inside your function. Such a variable is called *local* to the function A local variable is not available outside of the function, so it's not available to the main script. (If you want to use the variable outside the function, you have to make the variable *global,* rather than local, by using a `global` statement.) For example, the variable `$name` is created in the following function:

```
function format_name($first_name,$last_name)
{
   $name = $last_name.", ".$first_name;
}
```

You can then call the function, passing it values, and attempt to echo the value of the variable `$name`:

```
format_name("Jess","Jones");
echo "$name";
```

However, these statements do not produce any output. In the `echo` statement, `$name` doesn't contain any value. The variable `$name` was created inside the function, so it doesn't exist outside the function.

You can create a variable inside a function that does exist outside the function by using the `global` statement. The following statements contain the same function with a `global` statement added:

```
function format_name($first_name,$last_name)
{
   global $name;
   $name = $last_name.", ".$first_name;
}
```

You can now call the function, passing it the same values, and echo the value of the variable `$name`:

```
format_name("Jess","Jones");
echo "$name";
```

The script now echoes the value of the variable `$name`:

```
Jones, Jess
```

You must make the variable global before you can use it. If the `global` statement follows the `$name` assignment statement, the script does not produce any output. That is, in the preceding function, if the `global` statement followed the `$name = statement`, the function wouldn't work correctly.

Similarly, if a variable is created outside the function, you can't use it inside the function unless it is global. You can make the variable global as shown in the following statements:

```
$first_name = "Jess";
$last_name = "Jones";
function format_name()
{
   global $first_name, $last_name;
   $name = $last_name.", ".$first_name;
   echo "$name";
}
format_name();
```

If you don't use the `global` statement, `$last_name` and `$first_name` inside the function are different variables than `$last_name` and `$first_name` created outside the script. The local variables `$last_name` and `$first_name` inside the function are created when you name them and have no values. Therefore, `$name` would echo only a comma.

You need the `global` statement for the function to work correctly.

Passing values to a function

You pass values to a function by putting the values between the parentheses when you call the function, as follows:

```
functionname(value1,value2,...);
```

Of course, the variables can't just show up. The function must be expecting them. The `function` statement includes variable names for the values it's expecting, as follows:

```
function functionname($varname1,$varname2,...)
{
    statements
    return;
}
```

Passing the right type of values

Values can be variables or values, including values that are computed. The values passed can be any type of data, including arrays or objects (objects are discussed in Chapter 9).

The following statements call a function that computes the sales tax. A `salestax` function needs to know the amount of the purchase, so it can compute the amount of tax. It also needs to know the state, so it can use the correct tax rate to compute the sales tax. The values you need to pass are a number (the purchase amount) and a string (the state's name). The following calls are valid:

- `compute_salestax(2000,"CA");` This function is being passed two values, `2000` and `CA`, CA.
- `compute_salestax(2*1000,"");` This function is being passed two values, `2000` and `???`, an empty value. The function must include code that handles the empty variable.
- `compute_salestax(2000,"C"."A");` This function is being passed two values, `2000` and `???`, CA.

You can pass arrays to functions. (Arrays are discussed in Chapter 6.) For example, the following function uses an array that is passed to it:

```
function add_numbers($numbers)
{
   for($i=0;$i <sizeof($numbers);$i++)
   {
      @$sum = $sum + $numbers[$i];
   }
   return $sum;
}
```

This function adds all the numbers passed to it in an array of numbers. If the value passed to it is not an array, PHP stores the value in `$numbers` as its correct data type — an integer or a string. When the function gets to the statement `sizeof($numbers)`, it fails because `$numbers` is not an array and `sizeof` requires an array. A well-written function checks the values that are passed to it make sure they are the type of value needed before executing the statements in the function. For example, the following statement can be added to the function block, immediately before the `for` statement:

```
If(!is_array($numbers)
{
   echo "The value passed is not an array";
   exit();
}
```

Similarly, this function should check whether the elements of the array are numbers, using some of the functions described in Chapter 5.

You can use the following statements to define an array that is then passed to the `add_numbers` function:

```
$arrayofnumbers = array(100,200);
$total = add_numbers($arrayofnumbers);
```

After these statements, `$total` equals 300.

Passing values in the correct order

The function receives the values in the order they are passed. That is, suppose you have the following function:

```
function functionx($x,$y,$z)
{
   do stuff
}
```

You call the function as follows:

```
functionx($var1,$var2,$var3);
```

The function sets `$x=$var1`, `$y=$var2`, and `$z=$var3`.

If the values you pass aren't in the expected order, the function uses the wrong value when performing the task. For example, suppose that your definition for a function to compute sales tax looks like the following:

```
function compute_salestax($orderCost,$custState)
{
   compute tax
}
```

But suppose you call it by using the following call:

```
compute_salestax($custState,$orderCost);
```

The function uses the state as the cost of the order, which it sets to 0 because it is a string. It sets the state to the number in `$orderCost`, which would not match any of its categories. The output would be `0`.

Passing the right number of values

A function is designed to expect a certain number of values to be passed to it. If you don't send enough values, the function sets the missing one(s) to NULL. If you have your warning message level turned on, a warning message is displayed. (See Chapter 4 for a description of error levels.) For example, you might see a message similar to the following:

```
Warning: Missing argument 2 for format_name() in testing.php
        on line 9
```

Remember, warnings don't stop the script; it continues to run. Suppose that you call the `format_name` function described in the section "Using variables in functions," earlier in this chapter, by using the following statement:

```
format_name("Jess");
```

The output is as follows:

```
Jess,
```

If you send too many values, the function ignores the extra values. In most cases, you do not want to pass the wrong number of values.

You can set default values to be used when a value isn't passed. The defaults are set when you write the function, be assigning a default value for the value(s) it is expecting, as follows:

```
function add_2_numbers($num1=1,$num2=1)
{
   $total = $num1 + $num2;
   return $total;
}
```

If one or both values are not passed, the function uses the assigned defaults. But if a value is passed, it is used instead of the default. For example, you could use one of the following calls:

```
add_2_numbers(2,2);
add_2_numbers(2);
add_2_numbers();
```

The result are, in consecutive order:

```
$total = 4
$total = 3
$total = 2
```

The first $total is 4, because 2 and 2 are passed. The second $total is three because 2 is passed and the default 1 is used for $num2. The third $total is 2 because neither value is passed and, therefore, the defaults of 1 are used for both $num1 and $num2.

Passing values by reference

When you pass values into variables in the function definition, you are passing by value. Passing by value is the most common way to pass values to a function, as in the following example:

```
function add_1($num1)
{
      $num1 = $num1 + 1;
}
```

When passing by value, a copy is made of a value and the copy is passed to the function. The value passed into the function is stored in the variable $num1, and 1 is added to it in the function. However, the value of the variable outside the function is not changed. Suppose that you call the function with the following statements:

```
$orig_num = 3;
add_1($orig_num);
echo $orig_num;
```

The output from the echo statement is 3. A copy of the value stored in $orig_num was passed to add_1, but nothing in the function affected $orig_num. It is unchanged. You can change $orig_num by adding a return statement to the function, as follows:

```
return $num1;
```

You then store the returned value in $orig_num as follows:

```
$orig_num = 3;
$orig_num = add_1($orig_num);
echo $orig_num;
```

Now, the echo statement outputs 4.

In some cases, you may want to change the values of variables directly, changing their values outside the function. That is, in the first example above, you may want $orig_value changed from inside the function, without having to pass it back. In this simple case, you could make the variable global, but you can also do it using a technique called *passing by reference.* To pass a variable by reference, add & before the variable name, as follows:

```
function add_1(&$num1)
{
     $num1 = $num1 + 1;
}
```

When you call this function, a value is passed that tells PHP where the variable is stored, (that is, a pointer to the container called $orig_num where the value 3 is stored) rather than a copy of the value. The variable $num1 then becomes another name for $orig_num, rather than a different variable that contains 3. When you assign something to $num1, it is stored in $orig_num. $num1 and $orig_num are two names for the same storage location. When you change the variable by using statements inside the function, the value at the original location is changed as well. For example, suppose you call the function by using the following statements:

```
$orig_num = 3;
add_1($orig_num);
echo $orig_num;
```

The output of the echo statement is 4.

Because you're passing a pointer to a variable, the following doesn't make sense:

```
add_1(&7);
```

Passing by reference is used mainly when passing really large values, such as an object or a large array. It's more efficient to pass a pointer than to pass a copy of really large values.

Returning a value from a function

If you want a function to send a value back to the main script, you use the return statement. The main script can put the returned value in a variable or use it in any manner it would use any value.

A return statement returns any values specified and ends the function, returning to the main script. The general format is as follows:

```
return value;
```

For example, the add2numbers function looks like this:

```
function add_2_numbers($num1,$num2)
{
    $total = $num1 + $num2;
    return $total;
}
```

The total of the two numbers is returned and the function ends. You call the function as follows:

```
$sum = add_2_numbers(5,6);
```

$sum then equals the value in $total that was returned from the function, which is 11 in this case. In fact, you could use a shortcut when defining the function and send the total back to the main script with one statement:

```
return $num1 + $num2;
```

The main script can use the value in any of the usual ways. The following statements use the function call in valid ways:

```
$total_height = add_2_numbers($height1,$height2);
```

```
$totalSize = $current_size + add_2_numbers($size1,$size2);
```

```
if (add_2_numbers($costSocks,$costShoes) > 200.00 )
         $echo "No sale";
```

A return statement can return only one value. However, the value returned can be an array, so you can actually return many values from a function.

You can use a return statement in a conditional statement to end a function, as follows:

```
function find_value($array,$value)
{
   for($i=1;$i<sizeof($array);$i++)
   {
      if($array[$i] = $value)
      {
        echo "$i. $array[$i]<br>";
        return;
      }
   }
}
```

The function checks an array to see if it contains a particular value. For example, you can call the function with the following statements:

```
$names = array("Joe","Sam","Juan");
find_value($names,"Sam");
```

The function searches through the values in the array looking for Sam. If it finds Sam, it stops searching. The output shows the array item where Sam is found, as follows:

```
1. Sam
```

Often functions are designed to return Boolean values, as in the following function:

```
function is_over_100($number)
{
  if($number > 100)
  {
     return TRUE;
  }
  else {
     return FALSE;
  }
}
```

Numbers 100 or less return `FALSE`; numbers over 100 return `TRUE`.

Another common function design returns a value if the function succeeds, but returns `FALSE` if the function does not succeed. For example, you could design the `find_value` function as follows:

```
function find_value($array,$value)
{
  for($i=1;$i<sizeof($array);$i++)
  {
     if($array[$i] == $value)
     {
       return i$;
     }
  }
  return FALSE;
}
```

If the function finds the value in the array, it returns the number of the array element where it found `$value`. However, if it does not find the value anywhere in the array, it returns `FALSE`.

Using built-in functions

PHP's built-in functions are one reason why PHP is so powerful and useful. The functions included with PHP are normal functions. They are no different than functions you create yourself. It's just that PHP has already done all the work for you.

Rather than discussing built-in functions here, out of context, I discuss specific PHP functions where I describe tasks in which functions can be very helpful. For example, in Chapter 7, I discuss several functions that can be used to check whether a variable exists or whether it is empty. Here are a couple of those functions:

```
isset($varname)
empty($varname)
```

Also, in Chapter 5 I describe several functions that are useful for formatting and manipulating numbers and strings. And other PHP built-in functions are discussed throughout the book.

Appendix B is a reference list of many useful functions. Keep this list handy when writing scripts so you can quickly look up PHP built-in functions. Although you could write functions yourself to perform the tasks, take advantage of PHP's functions whenever possible. The reference in Appendix B does not include all the functions, of course — there are hundreds — but it includes the functions I have found to be most useful. All the functions are listed and described in the PHP documentation on the PHP Web site at `www.php.net/docs.php`.

Handling Errors

Sometimes functions fail. Sad, but true. You write them to carefully handle all possibilities, but something can still go wrong. For example, a function that connects to a database might fail because the database is currently down. It's not the function's fault; the situation is beyond its control. A well-written function tries to anticipate all possible situations, but recognizes that the unexpected can happen by including a statement that returns FALSE when the function is unable to carry out its mission for unexpected reasons.

Your script should anticipate any possible function failure and handle the situation. One possible action is to display your own message, rather than allow the user to see the warning message provided by PHP. PHP provides the `die` statement, which displays the message you specify. The format of the `die` statement is as follows:

```
die("message");
```

The `die` statement stops the script and prints out whatever you have entered in the place of *message*. When you use it with a function, you use it with `or`, as follows:

```
functionname()   or   die("message");
```

If the function returns FALSE, the `die` statement stops the script and prints out the message.

For example, if you use a function to connect to a MySQL database, you could use the following statement:

```
mysql_connect("host","user","password")
      or die("Database is not available. Try again later.");
```

Remember, if the function fails, PHP will display a warning message. If you want your message to be displayed instead of the PHP warning message, you need to change your error-reporting level so that warning messages are not displayed, or shut off the display of all error messages, as described in Chapter 4. Otherwise, both the PHP warning and your message will be displayed.

You can use `die` with any function, but it doesn't make sense to use it when `FALSE` is a legitimate return value. Remember, `die` stops the script dead in its tracks.

You can also handle possible function failures by using the function call as a condition. For example, you can get the same result as the previous example by using the following statements instead:

```
if(!mysql_connect("host","user","password"))
{
    echo "Database is not available. Try again later\n";
    exit();
}
```

Notice the exclamation point before the function call, making it a negative condition. The condition is `TRUE` if the function returns `FALSE`.

The `exit` statement does the same thing as the `die` statement. Keep in mind that you can use any statement in the `if` block; you can even have the script send you an e-mail if the database is unreachable.

Chapter 9

Object-Oriented Programming Meets PHP

In This Chapter

- Understanding object-oriented programming
- Identifying objects
- Writing classes
- Using classes

PHP began life as a simple set of scripts. Over the course of its life, PHP has added some object-oriented programming features, and object-oriented programming became possible with PHP 4. With the introduction of PHP 5, the PHP developers have really beefed up the object-oriented features of PHP, resulting in both more speed and added features. Much of this improvement is invisible — changes introduced with the Zend 2 engine that powers PHP 5, that make scripts using objects run much faster and more efficiently than they did in PHP 4. In addition, to speeding up scripts, object-oriented functionality has been added to PHP that object-oriented programmers have been waiting for.

Introducing Object-Oriented Programming

Object-oriented programming is an approach to programming that uses objects and classes, which are discussed in more detail later in this chapter. Object-oriented programming is widespread today, and many universities teach object-oriented programming in beginning programming classes. Currently, Java and C++ are the most prevalent languages used for object-oriented programming.

Object-oriented programming is not just a matter of using different syntax. It's a different way of analyzing programming problems. The program is designed by modeling the programming problem. For example, a programmer designing a program to support a company's sales department may look at the programming problem in terms of the relationships between customers and sales and credit lines — in other words, in terms of the design of the sales department itself.

In object-oriented programming, the elements of a program are *objects.* The objects represent the elements of the problem your program is meant to solve. For example, if the program is related to a used-car lot, the objects are probably cars and customers. Or if the program is related to outer space, the objects would probably be stars and planets.

Object-oriented programming developed new concepts and new terminology to represent those concepts. Understanding the terminology is the road to understanding object-oriented programming.

Objects and classes

The basic elements of object-oriented programs are *objects.* It's easiest to understand objects as physical objects. For example, a car is an object. A car has properties, such as color, model, engine, and tires, also called attributes. A car has things it can do, too, such as move forward, move backward, park, roll over, and play dead (well, mine does anyway).

In general, objects are nouns. A person is an object. So are animals, houses, offices, customers, garbage cans, coats, clouds, planets, and buttons. However, objects are not just physical objects. Often objects, like nouns, are more conceptual. For example, a bank account is not something you can hold in your hand, but it can be considered an object. So can a computer account. Or a mortgage. A file is often an object. So is a database. Orders, e-mail messages, addresses, songs, TV shows, meetings, and dates can all be objects.

A *class* is the script that serves as the template, or the pattern, that is used to create an object. The class defines the properties, the attributes, of the object. It also defines the things the object can do — its responsibilities. For example, you write a class that defines a car as four wheels and an engine and lists the things it can do, such as move forward and park. Then, given that class, you can write a statement that creates a car object. Your new car is created following the pattern in your class. When you use your car object, you may find that it is missing a few important things, like a door or a steering wheel or a reverse gear. That's because you left those out of the class when you wrote it.

As the person who writes a class, you know how things work inside the class. But it's not necessary to know how an object accomplishes its responsibilities in order to use it; anyone can use a class. I have no clue how a telephone object works, but I can use it to make a phone call. The person who built the telephone knows what's happening inside it. When there's new technology, the phone builder can open my phone and improve it. As long as he doesn't change the interface — the keypad and buttons — it doesn't affect my use of the phone at all.

Properties

Objects have *properties,* also sometimes called *attributes.* A car may be red, green, or covered in polka dots. Properties — such as color, size, or model for a car — are stored inside the object. Properties are set up in the class as variables. For example, the color attribute is stored in the object in a variable, given the descriptive name such as `$color`. Thus, the car object may contain `$color = red`.

The variables that store properties can have default values, can be given values when the object is created, or values can be added or modified later. For example, a car is created red, but when it is painted later, `$color` is changed to chartreuse.

Methods

The things objects can do are sometimes referred to as responsibilities. For example, a car object can move forward, stop, backup, and park. Each thing an object can do — each responsibility — is programmed into the class and called a method.

In PHP, methods use the same syntax as functions. Although the code looks like the code for a function, the distinction is that methods are inside a class. It can't be called independently of an object. PHP won't allow it. This type of function can perform its task only when called with an object.

When creating methods, give them names that are descriptive of what they do. Methods often have names like `parkCar` or `getColor`. Methods, like other PHP entities, can be named with any valid name, but are often named with camel caps, by convention.

The methods are the interface between the object and the rest of the world. The object needs methods for all its responsibilities. Objects should interact with the outside world only through their methods. If your neighbor object wants to borrow a cup of sugar, you want him to knock on your door and request the sugar. You don't want him to just climb in the kitchen window and help himself. Your `house` object should have a `front door`, and `neighbor` objects should not be able to get into your house without using the `front door`. In other words, your house object has a method for openFrontDoor that the neighbor must use. There should not be any other way the neighbor can get into the house. Opening the `front door` is something your `house` object can do, via a method called `openDoor`. Don't leave any open windows in your object design.

A good object should contain all it needs to perform its responsibilities, but not a lot of extraneous data. It should not perform actions that are another object's responsibility. The car object should travel and should have everything it needs to perform its responsibilities, such as gas, oil, tires, engine, and so on. The car object should not cook and does not need to have salt or frying pans. Nor should the cook object carry the kids to soccer practice.

Inheritance

Objects should contain only the properties and methods they need. No more. No less. One way to accomplish that is to share properties and methods between classes by using *inheritance.* For example, suppose you have two rose objects: one with white roses and one with red roses. You could write two classes: a `redRose` class and a `whiteRose` class. However, a lot of the information is the same for both objects. Both are bushes, both are thorny, and both bloom in June. Inheritance enables you to eliminate the duplication.

You can write one class called `Rose`. You can store the common information in this class, such as `$plant = bush`, `$stem=thorns`, and `$blooms=June`. Then you can write subclasses for the two rose types. The `Rose` class is called the *master class* or the *parent class.* `redRose` and `whiteRose` are the *subclasses,* which are referred to as *child classes,* or the *kids,* as my favorite professor fondly referred to them.

Child classes inherit all the properties and methods from the parent class. But they can also have their own individual properties, such as `$color=white` for the `whiteRose` class and `$color=red` for the `redRose` class.

A child class can contain a method with the same name as a method in a parent class. In that case, the method in the child class takes precedence for a child object. You can specify the method in the parent class for a child object if you want, but if you don't, the child class method is used.

Object-oriented concepts PHP 5 omits

If you're familiar with object-oriented programming in other languages, you may find that some features you're accustomed to using aren't available in PHP. Things are getting better — many of the features missing in PHP 4 have been added in PHP 5. The still-missing features include the following:

- **Polymorphism:** PHP does not allow more than one method, even a constructor, to have the same name in a class. Therefore, you can't implement polymorphism as you're used to doing. You can't have two or more methods with the same name in the same class that accept different types or number of variables. Some people use switches and other mechanisms to implement the functionality of polymorphism.
- **Multiple inheritance:** PHP does not allow multiple inheritance. A class can inherit from only one parent class.

Developing an Object-Oriented Program

Object-oriented programs require a lot of planning, even more than procedural programs that process statement from beginning to end, without using classes. You need to plan your objects and their properties and what they can do. Your objects need to cover all their responsibilities without encroaching on the responsibilities of other objects. For complicated projects, you may have to do some model building and testing before you can feel reasonably confident that your project plan includes all the objects it needs.

Choosing objects

Your first task is to develop the list of objects needed for your programming project. If you're working alone and your project is small, the objects may be obvious. However, if you're working on a large, complex project, selecting the list of objects can be more difficult. For example, if your project is developing the software for a bank, your list of possible objects is large: account, teller, money, checkbook, wastebasket, guard, vault, alarm system, customer, loan, interest, and so on. But, do you need all those objects? What is your program going to do with the wastebasket in the front lobby? Or the guard? Well, perhaps your program needs to schedule shifts for the guards.

One strategy for identifying your objects is to list all the objects you can think of — that is, all the nouns that may have anything to do with your project. Sometimes programmers can take all the nouns out of the project proposal documentation to develop a pretty comprehensive list of possible objects.

After you have a long list of possible objects, your next task is to cross off as many as possible. You should eliminate any duplicates, objects that have overlapping responsibilities and objects that are unrelated to your project. For example, if your project relates to building a car, your car project probably needs to have objects for every part in the car. On the other hand, if your project involves traffic control in a parking garage, you probably only need a car object that you can move around; the car's parts don't matter for this project.

Selecting properties and methods for each object

After you have a comprehensive list of objects, you can begin to develop the list of properties for each object. Ask yourself what you need to know about each object. For example, for your car repair project, you probably need to know things like when the car was last serviced, its repair history, any accidents, details about the parts, and so on. For your parking garage project, you probably need to know only the car's size. How much room does the car take up in the parking garage?

You need to define the responsibilities of each object, and each object needs to be independent. It needs methods for actions that handle all of its responsibilities. For example, if one of your objects is a bank account, you need to know what a bank account needs to do. Well, first, it needs to be created, so you can define an `openNewAccount` method. It needs to accept deposits and disburse withdrawals. It needs to keep track of the balance. It needs to report the balance when asked. It may need to add interest to the account periodically. Such activities come to mind quickly.

However, a little more thought, or perhaps testing, can reveal activities that were overlooked. For example, the account stores information about its owner, such as name and address. Did you remember to include a method to update that information when the customer moves? It may seem trivial compared to moving the money around, but it won't seem trivial if you can't do it.

Creating and using the class

After you have decided on the design of an object, you can create and then use the object. The steps for creating and using an object are shown below:

1. **Write the `class` statement.**

   The `class` statement is a PHP statement that is the blueprint for the object. The `class` statement has a statement block that contains PHP code for all the properties and methods that the object has.

2. **Include the class in the script where you want to use the object.**

   The class statement can be written in the script itself. However, it is more common to save the `class` statement in a separate file and use an `include` statement to include the class at the beginning of the script that needs to use the object.

3. **Create an object in the script.**

   You use a PHP statement to create an object based on the class. This is called instantiation.

4. **Use the new object.**

   After you create a new object, you can use it to perform actions. You can use any method that is inside the class statement block.

The rest of this chapter provides the details needed to complete these steps.

Defining a Class

After you've determined the objects, properties, and methods your project requires, you're ready to define classes. The class is the template (pattern) for the object.

Writing a class statement

You write the `class` statement to define the properties and methods for the class. The `class` statement has the following general format:

```
class className
{
    Add statements that define the properties
    Add all the methods
}
```

You can use any valid PHP identifier for the class name, except the name `stdClass`. PHP uses the name `stdClass` internally, so you can't use this name.

All the property settings and method definitions are enclosed in the opening and closing curly brackets. If you want a class to be a subclass that inherits properties and methods, use a statement similar to the following:

```
class whiteRose extends Rose
{
    Add the property statements
    Add the methods
}
```

The object created from this class has access to all the properties and methods of both the `whiteRose` class and the `Rose` class. The `Rose` class, however, does not have access to properties or methods in the child class, `whiteRose`. Imagine, the child owns everything the parent owns, but the parent owns nothing of the child's. What an idea.

The next few sections show you how to set properties, and define methods, within the `class` statement. For a more comprehensive example of a complete class statement, see the section, "Putting it all together," later in this chapter.

Setting properties

When you're defining a class, you declare all the properties in the top of the class, as follows:

```
class Car
{
    var $color;
    var $tires;
    var $gas;


    Method statements
}
```

PHP does not require you to declare variables. In the other PHP scripts discussed in this book, variables are not declared; they're just used. You can do the same thing in a class. However, it's much better to declare the properties in a class. By including declarations, classes are much easier to understand. It's poor programming practice to leave this out.

If you want to set default values for the properties, you can, but the values allowed are restricted. You can declare a simple value, but not a computed one, as detailed in the following examples:

- The following variable declarations are allowed as default values:

  ```
  var $color = "black";
  var $gas = 10;
  var $tires = 4;
  ```

- The following variable declarations are *not* allowed as default values:

  ```
  var $color = "blue"." black";
  var $gas = 10-3;
  var $tires = 2*2;
  ```

An array is allowed in the variable declaration, as long as the values are simple, as follows:

```
var $doors = array("front","back");
```

You can set or change a variable's value when you create an object, by using the constructor (described in "Writing the constructor," later in this chapter) or a method you write for this purpose.

Using $this

Inside a class, `$this` is a special variable that refers to the properties of the same class. `$this` can't be used outside of a class. It's designed to be used in statements inside a class to access variables inside the same class.

The format for using $this is the following:

```
$this->varname
```

For example, in the Car class that has an attribute `$gas`, you would access `$gas` in the following way:

```
$this->gas
```

Using `$this` refers to `$gas` inside the class. You can use `$this` in any of the following statements as shown:

```
$this->gas = 20;
if($this->gas > 10)
$product[$this->size] = $price
```

As you can see, you use `$this->`*`varname`* in all the same ways you would use `$`*`varname`*.

Notice that a dollar sign ($) appears before `this` but not before `gas`. Don't use a dollar sign before `gas` — as in `$this->$gas` — because it changes your statement's meaning. You may or may not get an error message, but it isn't referring to the variable `$gas` inside the current class.

Adding methods

Methods define what an object can do and are written in the class by using the function format. For example, your car may need a method that puts gas in the gas tank. You can have a variable called gas that contains the amount of gas currently in the gas tank. You can write a method that adds an amount of gas to `$gas`. You could add such a method to your class as follows:

```
class Car
{
  var $gas = 0;
  function addGas($amount)
  {
     $this->gas = $this->gas + $amount;
     echo "$amount gallons added to gas tank";
  }
}
```

This looks just like any other function, but it's a method because it's inside a class.

PHP provides some special methods with names that begin with __ (two underscores). These methods are handled differently by PHP internally. This chapter discusses three of these methods: `construct`, `destruct`, and `clone`. Don't begin the names of any of your own methods with two underscores unless you are taking advantage of a PHP special method.

Writing the constructor

The *constructor* is a special method that is executed when an object is created using the class as a pattern. A constructor is not required, and you don't need to use a constructor if you don't want to set any property values or perform any actions when the object is created. Only one constructor is allowed.

The constructor has a special name so that PHP knows to execute the method when an object is created. Constructors are named `__construct`. (Note the two underscores.) A constructor method looks similar to the following:

```
function __construct()
{
    $this->gas = 10;   # starts with a full gas tank
    $this->openDoor();
}
```

This constructor defines the new car. When the car is created, it has a full gas tank and an open door.

Prior to PHP 5, constructors had the same name as the class. You may run across classes written in this older style. PHP 5 looks first for a method called `__construct()` to use as the constructor. If it doesn't find one, it looks for a method that has the same name as the class and uses that method for the constructor. Thus, older classes still run under PHP 5.

Putting it all together

Your class can have as few or as many properties and methods as it needs. These methods can be very simple or very complicated, but the goal of object-oriented programming is to make the methods as simple as is reasonable. Rather than cram everything into one method, it's better to have several smaller methods and have one method call another.

The following is a simple class:

```
class MessageHandler
{
   var $message = "No message";
   function __construct($message)
   {
      $this->message = $message;
   }
   function displayMessage()
   {
      echo $this->message."\n";
   }
}
```

The class has one property — `$message` — that stores a message. The message is stored in the constructor.

The class has one method — `displayMessage`. This is the only thing the `messageHandler` object is able to do — echo the stored message.

Suppose you want to add a method that changes the message to lowercase and then automatically displays the message. The best way to write that expanded class is as follows:

```
class MessageHandler
{
   var $message = "No message";
   function __construct($message)
   {
      $this->message = $message;
   }
   function displayMessage()
   {
      echo $this->message."\n";
   }
   function lowerCaseMessage()
   {
      $this->message = strtolower($this->message);
      $this->displayMessage();
   }
}
```

Note the `lowerCaseMessage()` method. Because the class already has a method to display the message, this new method uses the existing `displayMessage()` method rather than include the statements in the new method. Any time you write a method and find yourself writing code that you have already written elsewhere in a different method in the same class, you need to redesign the methods. In general, you should not have any duplicate code in the same class.

The Listing 9-1 example is a more complicated class that can be used to create an HTML form. To simplify the example, the form contains only text input fields.

Listing 9-1: A Script That Contains a Class for a Form Object

```
<?php
/* Class name: Form
 * Description: A class that creates a simple HTML form
 *              containing only text input fields. The
 *              class has 3 methods.
 */
class Form
{
  var $fields=array();  # contains field names and labels
  var $processor;       # name of program to process form
  var $submit = "Submit Form"; # value for the submit button
  var $Nfields = 0; # number of fields added to the form

/* Constructor: User passes in the name of the script where
 * form data is to be sent ($processor) and the value to show
 * on the submit button.
 */
  function __construct($processor,$submit)
  {
     $this->processor = $processor;
     $this->submit = $submit;
  }

/* Display form function. Displays the form.
 */
  function displayForm()
  {
     echo "<form action='{$this->processor}' method='post'>";
     echo "<table width='100%'>";
     for($j=1;$j<=sizeof($this->fields);$j++)
     {
        echo "<tr><td align=\"right\">
              {$this->fields[$j-1]['label']}: </td>\n";
        echo "<td>
              <input type='text'
                name='{$this->fields[$j-1]['name']}'>
              </td></tr>\n";
     }
```

```
      echo "<tr><td colspan=2 align='center'>
            <input type='submit'
                value='{$this->submit}'></td></tr>\n";
      echo "</table>";
   }

/* Function that adds a field to the form. The user needs to
 * send the name of the field and a label to be displayed.
 */
   function addField($name,$label)
   {
     $this->fields[$this->Nfields]['name'] = $name;
     $this->fields[$this->Nfields]['label'] = $label;
     $this->Nfields = $this->Nfields + 1;
   }
}
?>
```

This class contains four properties and three methods. The properties are as follows:

- `$fields`: An array that holds the fields as they are added by the user. The fields in the form are displayed from this array.
- `$processor`: The name of the script that the form is sent to. This variable is used in the action attribute when the form tag is displayed.
- `$submit`: The text that the user wants displayed on the submit button. This variable's value is used when the submit button is displayed.
- `$Nfields`: The number of fields that have been added to the form so far.

The methods in this class are as follows:

- `__construct`: The constructor, which sets the values of `$processor` and `$submit` from information passed in by the user.
- `addField`: Adds the name and label for the field to the `$fields` array. If the user added fields for first name and last name to the form, the array may look as follows:

  ```
  $fields[1][name]=first_name
  $fields[1][label]=First Name
  $fields[2][name]=last_name
  $fields[2][label]=Last Name
  and so on
  ```

- `displayForm`: Displays the form. It echoes the HTML needed for the form and uses the values from the stored variables for the name of the field and the label that the user sees by the field.

The next section describes how to use a class, including the form class shown in Listing 9-1.

Using a Class

The class code needs to be in the script that uses the class. Most commonly, the class is stored in a separate include file and is included in any script that uses the class.

To use an object, you first create the object from the class. Then that object can perform any methods that the class includes. Creating an object is called *instantiating* the object. Just as you can use a pattern to create many similar but individual dresses, you can use a class to create many similar but individual objects. To create an object, use statements that have the following format:

```
$objectname = new classname(value,value,...);
```

```
$Joe = new Person("male");
$car_Joe = new Car("red");
$car_Sam = new Car("green");
$customer1 = new Customer("Smith","Joe",$custID);
```

The object is stored in the variable name, and the constructor method is executed. You can then use any method in the class with statements of the following format:

```
$Joe->goToWork();
$car_Joe->park("illegal");
$car_Sam->paintCar("blue");
$name = $customer1->getName();
```

Different objects created from the same class are independent individuals. Sam's car gets painted blue, but Joe's car is still red. Joe gets a parking ticket, but it doesn't affect Sam.

The script shown in Listing 9-2 shows how to use the form class that was created in the previous section and shown in Listing 9-1.

Listing 9-2: A Script That Creates a Form By Using the Form Class

```
<?php
/* Script name: buildForm
 * Description: Uses the form to create a simple HTML form
 */
require_once("form.inc");
echo "<html><head><title>Phone form</title></head><body>";
$phone_form = new Form("process.php","Submit Phone");
$phone_form->addField("first_name","First Name");
$phone_form->addField("last_name","Last Name");
$phone_form->addField("phone","Phone");
```

```
echo "<h3>Please fill out the following form:</h3>";
$phone_form->displayForm();
echo "</body></html>";
?>
```

First, the script included the file containing the class into the script. The class is stored in the file form.inc. The script creates a new form object called `$phone_form`. Three fields are added. The form is displayed. Notice that some additional HTML code was output in this script. That HTML could have been added to the `displayForm` method just as easily.

The script creates a form with three fields, using the form class. Figure 9-1 shows the resulting Web page.

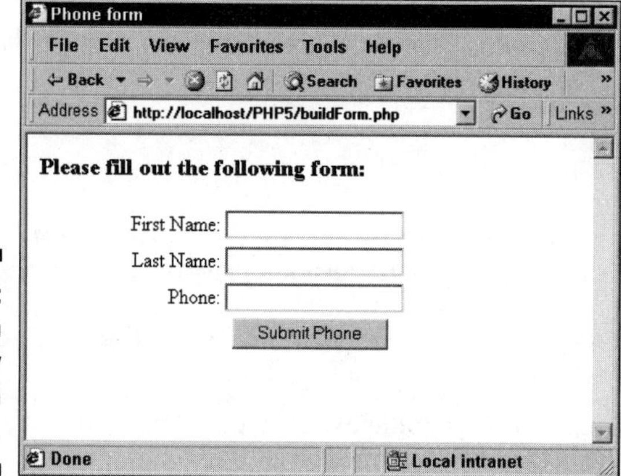

Figure 9-1: The form displayed by the script in Listing 9-2.

Making Properties and Methods Private

Properties and methods can be public or private. Public means that methods or properties inside the class can be accessed by the script that is using the class or from another class. For example, the following class has a public attribute and a public method as shown:

```
class Car
{
  var $gas = 0;
  function addGas($amount)
  {
     $this->gas = $this->gas + $amount;
     echo "$amount gallons added to gas tank";
  }
}
```

The public attribute in this class can be accessed by a statement in the script outside the class, as follows:

```
$mycar = new Car;
$gas_amount = $mycar->gas;
```

After these statements are run, `$gas_amount` contains the value stored in `$car` inside the object. The attribute can also be modified from outside the class, as follows:

```
$mycar->gas = 20;
```

Allowing script statements outside the class to directly access the properties of an object is poor programming practice. All interaction between the object and the script or other classes should take place using methods. The example class has a method to add gas to the car. All gas should be added to the car using the `addGas` method, which is also public, using statements similar to the following:

```
$new_car = new Car;
$new_car->addGas(5);
```

You can prevent access to properties by making them private. PHP provides two options for making properties and methods private, as follows:

- **private:** No access from outside the class, either by the script or from another class.
- **protected:** No access from outside except from a class that is a child of the class with the protected attribute or method.

You can make an attribute private as follows:

```
private $gas = 0;
```

With the attribute specified as private, a statement like the previous statement that attempts to access the attribute directly gets the following error message:

```
Fatal error: Cannot access private property car::$gas in
            c:\testclass.php on line 17
```

Now, the only way gas can be added to the car is using the `addGas` method. Because the `addGas` method is part of the `class` statement, it can access the private attribute.

In the same way, you can make methods private or protected. In this case, you want the outside world to use the `addGas` method. However, you may want to be sure that people buy the gas that is added. You don't want any stolen gas in your car. You could write the following class:

```
class Car
{
   private $gas = 0;
   private function addGas($amount)
   {
      $this->gas = $this->gas + $amount;
      echo "$amount gallons added to gas tank";
   }
   function buyGas($amount)
   {
      $this->addGas($amount);
   }
}
```

With this class, the only way gas can be added to the car from the outside is with the `buyGas` method. The `buyGas` method uses the `addGas` method to add gas to the car, but the `addGas` method can't be used outside the class because it is private. If a statement outside the class attempts to use `addGas`, as follows, a fatal error is displayed, as it was for the private attribute:

```
$new_car = new Car;
$new_car->addGas(5);
```

However, you can now add gas to the car using the `buyGas` method, as follows:

```
$new_car = new Car;
$new_car->buyGas(5);
```

You see the following output:

```
5 gallons added to gas tank
```

It's good programming practice to hide as much of your class as possible. Make all properties private. Only make methods public that absolutely need to be public.

PHP also provides an option to make properties and methods public. Although you don't need to use the public option, because public is the default, it helps to make the class more readable. The following statement:

```
public $gas = 0;
```

has the same effect as:

```
var $gas = 0;
```

Using Exceptions

PHP provides an error-handling class called `Exception`. You can use this class to handle undesirable things that happen in your script. When the undesirable thing that you define happens, a routine you have written is performed. In object-oriented talk, this is called *throwing an exception.*

In the `car` class, you keep track of the gas in the car and stop the car when it runs out of gas. You expect your program to detect 0 gallons and react. You don't expect the gas in the gas tank to be a negative amount. You consider that to be an exception, and you want to be sure that won't happen in your script. To deal with this, you can write a routine that uses the `Exception` class to watch for a negative gas amount. The following statements check for this situation:

```
$this->gas = $this->gas - 5;
  try
  {
     if ($this->gas < 0)
     {
       throw new Exception( "Negative amount of gas.");
     }
  }
  catch (Exception $e)
  {
     echo $e->getMessage();
     echo "\n<br />\n";
     exit();
  }
```

The preceding script contains a `try` block and a `catch` block:

- In the `try` block, you test a condition. If the condition is `TRUE`, you throw an exception — in other words, you create an `Exception` object. The `Exception` object has a property that stores the message you sent when you threw the exception.
- In the `catch` block, you catch the exception and call it `$e`. Then you execute the statements in the `catch` block. One of the statements is a call to a method called `getMessage` in the `Exception` class. The `getMessage` function returns the message that you stored, and your statement echoes the returned message. The statements then echo the end-of-line characters so the message is displayed correctly. The script stops on the `exit` statement.

  If no exception is thrown, the `catch` block has nothing to catch, and it is ignored. The script proceeds to the statements after the `catch` block.

Copying Objects

PHP provides a method you can use to copy an object. The method is __clone, with two underscores. You can write your own __clone method in a class if you want to specify statements to run when the object is copied. If you don't write your own, PHP uses it's default __clone method that copies all the properties as is. The two underscores indicate that the clone method is a different type of method, and thus is called differently, as shown in the following example.

For example, you could write the following class:

```
class Car
{
  private $gas = 0;
  private $color = "red";
  function addGas($amount)
  {
     $this->gas = $this->gas + $amount;
     echo "$amount gallons added to gas tank";
  }
  function __clone()
  {
     $this->gas = 0;
  }
}
```

Using this class, you could create an object and copy it as follows:

```
$firstCar = new Car;
$firstCar->addGas(10);
$secondCar=clone $firstCar;
```

After these statements, you have two cars:

- $firstCar: This car is red and contains 10 gallons of gas. The 10 gallons were added with the addGas method.
- $secondCar: This car is red, but contains 0 gallons of gas. The duplicate car is created using the __clone method in the Car class. This method sets gas to 0 and doesn't set $color at all.

If you did not have a __clone method in the Car class, PHP would use a default __clone method that would copy all the properties, making $secondCar both red and containing 10 gallons of gas.

Destroying Objects

You can destroy an object with the following statement:

```
unset($objName);
```

For example, you could create and destroy an object of the Car class with the following statements:

```
$myCar = new Car;
unset($myCar);
```

After `$myCar` is unset, the object no longer exists at all.

PHP provides a method that is automatically run when an object is destroyed. You add this method to your class and call it `__destruct`. For example, the following class contains a `__destruct` method:

```
class Bridge
{
  function __destruct()
  {
    echo "The bridge is destroyed";
  }
}
```

If you use the following statements, the object is created and destroyed:

```
$bigBridge = new Bridge;
unset($bigBridge);
```

The output from these statements is:

```
The bridge is destroyed
```

The output is echoed by the `__destruct` method when the object is unset.

The `__destruct` method is not required. It's just available for you to use if you want to execute some statements when the object is destroyed. For example, you might want to close some files or copy some information to your database.

Part IV
Common PHP Applications

"OK, I think I forgot to mention this, but we now have a Web management function that automatically alerts us when there's a broken link on the Aquarium's Web site."

In this part . . .

Part IV shows how to apply the features and functionality of PHP to common programming tasks. You find out how to write scripts to do the tasks that programmers most often need to do, and you also discover how PHP can interact with databases, operating systems, and e-mail applications. When you finish this part, you will know how to write scripts by using HTML forms to interact with your user, how to handle data, and many other tasks commonly performed with PHP.

Chapter 10

The Basics of Web Applications

In This Chapter

- Understanding Web site security
- Displaying static pages
- Collecting information from users with HTML forms
- Processing information received from users

PHP was originally designed for Web programming, and although its use for general-purpose scripts is growing, PHP is still used most frequently to develop dynamic Web sites. *Static* Web pages — pages where all users see the same Web page — don't allow for interaction between the user and the Web page. *Dynamic* Web pages, on the other hand, allow users to interact with the Web page. Users may see different Web pages, based on information they type into the Web page. For example, users might be required to type in valid usernames and passwords before they can see any Web pages on the Web site, allowing the site to customize Web pages based on users' previous preferences or profiles. Alternatively, users may select a type of product from an online catalog and see only the Web pages containing products of the type they select.

A dynamic Web page collects information from the user with an HTML form. The information that the user types into the form is then processed, depending on what the information will be used for. The information may be stored (see Chapter 12 for more on storing data using PHP) or used in a conditional statement to display alternative Web pages.

In this chapter, I do not tell you about the HTML required to display a form; I assume you already know HTML. (If you don't know HTML or need a refresher, check out *HTML 4 For Dummies,* 4th Edition, by Ed Tittel and Natanya Pitts [Wiley Publishing, Inc.].) What I do tell you is what you need to consider to keep your Web site secure and how to use PHP to display HTML forms and to process the information that users type into the form.

Securing Your Web Site

Web applications are particularly vulnerable to attacks from the outside. Most Web sites are open to the public, offering services, products, or information to anyone who visits. Dynamic Web sites are particularly vulnerable because they accept information from visitors to the site. Although the vast majority of visitors are good guys, trying to use the Web site for its intended purpose, a few people out have intentions that are not so pure, including the following groups:

- **People who want to steal things:** These are the folks who hope to find a file sitting around full of valid credit card numbers or a map to the pot of gold at the end of the rainbow.
- **People who want to destroy your Web site:** These saboteurs may think it's funny to wreck your site, or they may cause damage just to prove how smart they are.
- **People who want to harm your users:** These folks add things to your Web site that harm or steal from the people who visit your site.

This is not a security book. Security is a large, complex issue, and I am not a security expert. Nevertheless, I want to call a few issues to your attention and make some suggestions to help you protect your Web site. The following measures will increase the security of your Web site, but if your site handles really important, secret information, read some security books and talk to some experts:

- **Ensure the security of the computer that hosts your Web site.** This is the responsibility of the system administrator, which may or may not be you.
- **Keep information private.** Don't be more public than necessary. Store your information so it can't be easily accessed from the Web.
- **Be cautious of information from users.** Always clean any information that you didn't generate yourself.
- **Use a secure Web server.** This requires extra work, but it's important if you have top-secret information.

These topics are covered in more detail in the following sections.

Ensuring the security of the host computer

Your first line of defense is to make sure that the computer that hosts the Web site is secure. The computer's system administrator is responsible for keeping unauthorized visitors and vandals out of the system. Security measures include such things as firewalls, encryption, password shadowing, scan detectors, and so on. In most cases, the system administrator is not you. If it is, you need to do some serious investigation into security issues. If you're using a Web hosting company, you may want to discuss security with those folks, to reassure yourself that they're using sufficient security measures.

Keeping information private

Keep information as private as possible. Of course, the Web pages you want visitors to see must be stored in your public Web space directory. However, users don't need to see the names of the files stored there. You may have noticed that sometimes a site shows you a list of all the files in the directory. This is generally not a good idea. Your Web site isn't very secure if a visitor can look at any file on your site.

This list of files is displayed when the URL that the visitor types in points at a directory, rather than a specific file, and the directory doesn't contain a file with the default directory name. Most Web servers look first in a directory for a default name, specified in the server configuration, often `index.html`. If the directory doesn't contain a file with this default name, the server may display a list of files in the directory. A better choice is to have the Web server display a message telling visitors that they can't access the directory, similar to the following message:

```
Forbidden
You don't have permission to access /secretdirectory on this
          server.
```

A setting in the configuration of the Web server determines whether users see a list of files or a message. The Web server administrator can change the behavior. For example, in Apache, you control what is displayed by using an option called `Indexes`, which can be turned on or off in the `httpd.conf` file as follows:

```
Options Indexes          // turns file listing on
Options -Indexes         // turns file listing off
```

See the documentation for your Web server to allow or not allow directory listings in the user's Web browser.

It's also not wise to name a file an obvious, guessable name. For example, if you have a file containing secret passwords, it's not a good idea to name it `passwords.php`. You may want to call the file something odd or boring, such as `vegetableRecipes.php`. I know this suggestion violates other parts of the book where I promote informative filenames, but this is a special case. Malicious people sometimes do obvious things like typing `www.yoursite.com/passwords.html` into their browsers to see what happens.

Not everything needs to be public. For example, your database should not be stored in a public location. In fact, it can be stored on a totally different computer. Also, as discussed in Chapter 8, include files can be stored in a separate location, a space on the computer that can't be accessed from the Web.

Being cautious of information from users

Users can enter dangerous information into forms, either accidentally or with malicious intent. Therefore, never store or use information from forms without checking it first. Check it for reasonable formats and dangerous characters. Even characters entered accidentally can sometimes cause problems in your database or scripts. In particular, you don't want to accept HTML tags — such as `<script>` tags — from forms. Using script tags, a user can enter an actual script, perhaps a malicious one. If you accept the form field without checking it and store it in your database, you could have any number of problems, particularly if the stored script was sent in a Web page to a visitor to your Web site. For more on checking data from forms, see the section "Checking the information" later in this chapter.

Using a secure Web server

Communication between your Web site and its visitors is not totally secure. When the files on your Web site are sent to the user's browser, it is possible for someone on the Internet between you and the user to read the contents of these files as they pass by. For most Web sites, this isn't an issue, but if your site collects or sends credit card numbers or other secret information, use a secure Web server to protect this data.

Secure Web servers use SSL (Secure Sockets Layer) to protect communication sent to and received from browsers. This is similar to the scrambled telephone calls you hear about in spy movies. The information is encrypted (translated into coded strings) before it is sent across the Web. The receiving software decrypts it into its original content. In addition, your Web site uses a certificate that verifies your identity. Using a secure Web server is extra work, but it's necessary for some applications.

You can tell when you're communicating using SSL because the URL begins with `https` rather than `http`.

Information about secure Web servers is specific to the Web server you're using. To find out more about using SSL, look at the Web site for the Web server you're using. For example, if you're using Apache, check out two open source projects that implement SSL for Apache at `www.modssl.org` and `www.apache-ssl.org`. Commercial software is also available that provides a secure server based on the Apache Web server. If you're using Microsoft IIS, search for *SSL* on the Microsoft Web site at `www.microsoft.com`.

Displaying Static Web Pages

The simplest Web page design is a static Web page. If you need only static Web pages on your Web site, you don't need PHP. However, you may need static Web pages interspersed with your dynamic pages.

PHP can be used to display any Web pages, including static pages. You simply use `echo` statements to echo the appropriate HTML. If you have a Web page containing only HTML that needs to be displayed in a PHP script, the most efficient way to display the static Web page is to include it where it's needed with the following statement:

```
include("filename");
```

If you need to turn an existing static Web page into a PHP script, for some unlikely reason, you can add PHP tags at the beginning and end of the file. Then add `echo` at the top of the file and enclose the existing HTML code in single quotes.

Working with HTML Forms

For a Web page to be interactive, it must collect information from the user, which is done with HTML forms. The information collected may simply be a username and password for a user login. A form can also be long and elaborate, collecting a great deal of information from a user, such as shipping and credit card information for an online purchase application or a survey form asking many questions for research purposes.

To use HTML forms to collect information, your script displays the form on the Web site, and the user types information into text fields or selects items from a list. The user then clicks a button to submit the form information. When the form is submitted, the information in the form is passed to a second separate script, which processes the information.

This chapter provides basic information on using forms in a dynamic Web site. Often the information collected is stored in a database, or the form is displayed by using information retrieved from a database. If you're planning to use HTML forms teamed with a MySQL database, you can find more detailed information and more complex solutions in *PHP & MySQL For Dummies* by yours truly (Wiley Publishing, Inc.).

Collecting information from Web site visitors

HTML forms are used to collect information from Web site visitors. If you're unfamiliar with HTML forms, check out *HTML 4 For Dummies,* 4th Edition, by Ed Tittel and Natanya Pitts.

Displaying HTML Forms

To display a form by using PHP, you can do one of the following:

- **Use `echo` statements to echo the HTML for a form.** The following statements echo a form by using this method:

```
echo "<form action='processform.php' method='POST'>\n
     <input type='text' name='name'>\n
     <input type='submit' value='Submit Name'>\n
     </form>\n";
```

- **Use plain HTML outside the PHP sections.** For a plain static form, you don't need to include it in a PHP section. For example, the following statements produce the same form as the preceding example:

```
<?php
   statements in PHP section
?>
<form action="processform.php" method="POST">
<input type="text" name="fullname">
<input type="submit" value="Submit Name">
</form>
<?php
  statements in PHP section
?>
```

Both of these examples display the same form, which is shown in Figure 10-1.

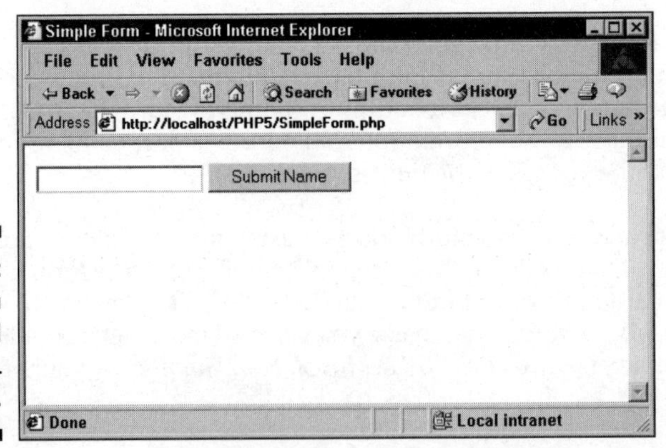

Figure 10-1: A form produced by HTML statements.

The form in Figure 10-1 has one text field, which is blank. It also has a button labeled Submit Name. The user types a name into the text field and clicks the button. When the user submits the form, the information in the form is passed to the script designated in the action attribute of the form tag. In this example, the action attribute is `action="processform.php"`, so when the user clicks the submit button, the script `processform.php` is called, and the information in the form is passed to it. (I am using `processform.php` as an example name here. You can name the script that processes the form with any name you want.)

PHP allows you to use variables in PHP forms, making the forms more powerful. Using variables, you can display information in the input text fields and build dynamic lists for selection boxes, radio buttons, and check boxes.

Displaying information in text fields

In some cases, you may want to display information in the text fields rather than just display blank fields. For example, you may want to display a default value in a field. Or, when displaying a form to a user to reenter incorrect information, you want to retain the correct information so that the user has to retype information only in the field with the error.

To display text fields that contain information, you use the following format for the input field HTML statements:

```
<input type="text" name="fieldname" value="content">
```

For example, suppose you're displaying a form to collect a customer's name and address. You know that most of your customers live in the U.S., so you decide to display the field with `US` as the default. If customers are from the U.S., you save them some typing and avoid errors they may type in. If customers are not from the U.S., they can just replace `US` with the correct country. You can display the country field with the following statement:

```
<input type="text" name="country" value="US">
```

In some cases, you may want to display variable information in a text field. You can use a PHP variable to display information. For example, suppose you have customer information (such as a phone number) stored in a database, and you want to display the information in a form so that the user can update any incorrect or outdated information. First, you retrieve the customer information from a database (see Chapter 12 for the lowdown on using a database) and store the information in variables. Next, you can display the form by using the information in the variables in one of two ways. You can create an input field in an HTML section by using a short PHP section for the value only, as follows:

```
<input type="text" name="phone" value="<?php echo $phone ?>">
```

Alternatively, you can create an input field by using an `echo` statement inside a PHP section:

```
echo "<input type='text' name='phone' value='$phone'>";
```

If you're using a long form with only an occasional variable, it's more efficient to use the first format. If your form uses many variables, it's more efficient to use the second format.

The script in Listing 10-1 displays a form containing customer information. Figure 10-2 shows the output from this script.

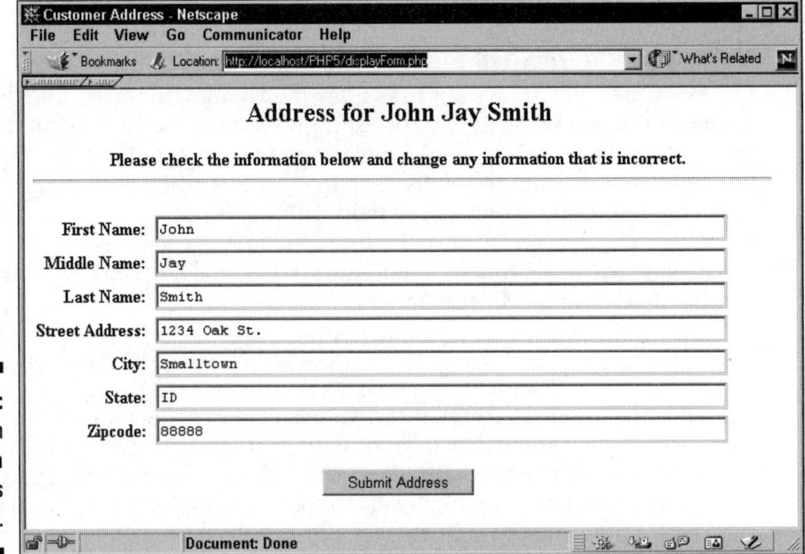

Figure 10-2: A form showing a customer's address.

Listing 10-1: A Script That Displays an HTML Form

```
<?php
/*  Script name:  displayForm
 *  Description:  Script displays a form and populates the
 *                form fields with the values of an array.
 */
  echo "<html>
        <head><title>Customer Address</title></head>
        <body>";
  $customer = array( "firstName"=>"John",
                     "midName"=>"Jay",
                     "lastName"=>"Smith",
                     "street"=>"1234 Oak St.",
                     "city"=>"Smalltown",
                     "state"=>"ID",
                     "zip"=>"88888");
```

```
   $labels = array( "firstName"=>"First Name:",
                    "midName"=>"Middle Name:",
                    "lastName"=>"Last Name:",
                    "street"=>"Street Address:",
                    "city"=>"City:",
                    "state"=>"State:",
                    "zip"=>"Zipcode:");
   echo "<h2 align='center'>Address for
           {$customer['firstName']}
           {$customer['midName']}
           {$customer['lastName']}</h2>\n";
   echo "<p align='center'>
         <b>Please check the information below and change any
            information that is incorrect.</b>
         <hr>
         <form action='processform.php' method='POST'>
         <table width='95%' border='0' cellspacing='0'
                                        cellpadding='2'>\n";
   foreach($customer as $field=>$value)
   {
     echo "<tr>
          <td align='right'> <B>{$labels[$field]} </br></td>
          <td><input type='text' name='$field' size='65'
             maxlength='65' value='{$customer[$field]}'></td>
          </tr>";
   }
   echo "</table>
         <div align='center'><p><input type='submit'
            value='Submit Address'> </p></div>
         </form>";
?>
</body></html>
```

Notice the following in displayForm.php, shown in Listing 10-1:

- **An array is created at the start of the script, which contains the information that is displayed in the form.** In real-life applications, you probably obtain this information from a database, a file, or other sources.
- **An array is created that contains the labels that are used in the form.**
- **The script processform.php is named as the script that runs when the form is submitted.** The information in the form is sent to processform.php, which processes the information.
- **The form is formatted with an HTML table.** Tables are an important part of HTML. If you're not familiar with HTML tables, check out *HTML 4 For Dummies,* 4th Edition, by Ed Tittel and Natanya Pitts.
- **The script loops through the $customer array with a foreach statement.** The HTML code for a table row is output in each loop. The appropriate array values are used in the HTML code.

For security reasons, always include maxlength — which defines the number of characters users are allowed to type into the field — in your HTML statement. Limiting the number of characters helps prevent the bad guys from typing malicious code into your form fields. If the information will be stored in a database, set maxlength to the same number as the width of the column in the database table.

Adding selection lists, radio buttons, and check boxes to forms

Other elements in HTML forms, such as selection lists, radio buttons, and check boxes, can be used with variables. To use one of these elements in your form, you echo the HTML that creates the form element and use variables for information that changes. For example, you can use a selection list in your form with the following statements:

```
echo "<select name='dinner' >
         <option>$dinner1</option>
         <option>$dinner2</option>
      </select>";
```

The selections in this selection list are the values in the variables. For example, $dinner1 could display chicken, and $dinner2 could display fish. When the user submits the form, the selected value is passed to the next script.

Similarly, you can use radio buttons in your form, as follows:

```
echo "<input type='radio' name='dinner'
          value='$dinner1'>$dinner1
      <input type='radio' name='dinner'
          value='$dinner2'>$dinner2";
```

The radio buttons that users can select are chicken and fish.

Check boxes allow users to check more than one box. Therefore, when you use check boxes, the name attribute must be an array, as in the following example:

```
echo "<input type='checkbox' name='dinner[]'
          value='$dinner1'>$dinner1
      <input type='checkbox' name='dinner[]'
          value='$dinner2'>$dinner2";
```

The form stores all the checked boxes in an array called $dinner. If both of the values above are selected, the form stores both values in the array as follows:

```
$dinner[0]=chicken
$dinner[1]=fish
```

The script in Listing 10-2 displays a Web page with a selection list that allows the user to select a date. In this form, the current date is selected by default.

Listing 10-2: A Script That Displays a Date Selection List

```
<?php
/*  Script name:  displayDate
 *  Description:  Script displays a selection list, with
 *                three parts--months, days, and years. The
 *                current date is selected by default.
 */
  echo "<html>
        <head><title>Date</title></head>
        <body>";
/* Create an array of month numbers and names */
  $monthName = array(1=> "January", "February", "March",
                         "April", "May", "June", "July",
                         "August", "September", "October",
                         "November", "December");
  $today = Time();  #stores today's date
  echo "<div align='center'><b>Select a date:</b>
        <form action='processform.php' method='POST'>\n";
 /* Build selection list for month */
  $todayMO = date("m",$today);  #get the month from $today
  echo "<select name='dateMO'>\n";
  for ($n=1;$n<=12;$n++)
  {
    echo "<option value=$n";
    if ($todayMO == $n)  #adds selected attribute if today
    {
      echo " selected";
    }
    echo "> $monthName[$n]\n";
  }
  echo "</select>";

  /* build selection list for the day */
  $todayDay= date("d",$today);   #get the day from $today
  echo "<select name='dateDay'>\n";
  for ($n=1;$n<=31;$n++)
  {
    echo " <option value=$n";
    if ($todayDay == $n )
    {
      echo " selected";
    }
    echo "> $n\n";
  }
  echo "</select>\n";

  /* build selection list for the year */
  $startYr = date("Y", $today);   #get the year from $today
  echo "<select name='dateYr'>\n";
  for ($n=$startYr;$n<=$startYr+3;$n++)
```

(continued)

Listing 10-2 *(continued)*

```
    {
      echo " <option value=$n";
      if ($startYr == $n )
      {
        echo " selected";
      }
      echo "> $n\n";
    }
    echo "</select>\n";
    echo "</form>\n";
  ?>
  </body>
  </html>
```

The script creates `$monthName`, an array with elements that have all the month numbers for keys and month names for values. Next it stores today's date in `$today`.

The rest of the script echoes a form that contains three selection lists, in drop down boxes, for the three parts of the date: month, day, and year. For the month, the `foreach` list creates a list of all the months, taken from the array `$monthName`. Each month is compared with the month of today's date stored in `$today`. If the month is the same as today's month, then the "selected" attribute is added to the selection, so the month is the default selection.

Similar lists are created for day and year. These lists are just numbers, so a `for` loop is used to create the list of numbers for the selection list. Again, each day and year are compared to the day and year in today's date and the current day and year are selected as the default.

The form displayed by the script in Listing 10-2 is shown in Figure 10-3.

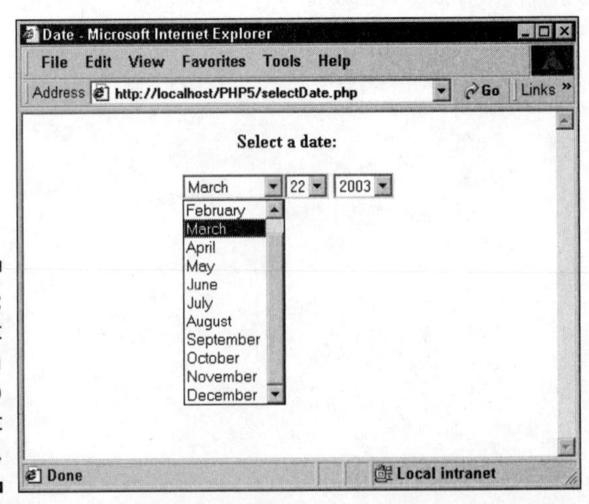

Figure 10-3: A form that allows a user to select a date.

Receiving the information

In the form tag, you tell PHP which script to run when the user clicks the submit button. You do this with the attribute `action="scriptname"` in the form tag. For example, in Listings 10-1 and 10-2 earlier in this chapter, I use `action="processform.php"`. When the user clicks the submit button, the script runs and receives the information from the form.

The form data is available in the processing script in the PHP built-in arrays, as described in Chapter 6. Information from forms that use the POST method is available in the built-in array called `$_POST`. If your form uses the GET method, the information is available in the array `$_GET`. Both types of form information are also stored in an array called `$_REQUEST`. Each array index is the name of the input field in the form. You get information from the array by using the form field name as the array key. For example, suppose that you echo the following field in your form that uses the POST method:

```
echo "<input type='text' name='firstName'>";
```

Setting `name` to `firstName` allows the processing script to use the variable `$_POST['firstName']`, which contains the text the user typed into the field. The information the user selects from selection drop-down lists or radio buttons is similarly available for use. Because the user can check more than one check box, information in check boxes is an array in the `$_POST` array and available as a multidimensional array. For example, if two check boxes for dinner choices (as described in the previous section) are both checked and submitted, the information is available in the following array:

```
$_POST['dinner'][0] = chicken
$_POST['dinner'][1] = fish
```

The script in Listing 10-3 displays the values for all the fields in a form displayed in Figure 10-2 earlier in the chapter.

Listing 10-3: A Script That Displays All the Fields from a Form

```
<?php
/*  Script name:  displayFormFields
 *  Description:  Script displays all the information passed
 *                from a form.
 */
  echo "<html>
        <head><title>Customer Address</title></head>
        <body>";
  foreach ($_POST as $field => $value)
  {
     echo "$field = $value<br>";
  }
?>
</body></html>
```

POST versus GET

You use one of two methods to submit form information. The methods pass the form data differently and have different advantages and disadvantages:

- **GET method:** The form data is passed by adding it to the URL that calls the form-processing script. For example, the URL may look like this:

  ```
  processform.php?lname=Smith&fname=Gol
        iath
  ```

  The advantages of this method are simplicity and speed. The disadvantages are that less data can be passed and the information is displayed in the browser, which can be a security problem in some situations.

- **POST method:** The form data is passed as a package in a separate communication with the processing script. The advantages of this method are unlimited information passing and security of the data. The disadvantages are the additional overhead and slower speed.

For CGI programs other than PHP, the program that processes the form must find the information and put the data into variables. In this case, the GET method is much simpler and easier to use. Many programmers use the GET method for this reason. However, PHP does all this work for you. The GET and POST methods are equally easy to use in PHP scripts. Therefore, when using PHP, it's almost always better to use the POST method, because you have the advantages of the POST method (unlimited data passing, better security) without its main disadvantage (more difficult to use).

You can use this script to process the information from the form displayed in Figure 10-2, which displays a customer's address. To do so, you must use the action attribute `action="displayFormFields.php"` in the script `displayForm.php`, which is shown in Listing 10-1. Then when the user clicks the Submit Address button in the form, the script in Listing 10-3 runs and produces the following output on a new Web page:

```
firstName = John
lastName = Smith
street = 1234 Oak St.
city = Smalltown
state = ID
zip = 88888
```

The script shown in Listing 10-3 displays all the values passed via the form in Figure 10-2. In most cases, you don't want to just display the values. Usually, you want to use the values for a purpose. Either you use the values in a conditional statement or you store the values, usually in a database.

Checking the information

Before you use the values in your script, you need to check the variables to make sure they contain what you expect them to contain. The user may have left required fields blank when entering information. The user may have made mistakes in typing information, so the information makes no sense. Or, the user may even have typed in malicious information that can cause problems for you or for visitors using your Web site. Thus, *never* trust information received from outside sources. *Always* check any information received in a form.

Validating information

Checking the information is called *validating* the information and includes checking for empty fields and checking the format of the information, as described in the following list:

- **Checking for empty fields:** You can require users to enter information in a field. If the field is blank, the user is told that the information is required, and the form is displayed again so the user can type the missing information.
- **Checking the format of the information:** Whenever users must type information in a form, you can expect a certain number of typos. You can detect some of these errors when the form is submitted and then point out errors to users and request that they type the information again. For example, *ab3&*xx* is clearly not a valid zip code.

You can check for empty fields by using the following function:

```
empty($_POST['fieldname'])
```

For example, you could use the following code in your processing script:

```
if(empty($_POST['fieldname']))
{
   echo "Field is blank";
   statements that redisplay the field
}
```

Checking the format of information passed into a form can help identify typos. For example, if the user types 8899776 in the zip code field, you know this is not a valid zip code. This information is too long to be a zip code and too short to be a zip + 4 code.

Checking the format also helps protect you from malicious users — users who want to damage your Web site or your database or steal information from you or your users. For example, you don't want users to enter HTML tags into a form field, something that can have unexpected results when sent to a browser. (A script tag that allows a user to enter a script into a form field is a particularly dangerous tag.)

If you check each field for its expected format, you can catch typos and prevent most malicious content. However, checking information is a balancing act. You want to catch as much incorrect data as possible, but you don't want to block legitimate information. For example, when you're checking a phone number, you limit it to numbers. The problem with this check is that it would screen out legitimate phone numbers in the form such as 555-5555 or (888) 555-5555. So, you also need to allow hyphens parentheses, and spaces. You could limit the field to a length of 14 characters, including parentheses, spaces, and hyphens, but this screens out overseas numbers or numbers that include an extension. The bottom line: You need to think carefully about what information you want to accept or screen out for any field.

Using regular expressions to check user input

You can check field information by using regular expressions, which are described in Chapter 7. You compare the information in the field to a pattern to see if it matches. If it does not match, you have determined that the information in the field is incorrect, and you can ask the user to reenter it.

For example, suppose you want to check an input field that contains the user's last name. You can expect names to contain letters, not numbers, and possibly apostrophes (O'Hara), hyphens (Smith-Jones), and spaces (Van Dyke). Also, it's difficult to imagine a name longer than 50 characters. Thus, you can use the following statements to check a name:

```
$last_name = trim($_POST['last_name']);
if ( !ereg("[A-Za-z' -]{1,50}",$last_name)
{
    do stuff to require user to reenter last name;
}
```

First, use the `trim` function to remove any beginning or trailing blank spaces — they're not needed. Notice that the condition in the `if` statement is negative. That is, the exclamation mark (`!`) means *not.* So, the `if` statement says: If the variable does *not* match the pattern, execute the `if` block.

If you want to list a hyphen (`-`) as part of a set of allowable characters surrounded by square brackets (`[ ]`), you must list the hyphen at the beginning or at the end of the list. Otherwise, if you put it between two characters, the script will interpret it as the range between the two characters, such as `A-Z`.

Using a script to create, display, and validate a form

The script in Listing 10-4 validates data received from a form. The script displays the empty form when it is first run. When the user submits the form, the same script is run again, and the form information is passed to it. The script checks the form fields for blank fields and for incorrectly formatted fields. If it finds errors, it displays an error message and redisplays the form. If all the form information passes the checks, the script displays the user's name and address.

The script requires two include files. One file, shown in Listing 10-5, creates an array that is used to build the form. The other include file, shown in Listing 10-6, displays the form.

Listing 10-4: A Script That Checks All the Data in the Form Fields

```
<?php
/*  Script name:   validateForm
 *  Description:   Displays and validates a form that
 *                 collects a name and address.
 */
  include("info.inc");                                     #6
  #################################
  ## First display of empty form ##
  #################################
  if(!isset($_POST['Submit']))                             #10
  {
    include("addressForm.inc");
  }
  ###########################################################
  ## Check information when form is submitted. Build      ##
  ## arrays of blank and incorrectly formatted fields.    ##
  ## If any errors are found, display error messages      ##
  ## and redisplay form. If no errors found, display      ##
  ## the submitted information.                           ##
  ###########################################################
  else                                                     #21
  {
    foreach($_POST as $field=>$value)                      #23
    {
      if(empty($_POST[$field]))                            #25
      {
        if($field != "midName")
        {
          $blanks[$field] = "blank";                       #29
        }
      }
```

(continued)

Listing 10-4 *(continued)*

```
      else                                                   #33
      {
        $value = trim($value);
        if($field != "zipcode")
        {
          if(!ereg("^[A-Za-z0-9' .-]{1,65}$",$value))
          {
            $formats[$field] = "bad";
          }
        }
        elseif($field == "zipcode")
        {
          if(!ereg("^[0-9]{5}(\-[0-9]{4})?",$value))
          {
            $formats[$field] = "bad";
          }
        }
      }
    }                                                         #51
    ### if any fields were not okay, display error ###
    ### message and redisplay form                 ###
    if (@sizeof($blanks) > 0 or @sizeof($formats) > 0)  #54
    {
      if (@sizeof($blanks) > 0)
      {
        echo "<b>You didn't fill in one or more
                 required fields. You must enter:</b><br>";
        foreach($blanks as $field => $value)
        {
          echo "   {$labels[$field]}<br>";
        }
      }
      if (@sizeof($formats) > 0)
      {
        echo "<b>One or more fields have information that
                 appears to be incorrect. Correct the
                 format for:</b><br>";
        foreach($formats as $field => $value)
        {
          echo "   {$labels[$field]}<br>";
        }
      }
      echo "<hr>";
      include("addressForm.inc");
    }
    else                                                      #78
    {
```

```
      ### If no errors in the form, display the ###
      ### name and address submitted by user    ###
       echo "<html><head><title>Name and Address
             </title></head><body>\n";
       foreach($_POST as $field=>$value)
       {
         if($field != "Submit")
         {
           echo "{$labels[$field]} $value<br>\n";
         }
       }
       echo "</body></html>";
     }
  }
?>
```

I have added line numbers at the end of some of the lines in Listing 10-4 to point out some important points in the script, as described in the following list:

- **Line 6:** This statement includes a file called `info.inc` that creates an array called `labels` with information used later in the script. The included file is shown in Listing 10-5. (See Chapter 8 for more on including files in scripts.)
- **Line 10:** This `if` statement checks for the existence of `Submit` in the `$_POST` array. The submit button in the form is given the name `Submit`. Therefore, if the form has been submitted, `Submit` will be in `$_POST`. The condition is negative, so if `Submit` does not exist, the block is executed. The block just includes a file called `addressForm.inc` that displays the form. The include file is shown in Listing 10-6. This block is executed the first time the script is called and displays a blank form.
- **Line 21:** This line starts the `else` block in which `Submit` does exist in `$_POST`. This section executes when the user submits a form and validates the data.
- **Line 23:** This line starts a loop through each element in `$_POST`. This `foreach` block checks each field in the form.
- **Line 25:** This `if` statement checks whether each field is empty. If the field is not blank, the script goes to line 33, which begins a block that checks the format of the field.
- **Line 29:** This statement adds an element to the array `$blanks` for each field that is blank. However, notice that this line does not execute if the field name is `midName`. That is because Middle Name is not a required field, so it can be blank.

- **Line 33:** This is an else statement. If a field is not blank, this else statement checks whether the format is acceptable. It checks all the fields, except zip code, to look for unacceptable characters. Acceptable characters are letters, numbers, an apostrophe, a space, a dot, and a hyphen. The zip code field is checked separately for its exact format. If any fields have unacceptable characters or the zip code doesn't have the correct format, an element for the field is added to the $formats array.
- **Line 51:** This is the end of the section that checks the form fields. At this point, the script has created two arrays, $blanks and $formats, that contain entries for any errors that were found. If no errors were found, the arrays were not created.
- **Line 54:** This if statement checks to see if any errors were found by checking to see if the arrays $blanks and $formats were created. If either array is found, the error message is displayed, and the form is redisplayed, retaining the information that the user typed so it can be corrected.
- **Line 78:** This else statement executes if no errors were found in the form information. The else block displays all the information that the user submitted in the form.

Notice that the script in Listing 10-4 is quite generic. That is, it processes information from any form, with the exception of the section that checks the format of the data in the fields. The section between lines 33 and 50 is customized for the specific form being validated. However, the other sections remain the same for most forms.

Listing 10-5 shows the file that is included, which creates the array used to display the form and the error messages.

Listing 10-5: An Include File That Creates the Array

```
<?php
/*  Script name:  info.inc
 *  Description:  creates an array of labels for use in a
 *                form.
 */
$labels = array( "firstName"=>"First Name:",
                 "midName"=>"Middle Name:",
                 "lastName"=>"Last Name:",
                 "street"=>"Street Address:",
                 "city"=>"City:",
                 "state"=>"State:",
                 "zipcode"=>"Zipcode:");
?>
```

Listing 10-6 shows the script that displays the form. This is based on the script shown in Listing 10-1 that displays the form shown in Figure 10-2.

Listing 10-6: An Include File That Displays the Form

```
<?php
/*  Script name:  addressForm.inc
 *  Description:  Script displays a form.
 */
  echo "<html>
        <head><title>Customer Address</title></head>
        <body>";
  echo "<p align='center'>
        <form action='validateForm.php' method='POST'>
        <table width='95%' border='0' cellspacing='0'
              cellpadding='2'>\n";
  foreach($labels as $field=>$value)
  {
    if(isset($_POST[$field]))                            #13
    {
       $value = $_POST[$field];
    }
    else
    {
       $value = "";
    }
    echo "<tr><td align='right'>{$labels[$field]}</br></td>
          <td><input type='text' name='$field' size='65'
                 maxlength='65'
                 value='$value'> </td> </tr>";
  }
  echo " </table>
         <div align='center'>
           <p><input type='Submit' name='Submit'
               value='Submit Address'></p></div>
         </form>";
?>
</body></html>
```

Notice that an `if-else` block begins on line 13. The block sets the values that are displayed in the form fields. The first time the form is displayed, the `$_POST` array does not exist, because the form has not been submitted yet. Therefore, the `if` statement on line 13 checks whether the `$_POST` element for the field exists. If it does not exist, `$value` is set to blank. If the `$_POST` entry does exist, `$value` is set to the information that the user typed in. The variable `$value` is then used when the form is displayed.

Notice that the line that creates the submit button includes a name attribute, in this case, name='Submit', as follows:

```
<p><input type='Submit' name='Submit'
             value='Submit Address'></p></div>
```

This causes the submit value to be included in the $_POST array. You can include two submit buttons in your form, with the same name but different values, and perform different actions based on which submit button the user clicked. That is, you can use an if statement such as if($_POST['Submit'] == "Submit Address").

The Web page in Figure 10-4 results when users accidentally type their first names into the middle name field and also type nonsense for their zip codes. Notice that two error messages appear, indicating that the First Name field is blank and that the zip code field contains incorrect information.

Cleaning information

If you check the format of the data carefully, you can often prevent the bad guys from typing malicious characters into your form fields. If you can limit the format of the input you accept, such as checking for a format for a zip code or a telephone number, or limit the input characters to letters and numbers, you can protect yourself fairly well. However, sometimes you need to accept anything the user enters. Your users might need to type in mathematical symbols or HTML code. For example, you might be writing a script for a bulletin board and want users to be able to enter anything into their messages.

When user input can't be restricted much, bad guys are able to enter malicious code into your form fields. For example, they could enter an actual script by using script tags. Depending on what you do with the information from the form, the malicious script can run on your system or be downloaded to run on the system of a visitor to your Web site.

PHP provides two functions that can clean the data, rendering it harmless:

- strip_tags: This function removes all tags from the text, although you can tell it to allow specific tags.
- htmlspecialchars: This function changes some special characters with meaning to HTML into an HTML format that allows them to be displayed without any special meaning. The changes are as follows:
    - < becomes <
    - > becomes >
    - & becomes &

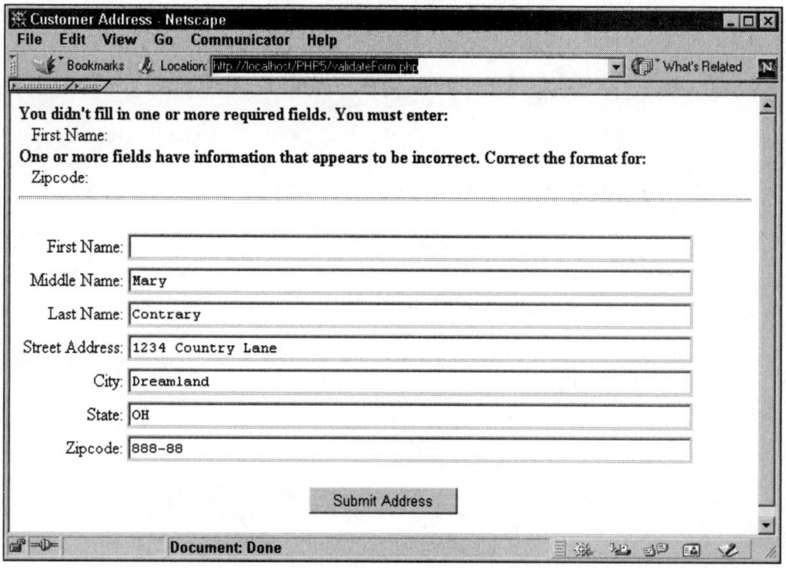

Figure 10-4: The result of processing a form with both missing and incorrect information.

It's safest to remove all tags from the user input. To remove all tags, use the following type of statement:

```
$last_name = strip_tags($last_name);
```

PHP looks for an opening < and removes it and everything else, until it finds a closing > or reaches the end of the string. You can tell PHP that specific tags are okay by using a statement like the following:

```
$last_name = strip_tags($last_name,"<b><i>");
```

This statement tells PHP to remove all tags from the string in $last_name except <b> and <i>.

You may need to allow users to enter < or > characters. For example, if users are entering text that will be displayed in a Web page and they need to display < or >, such as in a mathematical formula or to display HTML code, you don't want to remove the tags. You can change the tags to HTML entities, which HTML will display on a Web page as symbols and will not interpret as tags. You can change the tags with the following type of statement:

```
$message = htmlspecialchars($message);
```

The following example shows the difference between the two functions. Suppose $message contains the following text, typed into your form by a user:

```
Use the <?php ?> tags to enclose PHP statements.
```

You can use the following statements to strip the tags from `$message` and then echo the updated value:

```
$message = strip_tags($message);
echo $message;
```

The output of the `echo` statement is as follows:

```
Use the  tags to enclose PHP statements.
```

However, you can use the following statements instead:

```
$message = htmlspecialchars($message);
echo $message;
```

In this case, the output is different:

```
Use the &lt;?php ?&gt; tags to enclose PHP statements.
```

This output displays in the browser as follows:

```
Use the <?php ?> tags to enclose PHP statements.
```

This source is displayed correctly, but because the browser does not interpret it as a tag, the browser doesn't try to process the text as a PHP section. It just displays the source.

Another function useful for cleaning input is the `trim` function. Users often accidentally add spaces to the beginning or ending of a form field. These extra spaces sometimes cause problems, such as when you compare the input to a pattern. Use a statement like the following to remove these spaces:

```
$last_name = trim($last_name);
```

Chapter 11

Other Web Applications

In This Chapter

- Passing information from page to page
- Using cookies
- Using hidden fields in HTML forms
- Using PHP session functions
- Adding JavaScript to PHP scripts

The simplest Web applications collect information from users in HTML forms and then utilize the information by displaying it, storing it, or using it in conditional statements. (Some simple applications are shown in Chapter 10.) However, Web applications can be much more complex than this. For example, a shopping cart must collect different types of information; display this information; keep track of what users have ordered; calculate prices, taxes, and shipping; charge credit cards; and perform other tasks. Such complex applications consist of several scripts that share information. And applications may also accept complete files from users rather than just information in a form.

This chapter discusses the basics of these complex Web applications.

Overcoming Statelessness

HTML pages are *stateless.* That is, HTML pages are independent from one another. When a user clicks a link, the Web server sends a new page to the user's browser, but the browser doesn't know anything about the previous page. As far as the browser knows, this could be the first Web page ever in the history of the world. For static Web pages, where the user simply views a document, statelessness works fine. However, many dynamic Web applications need information to pass from page to page. For example, you may want to save a user's name and then display the name on another page.

The next few sections discuss methods of passing information from page to page.

Navigating Web Sites with Multiple Pages

Most Web sites consist of more than one Web page. A static multipage Web site provides a navigation system, consisting of links (which sometimes look like buttons) that users click to move around in the Web site and to find the desired page. A dynamic Web page can use links to move from one page to another, but uses additional methods as well. The following methods are used in PHP scripts to move users from one page to another on a Web site:

- **Echoing links:** Links send users to a new page when the user clicks the link.
- **Using forms:** Forms move users from one page to another when the user clicks the submit button.
- **Relocating users:** PHP provides the header function that takes the user to a new page without needing an action from the user.

These methods are described in more detail in the following sections.

Echoing links

Using PHP, you can echo HTML links, which the user can then click to see various pages in your Web site. This is no different than echoing any other HTML code. Just send the HTML for the links, as in the following:

```
echo "<a href='newpage.php'>New Page</a>";
```

Using forms

You can also use an HTML form to display another page, as described in Chapter 10. The `form` tag specifies a script that processes the form information. When the submit button is clicked, the specified script receives the data from the form and displays a new Web page.

The form does not have to collect information in order to display a new page. You can use an empty form on a Web page to provide a button that a user can click to move to another page. For example, you may want to provide a button labeled Cancel or Next for the user to click, even when you don't want to collect any information from the user. To do so, just use the HTML form tags and include only an `input` statement for a submit button. The button then appears by itself on the Web page, and the script specified in the `form` tag displays when the user clicks the submit button.

Statements that must come before output

Some PHP statements can only be used before sending any output to the browser. Header statements, setcookie statements, and session functions, all described in this chapter, must all come before any output is sent. If you use one of these statements after sending output, you may see the following message:

```
Warning: Cannot modify header
    information - headers
    already sent by (output
    started at /test.php:2) in
    /test.php on line 3
```

The message provides the name of the file and indicates which line sent the previous output. Or you may not see a message at all; the new page may just not appear. (Whether you see an error message depends on what error message level is set in PHP; see Chapter 4 for details.) The following statements fail because the header message is not the first output (an HTML section comes before the header statement):

```
<html>
<head><title>testing
    header</title></head>
<body>
<?php
   header("Location:
   http://janetscompany.com");
?>
</body></html>
```

As you can see, three lines of HTML code are sent before the header statement. The following statements work, although they don't make much sense, because the HTML lines are after the header statement — that is, after the user has already been taken to another page:

```
<?php
   header("Location:
   http://janetscompany.com");
?>
<html>
<head><title>testing
   header</title></head>
<body>
</body>
</html>
```

The following statements fail:

```
 <?php
   header("Location:
   http://company.com");
?>
<html>
<head><title>testing
   header</title></head>
<body>
</body></html>
```

The reason these statements fail is not easy to see, but if you look closely, you will notice a single blank space before the opening PHP tag. This blank space is output to the browser, although the resulting Web page looks empty. Therefore, the header statement fails because there is output before it. This is a common mistake and difficult to spot.

Relocating users

PHP also provides a method to move a user from one page to another in your Web site without requiring the user to click a link or a button. You can send a message to the Web server that tells it to send a new page by using the PHP header statement. The format of the header function that sends the user to a new page is as follows:

```
header("Location: URL");
```

The header statement sends the message, Location: URL, to the Web server. In response, the file located at *URL* is sent to the user's browser. Either of the following statements are valid header statements:

```
header("Location: newpage.php");
header("Location: http://company.com/catalog/catalog.php");
```

The header function has a major limitation. The header statement can only be used *before* any other output is sent. You can't echo output — such as some HTML code — to the Web page and then send a message requesting a new page in the middle of the script. The header statement is not the only PHP statement that has this restriction. See the nearby sidebar for a discussion of the header statement and other statements like it that must come before output.

In spite of its limitations, the header statement is useful. It's the only way to move users to a new page without requiring an action from the user. Therefore, it's really the only statement that can be used in conditional statements to display alternate pages to different users. The following example shows how to display alternate pages based on the type of user account:

```
<?php
    if ($typeAcct == "admin")
    {
       header("Location: AdminPage.php");
    }
    else
    {
       header("Location: SiteHomePage.php");
    }
?>
```

These statements run a script that displays an admin page for users with an admin account, but displays a general page for other users. You can have as many PHP statements as you want before the header function, as long as they don't send output. You can't have any HTML sections before the header, because HTML is always sent to the browser.

Moving Information from Page to Page

No matter how the user gets from one page to the next, you may need information from the first page to be available on the next page. With PHP, you can move information from page to page by using any of the following methods:

- **Adding information to the URL:** You can add specific information to the end of the URL of the new page. This method is most appropriate when you need to pass only a small amount of information.
- **Storing information via cookies:** You can store *cookies* — small amounts of information containing `variable=value` pairs — on the user's computer. After the cookie is stored, you can retrieve it from any Web page. However, users can refuse to accept cookies, so this method doesn't work in all environments.
- **Passing information using HTML forms:** You can pass information that is in a form. When the user clicks the submit button, the information in the form is sent to the next script. This method is useful when you need to collect information from users.
- **Using PHP session functions:** Beginning with PHP 4, PHP functions are available that set up a user session and store session information on the server; this information can be accessed from any Web page. This method is useful for sessions in which you expect users to view many pages.

The next few sections discuss these options in greater detail.

Adding information to the URL

A simple way to move any information from one page to the next is to add the information to the URL you're linking to. To do so, you put the information in the following format:

```
variable=value
```

In this case, the *variable* is a variable name, but you do not use a dollar sign ($) in it. The *value* is the value to be stored in the variable. You can add the `variable=value` pairs anywhere you use a URL. You signal the start of the information with a question mark (?). The following statements are all valid ways of passing information in the URL:

- `<a href="nextpage.php?age=14">go to next page</a>`
- `header("Location: nextpage.php?age=14");`
- `<form action="nextpage.php?age=14" method="POST">`

These examples all send the variable `$age` with the value `14` assigned to it. The variable/value pair is sent to `nextpage.php` by adding the pair to the end of the URL.

You can add several `variable=value` pairs, separating each pair with an ampersand (&) as follows:

```
<form action="nextpage.php?state=CA&city=Mall" method="POST">
```

Any information passed into a URL is available in the built-in array `$_GET`. In the preceding example, the script `nextpage.php` could use the following statements to display the information passed to it:

```
echo "{$_GET['city']}, {$_GET['state']};
```

The output is as follows:

```
Mall, CA
```

The information is also available in the built-in array `$_REQUEST`. You can use the following statements to get the same result:

```
echo "{$_REQUEST['city']}, {$_REQUEST['state']};
```

Passing information in the URL is easy, especially for small amounts of information. However, this method has some disadvantages, including some important security issues. Here are some reasons you may not want to pass information in the URL:

- **The whole world can see it.** The URL is shown in the address line of the browser, which means that the information you attach to the URL is also shown. If the information needs to be secure, you don't want it shown so publicly. For example, if you're moving a password from one page to the next, you probably don't want to pass it in the URL.
- **A user can send information in the URL, just as easily as you can.** For example, suppose that after a user logs into your restricted Web site, you add `auth=yes` to the URL. On each Web page, you check to see if `$_GET['auth'] = yes`. If so, you let the user see the Web page. However, any user can type `http://www.yoursite.com/page.php?auth=yes` into his browser and be allowed to enter without logging in.
- **The user can bookmark the URL.** You may not want your users to save the information you add to the URL.
- **The length of the URL is limited.** The limit differs for various browsers and browser versions, but a limit always exists. Therefore, if you're passing a lot of information, the URL may not have room for it.

Passing information via cookies

You can store information as *cookies,* which are small amounts of information containing `variable=value` pairs, similar to the pairs you can add to a URL. The user's browser stores cookies on the user's computer. Your scripts can then use the cookie information.

At first glance, cookies seem to solve the problem of moving data from page to page. Just stash a cookie on the user's computer and get it whenever you need it. In fact, the cookie can be stored so that it remains there after the user leaves your site and will still be available when the user enters your Web site a month later. Problem solved? Well, not exactly. Cookies are not under your control. They are under the user's control. The user can at any time delete the cookie. In fact, users can set their browsers to refuse to allow any cookies, and many users do refuse cookies or routinely delete them. Many users are not comfortable with the idea of a stranger storing things on their computers, especially files that remain after they leave the stranger's Web site. This is an understandable attitude. However, it definitely limits the usefulness of cookies. If your application depends on cookies and the user has cookies shut off, your application won't work for that user.

Cookies were originally designed for storing small amounts of information for short periods of time. Unless you specifically set the cookie to last a longer period of time, the cookie will disappear when the user leaves your Web site. Although cookies are useful in some situations, consider the following points before deciding to use them:

- **Users may set their browsers to refuse cookies.** Unless you know for sure that all your users will have cookies turned on or you can request that they turn on cookies and expect them to follow your request, cookies are a problem. If your application depends on cookies, it won't run if cookies are turned off.
- **PHP has features that work better than cookies.** Beginning with PHP 4, PHP sessions can store information that is available for the entire *session* — in other words, as long as the user stays at your Web site. Session functions store information on the server, where it is not at the mercy of the user. Sessions, however, don't work for long-term storage of information.
- **You can store data in a database.** If you have access to a database where you can store and retrieve data, this is often a better solution than cookies. Users can't delete the data in your database unexpectedly.

Storing and retrieving information in cookies

You store cookies by using the `setcookie` function. The general format is as follows:

```
setcookie("variable","value");
```

The *variable* is the variable name, but you do not include the dollar sign ($).This statement stores the information only until the user leaves your Web site. For example, the following statement stores the pair `state=CA` in the cookie file on the user's computer:

```
setcookie("state","CA");
```

When the user moves to the next page, the cookie information is available in the built-in array called `$_COOKIE`. The next Web page can display the information from the cookie by using the following statement.

```
echo "Your home state is ".$_COOKIE['state'];
```

The output from this statement is as follows:

```
Your home state is CA
```

The cookie is not available in the script where it is set. The user must go to another page or redisplay the current page before the cookie information is available.

Setting expiration dates

If you want the information stored in a cookie to remain in a file on the user's computer after the user leaves your Web site, set your cookie with an expiration time, as follows:

```
setcookie("variable","value",expiretime);
```

The *expiretime* value sets the time when the cookie expires. The value for *expiretime* is usually set by using either the `time` or `mktime` function as follows:

- `time`: This function returns the current time in a format the computer can understand. You use the `time` function plus a number of seconds to set the expiration time of the cookie, as shown in the following statements:

  ```
  setcookie("state","CA",time()+3600); #expires in one hour
  setcookie("Name",$Name,time()+(3*86400)) #expires 3 days
  ```

- `mktime`: This function returns a date and time in a format that the computer can understand. You must provide the desired date and time in the following order: hour, minute, second, month, day, and year. If any value is not included, the current value is used. You use the `mktime` function to set the expiration time of the cookie, as shown in the following statements:

```
setcookie("state","CA",mktime(3,0,0,4,1,2003)); #expires
                              at 3:00 AM on April 1, 2003
setcookie("state","CA",mktime(13,0,0,,,)); /#expires at
                                              1:00 PM
        today
```

You can remove a cookie by setting its value to nothing. Either of the following statements removes the cookie:

```
setcookie("name");
setcookie("name","");
```

The `setcookie` function has a major limitation, however. The `setcookie` function can only be used *before* any other output is sent. You *cannot* set a cookie in the middle of a script, after you have echoed some output to the Web page. For more information, see the see the sidebar in this chapter called “Statements that must come before output.”

Passing information using HTML forms

The most common way to pass information from one page to another is by using HTML forms. An HTML form is displayed with a submit button. When the user clicks the submit button, the information in the form fields is passed to the script included in the `form` tag. The general format is as follows:

```
<form action="processform.php" method="POST">
    tags for one or more fields
<input type="submit" value="string">
</form>
```

The most common use of a form is to collect information from users and pass it to the next page (discussed in detail in Chapter 10). However, forms can also be used to pass other types of information.

Hidden fields are fields in forms that send information to the next page without appearing in the form on the Web page. Hidden fields can be included in the form along with other types of fields, or can be the only type of field in the form. When the user clicks the submit button, the information in the hidden field is sent to the next page. For example, the following statements pass the user's account type to the next page when the user clicks a button that says *Next Page:*

```
<?php
  $acct = "admin";
  echo "<form action='nextpage.php' method='POST'>
        <input type='hidden' name='acct' value='$acct'>
        <input type='submit' value='Next Page'>
        </form>\n";
?>
```

The Web page shows a submit button that says `Next Page`, but it doesn't ask the user for any information. When the user clicks the button, `nextpage.php` runs, and the account type is available in `$_POST['acct']`. In this way, you can pass information that you need to use other places in the Web site from page to page. In this example, you could use this code as part of a script that displays some products. When the user clicks the Next Page button, the account type is sent to the new page for use in that script.

Using PHP sessions

A *session* is the time that a user spends at your Web site. Users may view many Web pages between the time they enter your site and leave it. Often you want information to be available for a complete session. Beginning with version 4.0, PHP provides a way to do this.

Understanding how PHP sessions work

PHP allows you to set up a session and store session variables. After you create a session, the session variables are available for your use on any other Web page. To make session information available, PHP does the following:

1. PHP assigns a session ID number.

   The number is a really long nonsense number that is unique for the user and that no one could possibly guess. The session ID is stored in a PHP system variable named `PHPSESSID`.

2. PHP stores the variables that you want saved for the session in a file on the server.

   The file is named with the session ID number. It's stored in a directory specified by `session.save_path` in the `php.ini` file. The session directory must exist before session files can be saved in it.

3. PHP passes the session ID number to every page.

If the user has cookies turned on, PHP passes the session ID by using cookies. If the user has cookies turned off, PHP behavior depends on whether `trans-sid` is turned on in `php.ini`. (You find out more about `trans-id` in the section "Using sessions without cookies," later in this chapter.)

4. PHP gets the variables from the session file for each new session page.

   Whenever a user opens a new page that is part of the session, PHP gets the variables from the file by using the session ID number that was passed from the previous page. The variables are available in the `$_SESSION` array.

For PHP 4.1.2 or earlier, `trans-sid` is not available unless it was enabled by using the option `--enable-trans-sid` when PHP was compiled.

Opening and closing sessions

You should open a session at the beginning of each Web page. Open the session with the `session_start` function, as follows:

```
session_start();
```

The function first checks for an existing session ID number. If it finds one, it sets up the session variables. If it doesn't find one, it starts a new session by creating a new session ID number.

Because sessions use cookies, if the user has them turned on, `session_start` is subject to the same limitation as cookies. That is, to avoid an error, the `session_start` function must be called before any output is sent. For complete details, see the sidebar in this chapter called "Statements that must come before output."

You can tell PHP that every page on your site should automatically start with a `session_start` statement. You can do this with a setting in the configuration file `php.ini`. If you're the PHP administrator, you can edit this file; otherwise, ask the administrator to edit it. Look for the variable `session.auto_start` and set its value to `1`. You may have to restart the Web server before this setting takes effect. With `auto_start` turned on, you do not need to add a `session_start` at the beginning of each page.

You may want to restrict your site to users with a valid user ID and password. For restricted sessions that users log into, you often want users to log out when they're finished. To close a session, use the following statement wherever to want to close the session:

```
session_destroy();
```

This statement gets rid of all the session variable information that is stored in the session file. PHP no longer passes the session ID number to the next page. However, the statement does *not* affect the variables set on the current page; they still hold the same values. If you want to remove the variables from the current page, as well as prevent them from being passed to the next page, unset them by using this statement:

```
unset($variablename1,$variablename2,...);
```

Using PHP session variables

To save a variable in a session so that it's available on later Web pages, store the value in the `$_SESSION` array, as follows:

```
$_SESSION['varname'] = "John Smith";
```

When you open a session on any subsequent Web page, the values stored in the `$_SESSION` array are available.

If you want to stop storing any variable at any time, you can unset the variable by using the following statement:

```
unset($_SESSION['varname'];
```

The following two scripts show how to use sessions to pass information from one page to the next. The script in Listing 11-1 shows the first page of a session. Listing 11-2 shows the second page in a session.

Listing 11-1: Starting a Session

```
<?php
 /* Script name: sessionTest1.php
  * Description: Starts a session. Saves a session variable.
  */
  session_start();
  $_SESSION['session_var'] = "testing";
?>
<html>
<head><title>Testing Sessions page 1</title></head>
<body>
  <p>This is a test of the sessions feature.
  <form action="sessionTest2.php" method="POST">
  <input type="text" name="form_var" value="testing">
  <input type="submit" value="Go to Next Page">
  </form>
</body>
</html>
```

In this script, a session is started and one session variable is stored called `session_var`. A form is also displayed with one text field where the user can enter some text. When the submit button from this form, labeled "Go to Next Page" is clicked, the `sessionTest2.php` script runs.

Listing 11-2: The Second Page of a Session

```
<?php
 /* Script name: sessionTest2.php
  * Description: Gets a variable from an existing session.
  */
  session_start();
?>
<html>
<head><title>Testing Sessions page 2</title></head>
<body>
<?php
  $session_var = $_SESSION['session_var'];
  $form_var = $_POST['form_var'];
  echo "session_var = $session_var<br>\n";
  echo "form_var = $form_var<br>\n";
?>
</body>
</html>
```

This script displays the variables that were passed from the previous script (`sessionTest1.php`).

If users pointed their browsers at `sessionTest1.php` and clicked the submit button that says Go to Next Page, they'd see the following output from `sessionTest2.php`:

```
session_var = testing
form_var = testing
```

As you can see, both the session variable, `session_var` and the form variable, `form_var` are available in the built-in arrays to be echoed from this script.

Using sessions without cookies

Many users turn off cookies in their browsers. PHP checks the user's browser to see whether cookies are allowed and behaves accordingly. If the user's browser allows cookies, PHP does the following:

- It sets the variable `$PHPSESSID` equal to the session ID number.
- It uses cookies to move `$PHPSESSID` from one page to the next.

If the user's browser is set to refuse cookies, PHP behaves differently:

- It sets a constant called SID. The constant contains a variable=value pair that looks like PHPSESSID=*longstringofnumbers*. (The long string of numbers is the session ID.)
- It may or may not move the session ID number from one page to the next, depending on whether trans-sid is turned on. If trans-sid is turned on, PHP passes the session ID number; if it is not turned on, PHP does not pass the session ID number.

trans-sid is turned off by default. You can turn it on by editing your php.ini file. Search for the line that begins with session.use_trans_id = . If the setting is 0, trans_id is off; if the setting is 1, trans_id is on. To turn the setting on when it is off, change 0 to 1. You may have to restart your Web server before the new setting takes effect.

Turning trans-sid on has advantages and disadvantages:

- **Advantages:** Sessions work seamlessly even when users turn cookies off. You can script sessions easier, without being concerned about the user's browser setting for cookies.
- **Disadvantages:** The session ID number is often passed in the URL. In some situations, for security reasons, the session ID number should not be shown in the browser address. Also, when the session ID number is in the URL, it can be bookmarked by the user. Then, if the user returns to your site by using the bookmark with the session ID number in it, the new session ID number from the current visit can get confused with the old session ID number from the previous visit and possibly cause problems.

Sessions with trans-sid turned on

When trans-sid is turned on and the user has cookies turned off, PHP automatically sends the session ID number in the URL or as a hidden form field. If the user moves to the next page by using a link, a header function, or a form with the GET method, the session ID number is added to the URL. If the user moves to the next page by using a form with the POST method, the session ID number is passed in a hidden field. PHP recognizes PHPSESSID as the session ID number and handles the session without any special programming on your part.

The session ID number is added only to the URLs for pages on your Web site. If the URL of the next page includes a server name, PHP assumes that the URL is on another Web site and does not add the session ID number. For example, suppose your link statement is as follows:

```
<a href="newpage.php">
```

PHP will add the session ID number. However, suppose your statement is as follows:

```
<a href="HTTP://www.janetscompany.com/newpage.php">
```

PHP will *not* add the session ID number.

Sessions without trans-sid turned on

When `trans-sid` is *not* turned on and the user has cookies turned off, PHP does *not* send the session ID number to the next page. Instead, you must send the session ID number yourself.

Fortunately, PHP provides a constant that you can use to send the session ID yourself. This constant is named `SID` and contains a `variable=value` pair that you can add to the URL, as follows:

```
<a href="nextpage.php?<?php echo SID?> > next page </a>
```

This link statement includes the question mark (?) at the end of the filename and the constant `SID` added to the URL. `SID` contains the session ID number. The output from `echo SID` looks something like this:

```
PHPSESSID=877c22163d8df9deb342c7333cfe38a7
```

Therefore, the URL of the next page looks as follows:

```
nextpage.php?PHPSESSID=877c22163d8df9deb342c7333cfe38a7
```

The session ID is added to the end of the URL. For one of several reasons (discussed earlier in this chapter), you may not want the session ID number to appear on the URL shown by the browser. To prevent this, you can send the session ID number in a hidden field in a form by using the POST method. First, get the session ID number, and then send it in a hidden field. The following statements do this:

```
<?php
  $PHPSESSID = session_id();
  echo "<form action='nextpage.php' method='POST'>
        <input type='hidden' name='PHPSESSID'
              value='$PHPSESSID'>
        <input type='submit' value='Next Page'>
        </form>";
?>
```

These statements do the following:

1. The function `session_id`, which returns the current session ID number, stores the session ID number in the variable `$PHPSESSID`.
2. `$PHPSESSID` is sent in a hidden form field.

On the new page, PHP automatically finds `PHPSESSID` without any special programming needed from you.

Creating sessions for members only

PHP session functions are ideal for Web sites that are restricted and require users to login with a login name and password. These types of Web sites undoubtedly have many pages, and you don't want the user to have to login to each page. PHP sessions can keep track of whether the user has logged in and refuse access to users who aren't logged in. Using PHP sessions, you can do the following:

1. Show users a login page.
2. If a user logs in successfully, set and store a session variable.
3. Whenever a user goes to a new page, check the session variable to see if the user has logged in.
4. If the user has logged in, show the page.
5. If the user has not logged in, bring up the login page.

To check whether a user has logged in, add the following statements to the top of every page:

```
<?php
  session_start()
  if ( @$_SESSION['login'] != "go" )
  {
    header("Location: loginPage.php");
    exit();
  }
?>
```

In these statements, PHP checks a session variable called `login` — which was set at login — to see whether `$_SESSION['login']` is equal to `"go"`. If it is not, it means the user is not logged in, and the user is sent to the login page. If `$_SESSION['login']` equals `"go"`, the script proceeds with the rest of the statements on the Web page.

Uploading Files

You may want users to upload files to your Web site. For example, you may want users to be able to upload resumes to your job-search Web site or pictures to your photo album Web site.

Using a form to upload a file

You can display a form that allows a user to upload a file by using an HTML form designed for that purpose. The general format of the form is as follows:

```
<form enctype="multipart/form-data"
        action="processfile.php" method="POST">
  <input type="hidden" name="MAX_FILE_SIZE" value="30000">
  <input type="file" name="user_file">
  <input type="submit" value="Upload File">
</form>
```

Notice the following points regarding the form:

- **The `enctype` attribute is used in the `form` tag.** You must set this attribute to `multipart/form-data` when uploading a file to ensure the file arrives correctly.
- **A hidden field is included that sends a value (in bytes) for `MAX_FILE_SIZE`.** If the user tries to upload a file that is larger than this value, it won't upload. When sending the value for MAX_FILE_SIZE in your form, you need to consider two size settings in php.ini, as follows
  - `upload_max_filesize`: The `MAX_FILE_SIZE` you send in your upload form can't be larger than the value of `upload_max_filesize`. If you are uploading a larger file and need to send a `MAX_FILE_SIZE` larger than the current value of `upload_max_filesize`, you need to increase the value of `upload_max_filesize` by editing the `php.ini` file. The default value for this setting is 2M.
  - `post_max_size`: The total amount of information you send in a POST form can't be larger than the value of `post_max_size`. The default value for this setting is 8M. You can increase this value if necessary by editing your `php.ini` file.
- **The input field that uploads the file is of type `file`.**

The value for `MAX_FILE_SIZE` must be sent before the file is uploaded if you want the file size limit to apply to the uploading file.

When the user submits the form, the file is uploaded to a temporary location. The script that processes the form needs to copy the file to another location because the temporary file is deleted as soon as the script is finished. You can use `phpinfo()` to see where the temporary files are stored. If you don't like the location of the temporary directory, you can change it by changing `upload_tmp_dir` in the `php.ini` file. If no directory is specified in `php.ini`, a default temporary directory is used. Because the temporary files are deleted almost immediately, the location of the temporary directory is not likely to be very important.

Accessing information about an uploaded file

Along with the file, information about the file is sent with the form. This information is stored in the PHP built-in array called `$_FILES`. An array of information is available for each file that was uploaded. As with any other form, you can obtain the information from the array by using the name of the field. For example, you can get information about the uploaded file from the following array:

```
$_FILES['fieldname']['name']
$_FILES['fieldname']['type']
$_FILES['fieldname']['tmp_name']
$_FILES['fieldname']['size']
```

For example, suppose you use the following field to upload a file:

```
<input type="file" name="user_file">
```

If the user uploads a file named `test.txt` by using the form, the resulting array that can be used by the processing script looks something like this:

```
$_FILES[user_file][name] = test.txt
$_FILES[user_file][type] = text/plain
$_FILES[user_file][tmp_name] = D:\WINNT\php92C.tmp
$_FILES[user_file][size] = 435
```

In this array, `name` is the name of the file that was uploaded, `type` is the type of file, `tmp_name` is the path/filename of the temporary file, and `size` is the size of the file. Notice that `name` contains only the filename, while `tmp_name` includes the path to the file as well as the filename.

If the file is too large to upload, the `tmp_name` in the array is set to `none`, and the size is set to 0.

By default, PHP stores the temporary uploaded file in your system directory on Windows (`Windows` for Win98/XP and `Winnt` for Win2000) or `/tmp` on Unix/Linux. You can change the location where the temporary files are stored by setting the location in `php.ini`. Look in your `php.ini` file for the following line:

```
;upload_tmp_dir =
```

Remove the semicolon at the beginning of the line so that the line becomes active. Add the path to the directory where you want the temporary files to be stored. Your active line looks similar to the following:

```
upload_tmp_dir = d:\tempfiles
```

The directory `tempfiles` must exist. If it doesn't, PHP ignores the setting and continues to save the files in the default location.

Moving uploaded files to their destination

The general format of the statement that moves the file is as follows:

```
move_uploaded_file(path/tempfilename,path/permfilename);
```

The `tmp_file` element in `$_FILES` stores the temporary filename and location, so you can use the following statement to move the file to your desired location, in this case, `c:\data\new_file.txt`:

```
move_uploaded_file($_FILES['user_file']['tmp_name'],
    'c:\data\new_file.txt');
```

The destination directory (in this case, `c:\data`) must exist before the file can be moved to it. This statement doesn't create the destination directory.

Security can be an issue when uploading files. Allowing strangers to load files onto your computer is risky; malicious files are possible. So, you probably want to check the files for as many factors as possible after they are uploaded, using conditional statements to check file characteristics, such as checking for the expected file type and for the size. In some cases, for even more security, it may be a good idea to change the name of the file to something else so users don't know where their files are or what they're called.

Putting it all together

A complete example script is shown in Listing 11-3. This script displays a form for the user to upload an image file, saves the uploaded file, and then displays a message after the file has been successfully uploaded. This script expects the uploaded file to be an image file, and tests to make sure that it is an image file, but any type of file can be uploaded. The form displayed by this script is shown in Figure 11-1.

Listing 11-3: A Script That Uploads a File Using a POST Form

```
<?php
 /* Script name: uploadFile.php
  * Description: Uploads a file via HTTP using a POST form.
  */
  if(!isset($_POST['Upload']))                          #5
  {
    include("form_upload.inc");
  } # endif
  else                                                  #9
  {
    if($_FILES['pix']['tmp_name'] == "none")            #11
    {
      echo "<b>File did not successfully upload. Check the
            file size. File must be less than 500K.<br>";
      include("form_upload.inc");
      exit();
    }
    if(!ereg("image",$_FILES['pix']['type']))           #16
    {
      echo "<b>File is not a picture. Please try another
            file.</b><br>";
      include("form_upload.inc");
      exit();
    }
    else                                                #23
    {
      $destination = 'c:\data'."\\".$_FILES['pix']['name'];
      $temp_file = $_FILES['pix']['tmp_name'];
      move_uploaded_file($temp_file,$destination);
      echo "<p><b>The file has successfully uploaded:</b>
            {$_FILES['pix']['name']}
            ({$_FILES['pix']['size']})</p>";
    }
  }
?>
```

I have added line numbers at the end of some of the lines in the script. The script is discussed below with reference to these line numbers:

- **Line 5:** This line is an `if` statement that tests whether the form has been submitted. If not, the form is displayed by including the file containing the form code. The `include` file is shown in Listing 11-4.
- **Line 9:** This line starts an `else` block that executes if the form has been submitted. This block includes the rest of the script and processes the submitted form and uploaded file.
- **Line 11:** This line is an `if` statement that tests whether the file was successfully uploaded. If not, an error message is displayed, and the form is redisplayed.

- **Line 16:** This line is an `if` statement that tests whether the file is a picture. If not, an error message is displayed, and the form is redisplayed.
- **Line 23:** This line starts an `else` block that executes if the file has been successfully uploaded. The file is moved to its permanent destination, and a message is displayed that the file has been uploaded.

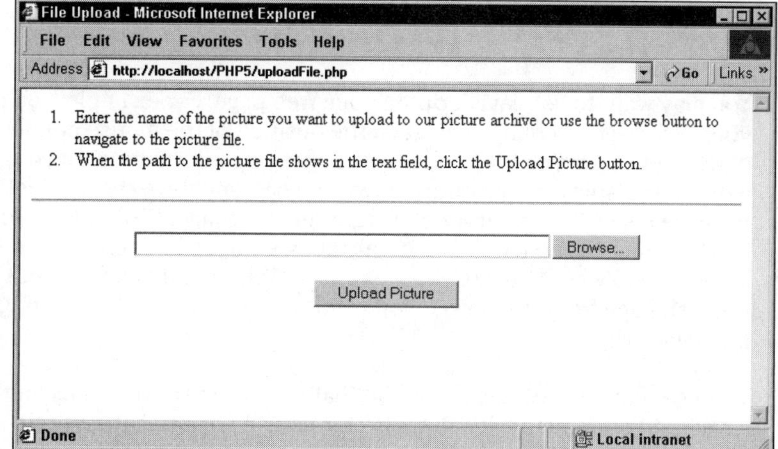

Figure 11-1: A form that allows users to upload an image file.

Listing 11-4 shows the include file used to display the upload form.

Listing 11-4: An Include File That Displays the File Upload Form

```
<!-- Script Name: form_upload.inc
     Description: Displays a form to upload a file -->
<html>
<head><title>File Upload</title></head>
<body>
<ol><li>Enter the name of the picture you want to upload
        to our picture archive or use the browse button
        to navigate to the picture file.</li>
    <li>When the path to the picture file shows in the text
        field, click the Upload Picture button.</li>
</ol>
<div align="center"><hr>
<form enctype="multipart/form-data"
        action="uploadFile.php" method="POST">
  <input type="hidden" name="MAX_FILE_SIZE" value="500000">
  <input type="file" name="pix" size="60">
  <p><input type="submit" name="Upload"
        value="Upload Picture">
</form>
</body></html>
```

Notice that the include file doesn't contain PHP code, just HTML code.

The form that allows users to select a file to upload is shown in Figure 11-1. The form has a text field for inputting a filename and a browse button that enables the user to navigate to the file and select it.

Using JavaScript with PHP

You may want to use JavaScript in your Web page. For example, you may want your Web page to change based on the position of the mouse pointer or a click of the mouse. Or you may want to modify some information on your Web page without redisplaying the entire page. You can't achieve these effects with PHP because it's strictly a server-side scripting language. PHP doesn't know what is happening on the user's PC; it only knows what's happening on the Web site server. If you want to make changes to the Web page display without resending the Web page from the server, you need to use a client-side scripting language, like JavaScript.

The user can turn off JavaScript so that the browser doesn't execute the JavaScript statements. It's not wise for your Web application to depend on JavaScript unless you can ensure that all your users have JavaScript enabled in their browsers.

I don't talk about the JavaScript language in this chapter. I assume that you either know JavaScript or can learn the actual JavaScript code elsewhere. In this chapter, I talk about how to use JavaScript in a PHP script. (For more information on JavaScript, check out *JavaScript For Dummies,* 3rd Edition, by Emily A. Vander Veer.)

Adding JavaScript code to a PHP script

JavaScript code, just like HTML code, is understood and executed by the browser on the user's computer (the client side). Therefore, you add JavaScript to a PHP script in the same way that you add HTML to a PHP script. In fact, JavaScript is basically part of the HTML code for the Web page. You add JavaScript to the HTML by using an HTML tag, as follows:

```
<script language="JavaScript">
    JavaScript code
</script>
```

JavaScript code is used in your PHP script in the same way HTML code is used — namely, it is echoed. For example, the following statements send some JavaScript to the browser:

```
<?php
  echo "<script language=\"JavaScript\">
          <!--
            document.write('This page last updated: '
              + document.lastModified + '<br>')
          // -->
        </script>";
?>
```

When a browser receives these JavaScript statements, it executes them and produces the following output:

```
This page last updated: 03/24/2003 12:01:47
```

This is the date and time that the file containing the script was last modified.

You can use JavaScript statements alone, outside of PHP tags, just as you can HTML code. You could add the preceding statements to a PHP file without using PHP tags or an `echo` statement. If the JavaScript statement is not added in a PHP section, it is sent to the browser exactly as is, without being passed to the PHP script, just as HTML code is when it's outside of a PHP section.

Using PHP variables with JavaScript

You can use PHP variables with JavaScript the same way you do with HTML. You can add the variable to the JavaScript code. For example, the JavaScript example in the preceding section can include a PHP variable, as follows:

```
<?php
  $string = "This page last updated: ";
  echo "<script language=\"JavaScript\">
          <!--
            document.write('$string'
              + document.lastModified + '<br>')
          // -->
        </script>";
?>
```

The JavaScript language itself uses variables. You can set a JavaScript variable to the value of a PHP variable to use in your JavaScript code. For example, the JavaScript could be sent as follows:

```
<?php
  $string = "This page last updated: ";
  echo "<script language=\"JavaScript\">
          <!--
            var message = \"$string\";
            document.write( message
              + document.lastModified + '<br>')
          // -->
        </script>";
?>
```

Because JavaScript code is not executed until it reaches the browser on the client side, passing values from JavaScript variables to PHP variables can't take place in the current page. The JavaScript value must be passed on to the next PHP script before PHP can receive it. JavaScript can pass the values on so that PHP can use them by adding them to the URL, by storing them in a cookie that PHP can read, or by sending them as a form element.

Chapter 12

Storing Data with PHP

In This Chapter

- Writing and reading flat files
- Exchanging data between PHP and other programs
- Understanding database support in PHP
- Using PHP to interact with a database
- Handling database-connection errors

Many applications require the long-term storage of information. In PHP scripts, you can make information available within *sessions* — periods of time that users spend at your Web site — by using methods such as PHP session functions and by submitting forms. However, eventually you need to store information for use tomorrow or next week. You can store it in a cookie that you set to last after the session is ended (as discussed in Chapter 11), but the information is vulnerable. It's not under your control. The user can delete or change the information at any time or can refuse to accept the cookie. To be available and stable, the information needs to be stored somewhere secure, where no one can access or tamper with it. The information needs to be stored on the server.

Information can be stored on the server in flat files or in databases. *Flat files* are text files stored in the computer file system. Humans can read flat files by using the operating system commands that display files, such as `cat` in Linux and Unix. You can access and edit these files by using any text file editor, such as Notepad or vi. The information in the flat file is stored as strings, and the PHP script that retrieves the data needs to know how the data is stored. For example, to retrieve a customer name from a file, the PHP script needs to know that the customer name is stored in the first 20 characters of every line.

Using a database for data storage requires you to install and learn to use database software, such as MySQL or Oracle. The data is stored in files created by the database software and can only be accessed by the database software. Databases can store very complex information that you can retrieve easily.

You don't need to know how the data is stored, just how to interact with the database software. For example, to retrieve a customer name, the PHP script needs to know only how to tell the database software that it wants the customer name, using a standard communication language called SQL, The database software handles the storage and delivers the data, without the script needing to know exactly where or how the customer name is stored.

Flat files have some advantages over databases:

- **Available and versatile:** You can create and save data in any operating system's file system. You don't need to install any extra software. Additionally, text data stored in flat files can be read by a variety of software programs, such as word processors or spreadsheets.
- **Easy to use:** You don't need to do any extra preparation, such as install database software, design a database, create a database, and so on. Just create the file and store the data with statements in your PHP script.
- **Smaller:** Flat files store data by using less disk space than databases.

In summary, a flat file is quick and easy and takes less space than a database. It is ideal for storing small amounts of information quickly, such as a simple list or small piece of information. Flat files are particularly useful for making information available to other software, such as an editing program or a spreadsheet. Flat files can be looked at by anyone with access to the computer directory where they are stored, so they are useful when information needs to be made available to other people.

Databases have some advantages as well:

- **Security:** A database provides a security layer of its own, in addition to the security provided by the operating system. A database protects the data from outside intrusion better than a flat file.
- **Accessibility of data:** You can store data in a database by using a very complex data structure, specifying data types and relationships among the data. The organization of the data makes it easy to search the data and retrieve what you need.
- **Ability to handle multiple users:** When many users store or access data in a single file, such as a file containing names and addresses, a database ensures that users take their turn with the file to avoid overwriting each other's data.

In summary, databases require more start-up effort and use more space than a flat file, but are much more suitable for handling complex information. The database handles the internal organization of the data, making data retrieval much simpler. A database provides more security, making it more suitable for sensitive, private information. Databases can more easily and efficiently handle high traffic when many users may try to access the data almost simultaneously.

In PHP 5, SQLite, an extension for data storage that combines the main advantages of flat files and databases, is included by default. SQLite stores the data in a flat file, so you don't need to install database software, but you store data using SQL, the standard database communication language. SQLite is a quick option for storing and retrieving small amounts of data in a flat file using SQL. SQLite is not a good option for really huge, complicated databases.

Using Flat Files

Flat files are simple to use, simpler than databases. You don't need any other software, such as database software. You just use PHP statements to read from or write to the file.

Using a flat file requires three steps:

1. **Open the file.**
2. **Write data into the file or retrieve data from the file.**
3. **Close the file.**

These steps are discussed in detail in the following sections.

Accessing files

The first step, before you can write information into or read information from a file, is to open the file. The following is the general format for the statement that opens a file:

```
$fh = fopen("filename","mode")
```

The variable, `$fh`, referred to as a file handle, is used in the statements that write data to or read data from the open file so that PHP knows which file to write into or read from. `$fh` contains the information that identifies the location of the open file.

You use a mode when you open the file to let PHP know what you intend to do with the file. Table 12-1 shows the modes you can use.

Table 12-1 Modes for Opening a File

Mode	What it does	What happens when the file doesn't exist
`r`	Read only.	If the file does not exist, a warning message is displayed.
`r+`	Reading and writing.	If the file does not exist, a warning message is displayed.
`w`	Write only.	If the file does not exist, PHP attempts to create it. If the file exists, PHP overwrites it.
`w+`	Reading and writing.	If the file does not exist, PHP attempts to create it. If the file exists, PHP overwrites it.
`a`	Append data at the end of the file.	If the file does not exist, PHP attempts to create it.
`a+`	Reading and appending.	If the file does not exist, PHP attempts to create it.

The filename can be a simple filename (`filename.txt`), a path to the file (`c:/data/filename.txt`), or a URL (`http://yoursite.com/filename.txt`).

Opening files in read mode

You can open the file `file1.txt` to read the information in the file with the following statement:

```
$fh = fopen("file1.txt","r");
```

Based on this statement, PHP looks for `file1.txt` in the current directory, which is the directory where your PHP script is located. If the file can't be found, a warning message, similar to the following, may or may not be displayed, depending on the error level set, as described in Chapter 4:

```
Warning: fopen(file1.txt): failed to open stream: No such
         file or directory in d:\test2.php on line 15
```

Remember, a warning condition does not stop the script. The script continues to run, but the file doesn't open, so any later statements that read or write to the file aren't executed.

You probably want the script to stop if the file can't be opened. You need to do this yourself with a `die` statement, as follows:

```
$fh = fopen("file1.txt","r")
          or die("Can't open file");
```

As explained in Chapter 8, the die statement stops the script and displays the specified message.

Opening files in write mode

You can open a file in a specified directory to store information by using the following type of statement:

```
$fh = fopen("c:/testdir/file1.txt","w");
```

If the file does not exist, it is created in the indicated directory. However, if the directory doesn't exist, the directory is not created, and a warning is displayed. (You must create the directory first, before you try to write a file into the directory.)

You can check whether a directory exists before you try to write a file into it by using the following statements:

```
If(is_dir("c:/tester"))
{
    $fh = fopen("c:/testdir/file1.txt","w");
}
```

With these statements, the `fopen` statement is executed only if the directory exists and is a directory.

Opening files on another Web site

You can also open a file on another Web site by using a statement such as the following:

```
$fh = fopen("http://janet.valade.com/index.html","r");
```

You can use a URL only with a read mode, not with a write mode.

Closing a file

To close a file after you have finished reading or writing it, use the following statement:

```
fclose($fh);
```

In this statement, `$fh` is the file handle variable you created when you opened the file.

Writing to a file

After you open the file, you can write into it by using the fwrite statement, which has the following general format:

```
fwrite($fh,datatosave);
```

In this statement, $fh is the file handle that you created when you opened the file, containing the pointer to the open file, and *datatosave* is the information to be stored in the file. The information can be a string or a variable. For example, you can use the following statements:

```
$today = date("Y-m-d");
$fh = fopen("file2.txt","a");
fwrite($fh,$today);
fclose($fh);
```

These statements store the current date in a file called file2.txt. Notice that the file is opened in append mode. If the file doesn't exist, it is created, and the date is written as the first line. If the file exists, the data is added to the end of the file. In this way, you create a log file, which stores a list of the dates on which the script is run. The fwrite statement stores exactly what you send, so the second time these statements are run, file2.txt contains the following:

```
2003-04-222003-04-22
```

You probably want the two dates to be stored on separate lines. To do so, use the following fwrite statement rather than the previous one:

```
fwrite($fh,$today"\n");
```

With the new line character added, file2.txt contains the following:

```
2003-04-22
2003-04-22
```

Be sure to open the file with the a mode if you want to add information to a file. If you use a write mode, the file is overwritten each time it's opened.

Reading from a file

You can read from a file by using the fgets statement, which has the following general format:

```
$line = fgets($fh)
```

In this statement, `$fh` holds the pointer to the open file. This statement reads a string until it encounters the end of the line or the end of the file, whichever comes first, and stores the string in `$line`. To read an entire file, you keep reading lines until you get to the end of the file. PHP recognizes the end of the file, and provides a function `feof` to tell you when you reach the end of the file. The following statements read and display all the lines in the file:

```
while(!feof($fh))
{
   $line = fgets($fh);
   echo "$line;
}
```

In the first line, `feof($fh)` returns `TRUE` when the end of the file is reached. The exclamation point negates the condition being tested, so that the while statement continues to run as long as the end of the file is not reached. When the end of the file is reached, `while` stops.

If you use these statements to read the log file created in the preceding section, you get the following output:

```
2003-04-22
2003-04-22
```

As you can see, the new line character is included when the line is read. In some cases, you don't want the end of line included. If so, you need to remove it by using the following statements:

```
while(!feof($fh))
{
   $line = rtrim(fgets($fh));
   echo "$line;
}
```

The `rtrim` function removes any trailing blank spaces and the new line character. The output from these statements is as follows:

```
2003-04-222003-04-22
```

Reading files piece by piece

Sometimes you want to read strings of a certain size from a file. You can tell `fgets` to read a certain number of characters by using the following format:

```
$line = fgets($fh,n)
```

This statement tells PHP to read a string that is *n*-1 characters long until it reaches the end of the line or the end of the file.

For example, you can use the following statements:

```
while(!feof($fh))
{
   $char4 = fgets($fh,5);
   echo "$char4\n";
}
```

These statements read each four-character string until the end of the file. The output is as follows:

```
2003
-04-
22

2003
-04-
22
```

Notice that there is a new line at the end of each line of the file.

Reading a file into an array

It's often handy to have the entire file in an array. You can do that with the following statements:

```
$fh = fopen("file2.txt","r");
while(!feof($fh))
{
   $content[] = fgets($fh);
}
fclose($fh);
```

The result is the array `$content` with each line of the file as an element of the array. The array keys are numbers.

PHP provides a shortcut function for opening a file and reading the entire contents into an array, one line in each element of the array. The following statement produces the same results as the preceding five lines:

```
$content = file("file2.txt");
```

The statement opens `file2.txt`, puts each line into an element of the array `$content`, and then closes the file.

The `file` function can slow down your script if the file you're opening is really large. How large depends on the amount of available computer memory. If your script seems slow, try reading the file with `fgets` rather than `file` and see if that speeds up the script.

You can direct the file function to automatically open files in your include directory (described in Chapter 8) by using the following statement:

```
$content = file("file2.txt",1);
```

The 1 tells PHP to look for file2.txt in the include directory rather than in the current directory.

Reading a file into a string

Sometimes it's useful to put the entire contents of a file into one long string. For example, you may want to send the file contents in an e-mail message. PHP provides a function for reading a file into a string, as follows:

```
$content = file_get_contents("file2.txt",1);
```

The file_get_contents function works the same as the file function, except that it puts the entire contents of the file into a string rather than an array. After this statement, you can echo $content as follows:

```
echo $content;
```

The output is the following:

```
2003-04-22
2003-04-22
```

The output appears on separate lines because the end of line characters are read and stored as part of the string. Thus, when you echo the string, you also echo the end of line characters, which start a new line.

The file_get_contents function was introduced in version 4.3.0. It isn't available in older versions of PHP.

Exchanging data with other programs

Flat files are particularly useful for providing information to other programs or reading information into PHP from other programs. Almost all software has the ability to read information from flat files or write information into flat files. For example, by default your word processor saves your documents in its own format, which only the word processor can understand. However, you can choose to save the document in text format instead. The text document is a flat file containing text that can be read by other software. Your word processor can also read text files, even ones that were written by other software.

When your PHP script saves information into a text file, the information can be read by any software that has the capability of reading text files. For example, any text file can be read by most word processing software. However, some software requires a specific format in the text file. For example, an address book software application may read data from a flat file but require the information to be in specified locations — for example, the first 20 characters in a line are read as the name, and the second 20 characters are read as the street address, and so on. You need to know what format the software requires in a flat file. Then write the flat file in the correct format in your PHP script by using `fwrite` statements, as discussed in the section "Writing to a file," earlier in this chapter.

A CSV (comma-separated values) file — also called a comma-delimited file — is a common format used to transfer information between software programs. A CSV file is used to transfer information that can be structured as a table, organized as rows and columns. For example, spreadsheet programs organize data as rows and columns and can read and write CSV files. A CSV file is also often used to transfer data between different database software, such as between MySQL and MS Access. Many other software programs can read and write data in CSV files.

A CSV file is organized with each row of the table on a separate line in the file, and the columns in the row are separated by commas. For example, an address book can be organized as a CSV file as follows:

```
John Smith,1234 Oak St.,Big City,OR,99999
Mary Jones,5678 Pine St.,Bigger City,ME,11111
Luis Rojas,1234 Elm St.,Biggest City,TX,88888
```

Excel can read this file into a table with five columns. The comma signals the end of one column and the start of the next. Outlook can also read this file into its address book. And many other programs can read this file.

The following PHP statements create the CSV file:

```
$address[] = "John Smith,1234 Oak St.,Big City,OR,99999";
$address[] = "Mary Jones,5678 Pine St.,Bigger City,ME,11111";
$address[] = "Luis Rojas,1234 Elm St.,Biggest City,TX,88888";
$fh = fopen("addressbook.txt","a");
for ($i=0;$i<3;$i++)
{
   fwrite($fh,$address[$i]."\n");
}
fclose($fh);
```

PHP can read the CSV file by using either the `file` or the `fgets` function, as described in the section "Reading a file into an array," earlier in this chapter. However, PHP provides a function called `fgetcsv` that is designed specifically to read CSV files. When you use this function to read a line in a CSV file, the line is stored in an array, with each column entry in an element of the array.

For example, you can use the function to read the first line of the address book CSV file, as follows:

```
$address = fgetcsv($fh,1000);
```

In this statement, `$fh` is the file handle, and 1000 is the number of characters to read. To read an entire line, use a number of characters that is longer than the longest line. The result of this statement is an array as follows:

```
$address[0] = John Smith
$address[1] = 1234 Oak St.
$address[2] = Big City
$address[3] = OR
$address[4] = 99999
```

The CSV file works well for transferring data in many cases. However, if a comma is part of the data, commas can't be used to separate the columns. For example, suppose one of data lines is as follows:

```
Smith Company, Inc.,1234 Fir St.,Big City,OR,99999
```

The comma in the company name would divide the data into two columns — Smith Company in the first and Inc. in the second — making six columns instead of five. When the data contains commas, you can use a different character to separate the columns. For example, tabs are commonly used to separate columns. This file is called a TSV file or a tab-delimited file. You can write a tab-delimited file by storing `"\t"` in the output file rather than a comma.

You can read a file containing tabs by specifying the column separator in the statement, as follows:

```
$address = fgetcsv($fh,1000,"\t");
```

You can use any character to separate columns.

The script in Listing 12-1 contains a function that converts any CSV file into a tab-delimited file.

Listing 12-1: A Script That Converts a CSV File into a Tab-Delimited File

```
<?php
 /* Script name: Convert
  * Description: Reads in a CSV file and outputs a
  * tab-delimited file. The CSV file must have a .
  * CSV extension.
  */
  $myfile = "testing";                                #7
  function convert($filename)                         #8
```

(continued)

Listing 12-1 *(continued)*

```
  {
    if(@$fh_in = fopen("{$filename}.csv","r"))          #10
    {
      $fh_out = fopen("{$filename}.tsv","a");          #12
      while(!feof($fh_in))                             #13
      {
        $line = fgetcsv($fh_in,1024);                  #15
        if($line[0] == "")                             #16
        {
          fwrite($fh_out,"\n");
        }
        else {                                         #20
          fwrite($fh_out,implode($line,"\t")."\n"); #21
        }
      }
      fclose($fh_in);
      fclose($fh_out);
    }
    else {                                             #27
      echo "File doesn't exist\n";
      return FALSE;
    }
    echo "Conversion completed!\n";
    return TRUE;                                       #32
  }
  convert($myfile);                                    #34
?>
```

Listing 12-1 has numbers at the end of some lines. The following points refer to the line numbers in the listing:

- **Line 7:** This line defines the filename as `testing`.
- **Line 8:** This line defines a function named `convert()` with one parameter, `$filename`.
- **Line 10:** This line opens a file that has the filename that was passed to the function with a `.csv` extension. The file is opened in read mode. If the file is opened successfully, the conversion statements in the `if` block are executed. If the file is not found, the `else` block beginning on line 27 is executed.
- **Line 12:** This line opens a file that has the filename that was passed to the function with a `.tsv` extension. The file is opened in append mode. The file is in the current directory in this script. If the file is in another directory where you think there is any possibility the file might not open in write mode, use an `if` statement here to test where the file opened and perform some action if it did not.
- **Line 13:** This line starts a `while` loop that continues to the end of the file.

- **Line 15:** This statement reads one line from the input file into the array `$line`. Each column entry is stored in an element of the array.
- **Line 16:** This statement tests whether the line from the input file has any text on it. If the line doesn't have any text, a new line character is stored in the output file. Thus, any empty lines in the input file are stored in the output file.
- **Line 20:** If the line from the input file is not empty, it's converted to a tab-delimited format and written into the output file.
- **Line 21:** This statement converts the line and writes it to the output file in one statement. The `implode` function converts the array `$line` into a string, with the elements separated by a tab.
- **Line 27:** This `else` block executes when the input file can't be found. An error message is echoed, and the function returns `FALSE`.
- **Line 32:** The function has completed successfully, so it returns `TRUE`.
- **Line 34:** This line calls the function, passing a filename to the function in the variable `$myfile`.

Working with Databases

If you need to store complex information, keep the information very secure, or handle many users accessing the data at once, a database is much better than a flat file for long-term storage. Also, if you already know and use database software, it's almost as simple to use a database as a flat file.

Understanding database software

A *database* is an electronic file cabinet that stores information in an organized manner so that you can find it when you need it. A database can be small, with a simple structure, such as a database containing the names, addresses, and phone numbers of all your friends. Or a database can be huge with an extremely complex structure, such as the database Amazon must have to hold all its information.

Technically, the term *database* refers to the file or group of files that holds the actual data. The data is accessed by using a set of programs called a Database Management System (DBMS). Almost all DBMSs these days are Relational Database Management Systems (RDBMSs), in which data is organized and stored in a set of related tables.

One of PHP's strengths is its support for many different DBMSs. PHP supports over 20 databases. It supports the following popular RDBMSs, as well as others that are less well known:

- IBM DB2
- Informix
- Ingres
- Microsoft SQL Server (MS SQL)
- mSQL
- MySQL
- Oracle
- PostgreSQL
- Sybase

In addition, PHP offers support for ODBC, which stands for the Open Database Connectivity standard, a standard database access method developed by Microsoft. Many DBMSs understand ODBC, particularly Windows DBMSs. Using ODBC support in PHP, you can access some databases that are not specifically supported, such as DB2 and Access. Also, you can use ODBC to access several different databases with the same code. To use ODBC to communicate with a database, the database needs to have an ODBC driver installed. See the documentation for your database to find out how to install ODBC support for your database.

If you currently have a database set up and know how to use it, you can undoubtedly store and retrieve data from your existing database by using PHP scripts. If you don't have an existing database, you need to choose one. Selecting and installing a database is independent of PHP. You install the database, make sure it's working, and learn to use it. After your database is working, you can store and retrieve data with PHP scripts.

Choosing a RDBMS depends on your needs. The RDBMS that is right for you may not be the best option for someone else. You need to research your options and choose the one with the characteristics that suit your situation. You may need to consider some of the following issues:

- **Cost:** The cost of the RDBMS software ranges from free to quite pricey. MySQL, mSQL, and PostgreSQL are open source software, meaning they're free. Other RDBMSs, such as Sybase, MS SQL Server, and Oracle, are commercial software with prices that range from moderate to astronomical.

- **Features:** The features provided by an RDBMS vary. For example, mSQL has a small set of features, but this may be enough for some purposes. On the other hand, Oracle can do everything but drive your car. In general, the more features the RDBMS has, the more computer resources it requires and the higher its cost. Therefore, you may not want to install software with a huge feature set that you don't need.
- **Resources:** Some RDBMSs require more resources, such as disk space and memory, than others. For example, mSQL is very small and lightweight, requiring very little overhead. MySQL was also developed to be small. On the other hand, Oracle, depending on which products and tools you install, can require many resources.
- **Support:** Commercial software and open source software provide support differently:
    - **Commercial:** Commercial software provides a method for customers to get technical support from the company that sold them the software. Sometimes customers have to pay for the technical support or wait in phone queues, but the company answers their questions and assists with troubleshooting.
    - **Open source:** Open source software does not provide a direct phone line to a software company. Open source software is supported by the community of users. E-mail lists and forums offer access to many people who are using the software and who are willing to answer questions and assist each other with problems. Sometimes asking a question on an e-mail list gets you an answer faster than phoning a technical-support phone number at a software company.

After you choose which database you're going to use, you need to install the database software and figure out how to use it. You need to know how to design and create a database that you can then access from a PHP script. In general, a database has two parts: a structure to hold the data and the data itself.

The structure consists of the database itself and tables within the database that hold the data. You need to design the database structure before you can store data in it. RDBMS tables are organized like other tables you're used to — in rows and columns. For example, suppose you want to provide an online catalog, containing all your products, so users can see what you have and place orders. You create a database called Catalog. In the Catalog database, you create a table called Product that contains all your products. The Product table has a different product in each row. The columns of the row contain information about each product. For example, if the product is a shirt, each row of the table contains information about a different shirt you sell. The columns contain information about the shirt, such as the name of the shirt (T-shirt, dress shirt, polo shirt, and so on), the description, the size, the color, and so on.

When you create a table, you give each column a name, called the *field name.* For your Product table containing shirts, you name the columns as follows:

- Type
- Description
- Size
- Color
- Price

Your Catalog database can have other tables in it, such as a table containing shipping costs and a table containing sales tax information.

In addition to the database design and creation, you need to understand the security used by your RDBMS. One of the advantages of databases is the security provided for the data, but the security makes storing and retrieving data more complicated. The RDBMS doesn't allow just anyone to get data from your database. You need to have a valid account name and password before you can use the database. If you're using a database on a Web hosting company, those folks need to provide you with a valid account and password. If you're installing the database software yourself, you need to understand how to administer the accounts.

After you have designed and created the database structure, you can add data to the tables and retrieve stored data from the tables. PHP makes data storage and retrieval quite simple.

Understanding database support in PHP

PHP communicates with databases by using functions designed specifically to interact with databases. PHP includes a set of functions for each database it supports. For example, to communicate with MySQL 4.0 or earlier, you use functions such as `mysql_connect()` and `mysql_query()` and to communicate with MySQL 4.1 or later, you use functions such as `mysqli_connect()` and `mysqli_query()`. To communicate with Sybase, you use functions such as `sybase_connect()` and `sybase_query()`.

By default, PHP includes support for ODBC. For database support other than ODBC, you must add support for the database you plan to use. If you're using a Web hosting company, those folks must provide the database support. If you're running your Web site on your own computer, you need to add database support to PHP. You can include database support by using the methods described in the following sections.

Setting up database support in Unix/Linux/Mac

Support for a database is an installation option that is included in the configure step during installation. Appendix A includes a section that discusses the installation options. For example, to include support for mSQL, use the following command line options in the configuration step during installation:

```
./configure --with-msql=/usr/msql
```

Table 12-2 shows many of the database installation options available. If the database is installed in the default location, you don't need to include the DIR parameter. You can use the option without the parameter, as follows:

```
./configure --with-msql
```

Table 12-2 PHP Database Installation Options

Database	*Installation Option*	*Default DIR*
IBM DB2	with-ibm-db2=DIR	/home/db2instl/sqllib
Informix	with_informix=DIR	No default
Ingres II	with-ingres=DIR	/II/ingres
mSQL	with-msql=DIR	/usr/local/Hughes
MySQL 4.0 or earlier	with-mysql=DIR	/usr/local/mysql
MySQL 4.1 or greater	with-mysqli=DIR	No default. DIR must be the path to the file mysql_config that is installed with MySQL 4.1 or greater.
Oracle 7 and newer versions	with-oci8	Default DIR is contained in the environmental variable, ORACLE_HOME
Earlier versions of Oracle	with-oracle=DIR	Default DIR is contained in the environmental variable, ORACLE_HOME
PostgreSQL	with-pgsql=DIR	/usr/local/pgsql
Sybase	with-sybase=DIR	/home/sybase
Sybase-CT	with-sybase-ct=DIR	/home/sybase

After you compile PHP using the appropriate installation option, you can check that database support was correctly activated with the phpinfo function. The database support and settings appears in the output from phpinfo.

Setting up database support in Windows

Enabling PHP support for a database in Windows requires two steps:

1. **Copy the dll (Dynamic Link Library) file for the database into the main directory.**
2. **Activate the database support.**

After performing the steps, as described below, you can use the phpinfo function to check that the database support has been activated. Information and settings for the database are displayed in the output from phpinfo.

Copying the dll

The dlls are included in the zip file you download from the PHP Web site. Downloading and installing PHP manually from the zip file is described in Appendix A. After installing manually, a directory called ext is in the directory where PHP is installed. The path will be something like c:\php\ext, and the dlls for the databases are in this directory.

Copy the dll you need into the main directory where PHP is installed, such as c:\php. For example, to add support for PostgreSQL to PHP on a Windows 2000 system, copy c:\php\ext\php_pgsql.dll into the main directory where PHP is installed. To do this, CD into c;\php\ext and type:

```
copy php_pgsql.dll
```

If you used the installer to install PHP, the database dlls were not downloaded. You need to download the zip file, as described for installing PHP manually. Then unzip the file, find the appropriate dll, and copy it into the system directory.

Activating the database support

Database support is activated in the php.ini file. Look for a list of statements that have the following form:

```
;extension=php_pgsql.dll
;extension=php_msql.dll
```

This list includes a statement for every database that is supported. Notice the semicolon at the beginning of each line. The semicolon is the comment character in the php.ini file, so the statements in the list are comments and are not active. Find the statement for the database support you need and then remove the semicolon from the statement for the database support you want to activate, as in the following example

```
extension=php_pgsql.dll
```

This statement activates PostgreSQL support. After you save the php.ini file, you may need to restart your Web server before the database support goes into effect.

If you activate the database support line in php.ini, but haven't copied the dll into the main directory, you will see an error message similar to the following when you try to run a PHP script:

```
Unknown(): Unable to load dynamic library 'php_pgsql.dll'.
            The specified module could not be found.
```

If you perform both steps correctly (copy the dll into the main directory and activate the correct line in php.ini), but the database software isn't installed, you will get an error message similar to the following when you try to run a PHP script:

```
The dynamic link library msql.dll could not be found in the
            specified path
```

For MS SQL users only: You need to install the MS SQL Server Client Tools, as well as the database server. Microsoft provides these tools on the CD.

For MySQL users only: Be sure you use the correct dll: php_mysql.dll for MySQL 4.0 or earlier or php_mysqli.dll for MySQL 4.1 or later.

Communicating with your database

Most database software understands SQL (Structured Query Language), a computer language you use to communicate with a database. You send an SQL statement, called a query, to the RDBMS that tells it what you want to do. SQL queries can instruct the RDBMS to create a database, create tables in a database, store data, retrieve data, delete data, and perform many other actions.

Although most databases understand SQL, there may be differences in the SQL you can use with different databases. For example, mSQL understands a limited set of SQL queries, but Oracle and Sybase each have an extended set of SQL queries they understand, beyond the standard SQL.

A complete description of SQL is beyond the scope of this book. If you're using MySQL as your database, you may want to look at my other book, *PHP & MySQL For Dummies* (Wiley Publishing, Inc.). A description of the SQL you need to work with databases is contained in this book. Or, for a complete description of SQL and all its capabilities and features, see *SQL For Dummies,* 5th Edition, by Allen Taylor (Wiley Publishing, Inc.).

Although I do not discuss SQL in detail, I will describe a couple of simple SQL queries so that I can use some real examples in this book to show you how to use your database. To get data from your database, you can use the following query:

```
SELECT * FROM tablename
```

This query retrieves all the data that is contained in the table. The * is a special character called a *wild card* that selects all the fields in the table. Suppose you want to retrieve data from the Catalog database discussed in the section "Understanding database software," earlier in this chapter. This database has a table named Product that contains the information for all the products in the catalog. You can use the following SQL query to retrieve all the data from the Product table:

```
SELECT * FROM Product
```

To add a new record to a table, you can use the following query:

```
INSERT INTO tablename (fieldname1,fieldname2, ...) VALUES
            (value1,value2, ...)
```

This query creates a new row in the table with the specified values and adds the values provided to the named fields. For example, for the Catalog database discussed previously, you can add a new product with the following query:

```
INSERT INTO Product (Type,Description,Size,Color,Price)
            VALUES ("T-shirt","100% cotton","L","Black",20)
```

Notice that there are quotes around the strings, but not around the number. Also, notice that there is a value listed for every field named. The database gives an error message if the number of values is not equal to the number of fields.

In the next section, I discuss how to use a PHP script to interact with a database.

Using PHP with a database

Whichever database you're using, the steps to interact with a database are similar:

1. **Connect to the database.**
2. **Send an SQL query that contains instructions for the database software.**
3. **If you retrieved data from the database, process the data.**
4. **Close the connection to the database.**

These steps are discussed in more detail in the following sections.

Connecting to the database

The first step in a database interaction is connecting to the database. You use a PHP function to connect to the database. To make the connection, you need to supply the function with four things:

- **Location:** The database does not need to be on the same computer where PHP is installed. Therefore, you need to tell the PHP connect function the name of the computer where the database is located (the hostname). You can supply either a domain name (such as `mycompany.com`) or an IP address (such as `172.17.204.2`). If the database is on the same computer as PHP, you can use `localhost` for the hostname.
- **Account name:** You must provide a valid account name that can be used to access the database. The database administrator sets this up. If you're using a Web hosting company, you will be given a valid account name.
- **Password:** You have to have a valid password to access the database. The database administrator sets this up. If you're using a Web hosting company, you will be given a valid password for your account.
- **Database name:** An RDBMS can create and maintain many databases, so you need to tell it which database you want to use.

For security reasons, it's best to keep your database connection information in a separate file and use it in your PHP script with an `include` statement. As long as your include files are stored in a secure location, as discussed in Chapter 8, your information is more secure than if it were stored in the PHP script itself. For the following examples, I create an `include` file called `info.inc` with the following statements:

```
$host = "localhost";
$account = "admin";
$password = "secret";
$dbname = "Catalog";
```

Then I can include this file in any PHP script that needs to access the database by using the following statement:

```
include("info.inc");
```

The PHP function to connect to the database software is not the same for all RDBMSs. That would be too simple. However, although the functions may differ for different databases, the form is similar. For example, the most popular software for Web site database applications is MySQL. For MySQL 4.0 or earlier you use two statements as follows, to connect to the database,:

```
$connect = mysql_connect($host,$account,$password);
$db = mysql_select_db("Catalog",$connect);
```

The first statement connects to the database management software and the second statement tells it which database you want to access. For MySQL 4.1 or later, the format is slightly different, as follows:

```
$connect = mysqli_connect($host,$account,$password);
$db = mysqli_select_db($connect,"Catalog");
```

Notice that the order of the items passed in the function is reversed for the second line. Mysql passes (`"Catalog",$connect`) and mysqli passes (`$connect,"Catalog"`).

Several databases,require two separate functions to connect to the database, as shown for MySQL above. For example, mSQL and Sybase use similar statements, as shown in the following statements:

```
$connect = msql_connect($host,$account,$password);
$db = msql_select_db("Catalog",$connect);
```

```
$connect = sybase_connect($host,$account,$password);
$db = sybaseselect_db("Catalog",$connect);
```

For other databases, only one function is needed, as shown in the following statement for postgreSQL:

```
$connect = pg_connect("host=$host user=$user
          password=$password dbname=Catalog");
```

The format for connecting to other database management systems is similar with small variations. Connecting to Oracle using the OCI8 interface differs even more, as follows:

```
$connect = OCILogon($account,$password);
```

The Oracle connection also requires an environment variable `ORACLE_SID` set to the desired Oracle instance.

To determine the correct format to connect to the database that you're using, see the PHP manual on the PHP Web site (`www.php.net`) for the appropriate function for your RDBMS.

Sending a query to the database

After PHP has established a connection to the database, you can perform whatever action you desire, such as get data, change data, or insert new data. The SQL query tells the database what action you want to perform. You send the SQL query to the by using another PHP function for your RDBMS. Again, the format of these statements varies, but they are similar. For example, for MySQL, you can send the query by using the following statements:

```
$sql = "SELECT * FROM Product";
$result = mysql_query($sql,$connect);
```

The first statement stores the SQL query in a variable `$sql`. The `SQL` statement gets all the data in the table Product. The `mysql_query` function sends the query in `$sql` to the database over the database connection established earlier and stored in `$connect`. The data is stored in a temporary table `1`, with rows and columns, and `$result` (or whatever you chose to call this variable) contains a pointer to the temporary table.

For PostgreSQL, the statements are similar, as follows:

```
$sql = "SELECT * FROM Product";
$result = pg_query($connect,$sql);
```

The first statement creates the SQL query and stores it in `$sql`. The second statement executes the query and returns the data. For Oracle, two PHP functions are needed to execute a query, as follows:

```
$sql = "SELECT * FROM Product";
$query = OCIParse($connect,$sql);
$result = OCIExecute($query);
```

The first statement creates the SQL query. Notice that the first statement is the same for all three databases. For Oracle, the second two statements are required to execute the statement and return the results.

Any SQL query is sent by using the same functions. The query in these three examples returns data, but queries that don't return data are sent with the same function, as in the following example:

```
$first_name = "John";
$last_name = "Smith";
$sql = "INSERT INTO Customer (firstName,lastName) VALUES
        ('$first_name','$last_name')";
$result = mysql_query($sql);
```

When no data is returned by the query, `$result` contains `TRUE`, rather than a pointer to the retrieved data.

To determine the correct way to send the query, see the PHP manual on the PHP Web site (`www.php.net`) for the appropriate functions for your RDBMS.

Processing data

If you send a query that retrieves data, you undoubtedly intend to use that data in your PHP script. You may want to display a list of check boxes based on data taken from the database, display data in a Web page so users can edit it, use the data from the database as default text in an HTML form, and so on.

To process the returned data, you need to get it from the temporary table where it was placed when the SQL query was executed. You use PHP database functions to get the data from the temporary table.

The data is stored in the temporary table in rows and columns. You can use PHP functions to retrieve one row from the table and store it in an array, with the field names as the array keys. For MySQL, the statement is as follows:

```
$row = mysql_fetch_array($result);
```

In the previous section, we saved the results and stored the location in a variable named `$result`. In this statement, we tell PHP which results to fetch by using `$result`. The `mysql_fetch_array` returns one row of data from the temporary table specified by `$result`.

After this statement, `$row` is an array containing all the fields in the temporary table, such as the following:

```
$row['firstName'] = John
$row['lastName'] = Smith
```

To process all the data in the temporary table, you can use a loop to get one row at a time, processing each row until the end of the table is reached. For PostgreSQL, the `while` loop looks like this:

```
while($row=pg_fetch_asoc($result))
{
   foreach($row as $value)
   {
      echo "$value<br>";
   }
}
```

The `while` loop executes once for each row in the temporary table. An array called `$row` is created in each loop, containing the data in that row. The `foreach` loop travels through the `$row` array and displays each field name and the data in each field.

The following example for PostgreSQL uses a `for` loop to process the data, giving the same result as the preceding example that uses a `while` loop:

```
$Nrows = pg_num_rows($result);
for($i=0;$i<$Nrows;$i++)
{
   $row = pg_fetch_row($result,$i);
   foreach($row as $value)
   {
      echo "$value<br>";
   }
}
```

In this example, the function pg_num_rows returns the number of rows that are in the temporary table. (MySQL has a similar function, mysql_num_rows ($result).) The for loop is set up to loop once for each row in the temporary table. Inside the for loop, a row is selected from the table, and foreach is used to process each row. Notice that $i is passed to pg_fetch_row to tell it which row to fetch.

The following example produces the same results with Oracle:

```
$Nfields = OCINumCols($result);
while (OCIFetch($result))
{
    for($i=1;$i<=$Nfields;$i++)
    {
        $value = OCIResult($result,$i);
        echo "$value<br>";
    }
}
```

In this example, $Nfields is the number of fields in the result table. OCIFetch gets one row from the result table. The while loop continues looping until there are no more rows to get. OCIResult returns the value from one field in the row. The for loop travels through the row, getting the value for each field in the row and displaying it.

The previous examples show the bare-minimum PHP functions that you need for interacting with an RDBMS. PHP offers many functions for each RDBMS, such as mysql_affect_rows, which returns the number of rows changed by the query, or pg_field_name, which returns the names of the fields.

Although the PHP database functions are similar, they are different enough that you need to learn the correct functions to use for your RDBMS. Read through the documentation on the PHP Web site for the functions for your RDBMS. The documentation includes some examples. If you're using MySQL, *PHP & MySQL For Dummies* contains details and many examples.

Closing the connection

Any open database connections are closed when the script ends. However, it is good programming practice to close the connections in the script, to avoid any possible problems. You close database connections the same way you open them — with a PHP function. For example, for MySQL, use the following function to close a database connection:

```
mysql_close($connect);
```

The following are examples of other closing functions:

```
ocilogoff($connect);   # Oracle
pg_close($connect);    # PostgreSQL
mssql_close($connect); # MS SQL
```

Handling errors

When you use a `connect` function in PHP, the function attempts to make a connection to the database, but it is not always successful. For example, the database software may be down, or you may be using an invalid account name or password. For example, if you attempt to connect to a MySQL database with an invalid password, the following message is displayed:

```
Warning: mysql_connect(): Access denied for user:
         'root@localhost' (Using password: YES) in
         c:\test12.php on line 10
```

The message shows the account name you're attempting to use and indicates whether you're using a password. In this case, it shows that you used a password, but it doesn't show what password you used. The statement means that MySQL will not allow you to access the database because the account name and password are not valid.

The message is a warning, not an error. Therefore, after displaying the message, PHP continues to execute the rest of the script. This is not usually what you want. In general, if you are unable to connect to the database, the rest of the script will fail as well. So, you can use a `die` statement to stop the script if the script fails to connect to the database. The following example shows the use of a `die` statement when connecting to a PostgreSQL database:

```
$connect = pg_connect("host=$host user=$user
           password=$password dbname=Catalog")
   or die("Can't connect to database");
```

Using this statement, the script stops if the connection attempt fails, and the message in the `die` statement is displayed. It's a good idea to use a `die` statement with all the database functions so the script stops if the function is unable to execute successfully.

When you use a function to get data from the temporary result table, you may see a warning message. For example, suppose you include the following statements in your script:

```
$sql = "SELECT * FROM Productt";
$result = mysql_query($sql);
$row = mysql_fetch_array($result);
```

In this case, the typo in the table name (notice the tt in Product) results in the following message:

```
Warning: mysql_fetch_array(): supplied argument is not a
        valid MySQL result resource in test.php on line 9
```

The warning tells you that `$result` does not contain a valid result resource. That is, `$result` does not contain a pointer to a table with rows and columns. The warning usually means that the SQL query did not execute as intended or that the results were different than you expected. For this example, the incorrect table name caused the query to fail to execute, returning `FALSE`. Thus, `$result` contains `FALSE`, an invalid result when used in the `mysql_fetch_array` function.

No warning was displayed when the `mysql_query` function was executed, even though the SQL query failed. A MySQL error message is generated when the SQL fails, but it is not displayed unless your script specifically displays it. A better format for your script is to stop the script if the SQL query fails and display the MySQL error message to see what the problem is. You can display the MySQL error message by using the `mysql_error` function. Therefore, you might modify the previous statements as follows:

```
$sql = "SELECT * FROM Productt";
$result = mysql_query($sql)
       or die("Query failed: ".mysql_error());
$row = mysql_fetch_array($result);
```

The output from these statements is as follows:

```
Query failed: Table 'Catalog.productt' doesn't exist
```

With these statements, when the query fails to execute, the `die` statement displays its message, which includes the MySQL error message that is displayed by `mysql_error`, and the script stops.

The general error-handling procedures recommended for PHP apply to the database functions as well. For example, you may not want to display errors to users but send errors to a log file instead. (Error handling is described in Chapter 4.)

Putting it all together

The previous sections describe the separate functions needed to interact with a database in your PHP application scripts. This section provides examples that put the functions together into complete scripts.

For the first example, assume you have a PostgreSQL database called Sales with a table called Customer. The first name, last name, and phone number for each customer are stored in the table. The script in Listing 12-2 displays all the names and phone numbers in a Web page.

Listing 12-2: A Script That Displays a Customer List

```
<?php
/* Script name: DisplayCustomers
 * Description: Gets all customer records from a
 *              PostgreSQL database and displays the
 *              Customer list in a Web page.
 */
 include("info.inc");     # contains connect variables
 $connect = pg_connect("host=$host user=$user
           password=$password dbname=Sales")
    or die("Can't connect to database");
 $sql = "SELECT * from Customer";
 $result = pg_query($sql)
           or die("Query failed: ".mysql_error());
 $Nrows = pg_num_rows($result);
 echo "<html>
    <head><title>Customer List</title></head>
    <body>
    <table width=\"100%\" border=\"0\">\n";
 for($i=0;$i<$Nrows;$i++)
 {
    echo "<tr>";
    $row = pg_fetch_row($result,$i);
    echo "<td>{$row[1]}, {$row[0]}</td>
        <td>{$row[2]}</td>";
    echo "</tr>\n";
 }
 echo "</table></body></html>";
?>
```

The script gets all the customer information from the Customer table. It then uses a for loop to output the customer information to the Web page in an HTML table.

The second example creates a list of check boxes in a Web page where users can select the type of product they want to view. The script shown in Listing 12-3 gets the list of product types from a MySQL database. The table has two fields: `ProductType` and `Description`.

Listing 12-3: A Script That Creates Check Boxes

```
<html>
<head><title>Testing Files</title></head>
<body>
<?php
/* Script name: DisplayCheckboxes
 * Description: Gets all items for check boxes from a
 *              MySQL database and creates the list of
 *              check boxes in a Web page.
 */
 include("info.inc");      # contains connect variables
 $connection = mysql_connect($host,$user,$password)
       or die ("Couldn't connect to server");
 $db = mysql_select_db("Catalog",$connection)
       or die ("Couldn't select database");
 $query = "SELECT * FROM ProductType";
 $result = mysql_query($query)
       or die("Query failed: ".mysql_error());
 echo "<html><head><title>Product Type</title></head>
   <body><div style='margin-left: .2in'>
   <h3>Which product are you interested in?</h3>\n";
 ## create form containing check boxes ##
 echo "<form action='processform.php' method='post'>\n";
 echo "<hr><table width='100%'>";
 while ($row = mysql_fetch_array($result))
 {
    echo "<tr>";
    echo "<td width='20%'><b><input type='checkbox'
      name=\"interest['ProductType']\"
      value=\"{$row['ProductType']}\">{$row['ProductType']}
      </b></td>\n";
    echo "<td>{$row['Description']}</td>";
    echo "</tr>\n";
 }
 echo "</table>";
 echo "<p><input type='submit' value='Select Product'>
       </form>\n";
?>
</div></body></html>
```

The script creates an HTML form, containing an HTML table. A `while` loop creates each row of the table and populates the table with the information retrieved from the database. Notice the `while` condition etches a row from the temporary table stored at the location contained in `$result`. The `while` loop will continue to execute as long as there are rows in the table. When the loop reaches the last row, the `while` loop will end.

Notice the array variables that are echoed into the table cells. The name of the array elements needs to be enclosed in curly brackets; otherwise, a parse error results.

The script in Listing 12-3 produces the Web page shown in Figure 12-1. The list of check boxes contains all the types in the database table. If more product types are added to the database, they will be displayed by this script.

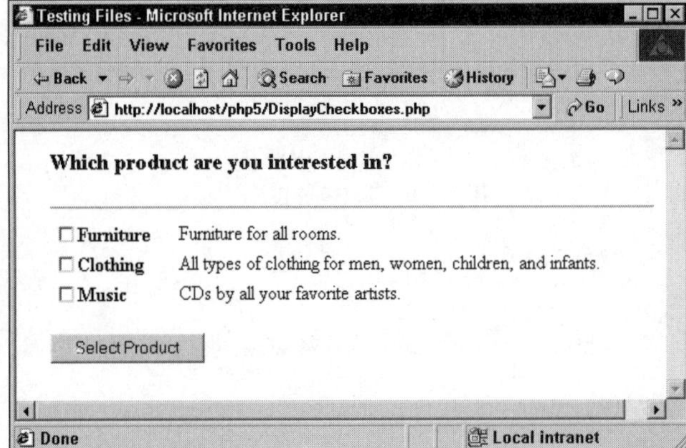

Figure 12-1: A Web page with check boxes produced by the script in Listing 12-3.

Using SQLite

SQLite allows you to interact with your data as if it were a database, using functions, without requiring you to install database software. You use SQL, as you do when you store your data in a database, but the data is actually stored in a flat file. Thus, SQLite has the advantages of a flat file — fewer resources required. In addition, it provides the advantage of using SQL — you don't need to learn the operating system commands required to open and manipulate a flat file directly. SQLite is also faster than a database for some of the most common tasks. However, it has the flat file disadvantages: poor security and inability to handle really complex data. In summary, SQLite provides a quick, easy way to store data in a flat file, but is not a replacement for a database if you have really large amounts or really complex data or need to keep your data secure.

Storing and retrieving data with SQLite is very similar to the methods described in the preceding section for using databases with PHP. You use SQL to communication with the data file and use PHP functions to send the SQL and retrieve the data. You interact with the data using the same steps that you use with a database, as follows:

1. **Connect to the data file.**

   As with a database, first you establish a connection to the data file. To connect to the data file, use the following PHP function:

   ```
   $db = sqlite_open("testdb");
   ```

   This statement opens the data file testdb. If the file doesn't exist, it is created.

2. **Send an SQL query.**

   To send an SQL query, use the sqlite_query function, as follows:

   ```
   $sql = "SELECT * FROM Product";
   $result = sqlite_query($db,$sql);
   ```

3. **If you retrieved data from the data file, process the data.**

   As with a database, the retrieved data is stored in ae temporary table in rows and columns. You can use PHP functions to retrieve one row from the temporary data table and store it in an array, with the field names as the array keys. The statement is as follows:

   ```
   $row = sqlite_fetch_array($result);
   ```

   After this statement, $row is an array containing all the fields in the temporary table, such as the following:

   ```
   $row['firstName'] = John
   $row['lastName'] = Smith
   ```

   To process all the data in the temporary table, you can use a loop to get one row at a time, processing each row until the end of the table is reached, as follows.

   ```
   while($row=sqlite_fetch_array($result))
   {
      foreach($row as $value)
      {
         echo "$value<br>";
      }
   }
   ```

4. **Close the connection to the data file.**

   When you finish storing and/or retrieving data, you can close the data file with the following statement:

   ```
   sqlite_close($db);
   ```

Error handling as discussed in the previous section refers to SQLite, as well as to databases. For instance, the die statement discussed in the Error Handling section is useful with SQLite. Also, as discussed, when the query fails, an

SQLite error message is generated, but not displayed unless you use a function developed specifically to display it. Thus, the following statements handle errors, as well as send the SQL query:

```
$sql = "SELECT * FROM Product";
$result = sqlite_query($sql)
       or die("Query failed: ".sqlite_error());
$row = sqlite_fetch_array($result);
```

Read the preceding section that describes using databases with PHP. Most of the information applies to the use of SQLite as well. What makes SQLite different is that the data is stored in a flat file, rather than stored by the database software in files that are unique to the specific database used.

Chapter 13

PHP and Your Operating System

In This Chapter

- Manipulating files
- Running programs outside PHP
- Transferring files from one machine to another
- Sending e-mail and e-mail attachments

PHP provides all the file-handling features that any full-featured language offers. Using PHP, you can do anything you need to do with the information on your system. You can manage your information in files — you can create, copy, delete, find, move, and more. You can run any program that's on your computer, regardless of whether it's a PHP program. You can transfer files between computers. Or you can send information via e-mail. This chapter gives you the information you need to use PHP to do pretty much anything you can think of on your computer.

Managing Files

The information you save on your hard disk is organized into *files.* Rather than storing files in one big "file drawer," making them difficult to find, files are stored in many drawers, called *directories* or *folders.* The system of files and directories is called a *file system.* A file system is organized in a hierarchical structure. A file system has a top level that is a single directory called *root,* such as `c:\` on Windows or / on Linux. The root directory contains other directories, and each directory can contain other directories, and so on. The file system's structure can go down as many levels as you want.

A directory is a specific type of file that you use to organize other files. A directory contains a list of files and the information needed for the operating system to find those files. A directory can contain both files and other directories.

PHP includes functions that allow you to open files and read what's in them or write information into them (as discussed in Chapter 12). Files also can be checked, copied, deleted, and renamed, among other things. Functions for performing these additional file-management tasks are described in the following sections. You also find out about functions that allow you to manage directories and discover what's inside them.

In this chapter, I cover the most useful functions for managing files, but more functions are available. When you need to perform an action on a file or directory, check the documentation on the PHP Web site to see if there's a function that does what you need to do. If such a function does not exist, you can use your operating system commands or a program in another language, as described in "Using Operating System Commands," later in this chapter.

Getting information about files

Often you want to know information about a file. PHP has functions that allow you to find out file information from within a script.

You can find out whether a file exists with the `file_exists` statement, as follows:

```
$result = file_exists("stuff.txt");
```

After this statement, `$result` contains either `TRUE` or `FALSE`. The function is often used in a conditional statement, such as the following:

```
if(!file_exists("stuff.txt"))
{
    echo "File not found!\n";
}
```

After you know the file exists, you can find out information about it.

Table 13-1 shows many of the functions that PHP provides for checking files.

Table 13-1 Functions That Get Information about a File

Function	*What It Does*	*Output*
`is_file ("stuff.txt")`	Tests whether the file is a regular file, rather than a directory or other special type of file	`TRUE` or `FALSE`
`is_dir ("stuff.txt")`	Tests whether the file is a directory	`TRUE` or `FALSE`
`is_executable ("do.txt")`	Tests whether the file is executable	`TRUE` or `FALSE`

Function	What It Does	Output
is_writable ("stuff.txt")	Tests whether you can write to the file	TRUE or FALSE
is_readable ("stuff.txt")	Tests whether you can read the file	TRUE or FALSE
fileatime ("stuff.txt")	Returns the time when the file was last accessed	UNIX timestamp (like 1057196122) or FALSE
filectime ("stuff.txt")	Returns the time when the file was created	UNIX timestamp or FALSE
filemtime ("stuff.txt")	Returns the time when the file was last modified	UNIX timestamp or FALSE
filegroup ("stuff.txt")	Returns the group ID of the file	Integer that is a group ID or FALSE
fileowner ("stuff.txt")	Returns the user ID of the owner of the file	Integer that is a user ID or FALSE
filesize ("stuff.txt")	Returns the file size in bytes	Integer or FALSE
filetype ("stuff.txt")	Returns the file type	File type (such as file, dir, file, dir, link, char), or FALSE if error or can't identify type
basename ("/t1/do.txt")	Returns the filename from the path	do.txt
dirname ("/t1/do.txt")	Returns the directory name from the path	/t1

Some of the information is relevant only for Linux/Unix/Mac, and some is returned on Windows as well.

A function that returns useful info about a path/filename is pathinfo(). You can use the following statement:

```
$pinfo = pathinfo("/topdir/nextdir/stuff.txt");
```

After the statement, $pinfo is an array that contains the following three elements:

```
$pinfo[dirname] = /topdir/nextdir
$pinfo[basename] = stuff.txt
$pinfo[extension] = txt
```

When you're testing a file with one of the `is_something` functions, any typing error, such as a misspelling of the filename, gives a `FALSE` result. For example, `is_dir("tyme")` returns `FALSE` if `"tyme"` is a file, not a directory. But, it also returns `FALSE` if `"tyme"` does not exist, because you meant to type `"type"`.

Unix timestamps are returned by some of the functions in the list. You can convert these timestamps to dates with the `date` function, as described in Chapter 5.

Copying, renaming, and deleting files

Chapter 12 describes how to create a file and write information into it. In this section, I describe some other things you can do with a file, such as copy it or delete it.

You can copy an existing file into a new file. After copying, you have two copies of the file with two different names. Copying a file is often useful for backing up important files. To copy a file, use the `copy` statement, as follows:

```
copy("fileold.txt","filenew.txt");
```

This statement copies `fileold.txt`, an existing file, into `filenew.txt`. If a file with the same name as `filenew.txt` already exists, it is overwritten. If you don't want to overwrite an existing file, you can prevent it by using the following statements:

```
If(!file_exists("filenew.txt"))
{
     copy("fileold.txt","filenew.txt");
}
else
{
     echo "File already exists!\n";
}
```

You can rename a file by using the `rename` statement, as follows:

```
rename("oldname.txt","newname.txt");
```

If you attempt to rename a file with the name of a file that already exists, a warning is displayed, as follows, and the file is not renamed.

```
Warning: rename(fileold.txt,filenew.txt): File exists in
         c:test.php on line 17
```

To remove an unwanted file, use the `unlink` statement, as follows:

```
unlink("badfile.txt");
```

After this statement, the file is deleted. However, if the file doesn't exist to start with, `unlink` doesn't complain. It acts the same as if it had deleted the file. PHP does not let you know if the file doesn't exist. So, watch out for typos.

Organizing files

Files are organized into *directories,* also called *folders.* This section describes how to create and remove directories and how to get a list of the files in a directory.

Creating a directory

To create a directory, use the `mkdir` function, as follows:

```
mkdir("testdir");
```

This statement creates a new directory named `testdir` in the same directory where the script is located. That is, if the script is `/test/test.php`, the new directory is `/test/testdir`. If a directory already exists with the same name, a warning is displayed, as follows, and the new directory is not created:

```
Warning: mkdir(): File exists in d:/test/test.php on line 5
```

You can check first to see whether the directory already exists by using the following statements:

```
If(!is_dir("mynewdir"))
{
   mkdir("mynewdir");
}
else
{
   echo "Directory already exists!";
}
```

After the directory is created, you can organize it's contents by copying files into and out of the directory. Copying files is described in the section "Copying, renaming, and deleting files," earlier in this chapter.

To create a directory in another directory, use the entire path name, as follows:

```
mkdir("/topdir/nextdir/mynewdir");
```

You can use a relative path to create a new directory, as follows:

```
mkdir("../mynewdir");
```

With this statement, if your script is /topdir/test/makedir.php, the new directory is /topdir/mynewdir.

To change to a different directory, use the following statement:

```
chdir("../anotherdir");
```

Building a list of all the files in a directory

It's often useful to get a list of the files in a directory. For example, you may want to provide a list of files for users to download or want to display images from files in a specific directory.

PHP provides functions for opening and reading directories. To open a directory, use the opendir statement, as follows:

```
$dh = opendir("/topdir/testdir");
```

If you attempt to open a directory that doesn't exist, a warning is displayed, as follows:

```
Warning: opendir(testdir): failed to open dir: Invalid
         argument in test13.php on line 5
```

In the previous statement, the variable $dh is a *directory handle,* a pointer to the open directory that you can use later to read from the directory. To read a filename from the directory, use the readdir function, as follows:

```
$filename = readdir($dh);
```

After this statement, $filename contains the name of a file. Only the filename is stored in $filename, not the entire path to the file. To read all the filenames in a directory, you can use a while loop, as follows:

```
while($filename = readdir($dh))
{
   echo $filename."\n";
}
```

The readdir function does not provide any control over the order in which filenames are read, so you don't always get the filenames in the order you expect.

Suppose you want to create a gallery that displays in a Web page all the images in a specified directory. You can use the opendir and readdir functions to do this. Listing 13-1 shows a script that creates an image gallery.

Listing 13-1: A Script That Creates an Image Gallery

```
<?php
 /* Script name: displayGallery
  * Description: Displays all the image files that are
  *              stored in a specified directory.
  */
 echo "<html><head><title>Image Gallery</title></head>
      <body>";
 $dir = "../test1/testdir/";                             #8
 $dh = opendir($dir);                                    #9
 while($filename = readdir($dh))                         #10
 {
   $filepath = $dir.$filename;                           #12
   if(is_file($filepath) and ereg("\.jpg$",$filename)) #13
   {
      $gallery[] = $filepath;
   }
 }
 sort($gallery);                                         #16
 foreach($gallery as $image)                             #17
 {
   echo "<hr>";
   echo "<img src='$image'><br>";
 }
?>
</body></html>
```

Notice the line numbers at the end of some of the lines in Listing 13-1. The following discussion of the script and how it works refers to the line numbers in the script listing:

- **Line 8:** This line stores the name of the directory in `$dir` for use later in the program. Notice that the / is included at the end of the directory name. Don't use \, even with Windows.
- **Line 9:** This line opens the directory.
- **Line 10:** This line starts a `while` loop that reads in each file name in the directory.
- **Line 12:** This line creates the variable `$filepath`, which is the complete path to the file.

  If the / is not included at the end of the directory name on line 8, `$filepath` will not be a valid path.

- **Line 13:** This line checks to see whether the file is a graphics file by looking for the `.jpg` extension. If the file has a `.jpg` extension, the complete file path is added to an array called `$gallery`.
- **Line 16:** This line sorts the array so the images are displayed in alphabetical order.
- **Line 17:** This line starts the `foreach` loop that displays the images in the Web page.

Using Operating System Commands

Your operating system has many commands you can use by typing the commands at the command-line prompt. If you want to see what files are in a directory, for example, you can use the `dir` command in a Windows command prompt window or the `ls` command in Unix/Linux. Or to make a copy of a file, you can use the `copy` command in the Windows command prompt window or the `cp` command in Unix/Linux. (To access the command prompt window in Windows 2000, choose Start➪Programs➪Accessories➪Command Prompt.)

In this section, I assume that you know the format and use of the system commands for your operating system. Describing operating system commands is outside the scope of this book. If you know that you need to run an operating system command from your PHP script, this section shows you how.

PHP has functions to perform the most widely used actions. For example, you can see what files are in a directory by using the `opendir` and `readdir` functions, as described earlier in the chapter. Or, you can make a copy of a file with the `copy` function.

Error messages from system commands

None of the methods for executing system commands displays or returns an informational error message when the system command fails. You know the system command didn't work because you didn't get the outcome you expected. But because the functions don't return error messages, you don't know what went wrong.

You can return or display the operating system error message by adding a few extra characters to the system command you're executing. On most operating systems, if you add the characters `2>&1` after the system command, the error message is sent to wherever the output is directed. For example, you can use the following statement:

```
$result = system("di c:\php");
```

The `system` function displays the directory when the system command executes. However, notice that `dir` is mistyped. It is `di` rather than `dir`. No system command called `di` exists, so the system command can't execute, and nothing is displayed. Suppose you used the following statement instead:

```
$result = system("di c:\php
    2>&1");
```

In this case, the error message is displayed. On Windows 2000, the error message displayed is as follows:

```
'di' is not recognized as an
    internal or external com-
    mand, operable program or
    batch file.
```

Be sure you don't include any spaces in `2>&1`. The format requires the characters together, without any spaces.

However, you may want to perform an action not provided by PHP, such as making a copy of an entire directory, including files; looking at or changing your path; or clearing the screen. Or, you may think it's easier to use a system command, such as using `ls` or `dir` to see your directory, rather than write the loop required with `opendir` and `readdir`. Or, you may want to run a program in another language. You may have a program written in Perl, for example, that does exactly what you need, and you don't want to write a new program in PHP to do the same thing. No problem. You can do all of these things through PHP.

PHP allows you to use system commands or run programs in other languages by using any of the following methods:

- **backticks:** PHP executes the system command that is between two backticks (`) and displays the result.
- `system` **function:** This function executes a system command, displays the output, and returns the last line of the output.
- `exec` **function:** This function executes a system command, stores the output in an array, and returns the last line of the output.
- `passthru` **function:** This function executes a system command and displays the output.

You can execute any command that you can type into the system prompt. The command is executed exactly as is. You can execute simple commands: `ls` or `dir`. `rename` or `mv`, `rm` or `del`. If your operating system allows you to pipe or redirect output, you can pipe or redirect in the system command you're executing in PHP. If your operating system allows you to enter two commands on one line, you can put two commands into the single command you're executing from PHP. The following sample commands are valid to execute from PHP, depending on the operating system:

```
dir
rm badfile.txt
dir | sort
cd c:\php ; dir      (Not valid in Windows)
"cd c:\php && dir"  (Windows 2000)
dir > dirfile
sort < unsortedfile.txt
```

On some occasions, you want to run a system command that takes a long time to finish. You can run the system command in the background (if your operating system supports such things) while PHP continues with the script. If you do this, you need to redirect the output to a file, rather than return it to the script, so that PHP can continue before the system command finishes.

The following sections describe the preceding methods in greater detail.

Using backticks

A simple way to execute a system command is to put the command between two backticks (`), as follows:

```
$result = `dir c:\php`;
```

The variable `$result` contains the statement's output, in this case a list of the files in the `c:\php` directory. If you echo `$result`, the following output is displayed:

```
Volume in drive C has no label.
 Volume Serial Number is 394E-15E5

 Directory of c:\php

02/25/2004  10:48a      <DIR>          .
02/25/2004  10:48a      <DIR>          ..
02/25/2004  04:30p      <DIR>          dev
02/25/2004  04:30p      <DIR>          ext
02/25/2004  04:30p      <DIR>          extras
02/25/2004  04:30p             417,792 fdftk.dll
02/25/2004  04:30p              90,112 fribidi.dll
02/25/2004  04:30p             346,624 gds32.dll
02/25/2004  04:30p                  70 go-pear.bat
02/25/2004  04:30p              32,081 install.txt
02/25/2004  04:30p             876,544 libeay32.dll
02/25/2004  04:30p              47,027 libintl-1.dll
02/25/2004  04:30p             165,643 libmhash.dll
02/25/2004  04:30p             233,472 libmysql.dll
02/25/2004  04:30p               3,208 license.txt
02/25/2004  04:30p              57,344 msql.dll
02/25/2004  04:30p              18,151 news.txt
02/25/2004  04:30p             278,800 ntwdblib.dll
02/25/2004  04:30p      <DIR>          PEAR
02/25/2004  04:30p              53,248 php-cgi.exe
02/25/2004  04:30p              28,672 php-win.exe
02/25/2004  04:30p              28,672 php.exe
02/25/2004  04:30p               3,872 php.gif
02/25/2004  04:30p              39,284 php.ini-dist
02/25/2004  04:30p              40,899 php.ini-recommended
02/25/2004  04:30p              40,960 php5activescript.dll
02/25/2004  04:30p              36,864 php5apache.dll
02/25/2004  04:30p              36,864 php5apache2.dll
02/25/2004  04:30p              53,248 php5apache_hooks.dll
02/25/2004  04:30p             503,320 php5embed.lib
02/25/2004  04:30p              28,672 php5isapi.dll
02/25/2004  04:30p              28,672 php5nsapi.dll
02/25/2004  04:30p           3,452,928 php5ts.dll
02/25/2004  04:30p               1,224 snapshot.txt
```

```
02/25/2004  04:30p             159,744 ssleay32.dll
02/25/2004  04:30p              49,152 php_mysql.dll
              30 File(s)      7,153,163 bytes
               6 Dir(s)    251,727,872 bytes free
```

The backtick operator is disabled when safe_mode is enabled. safe_mode is set to Off by default when PHP is installed. safe_mode is not set to On unless the PHP administrator deliberately turns it on.

Using the system function

The system function executes a system command, displays the output, and returns the last line of the output from the system command. To execute a system command, use the following statement:

```
$result = system("dir c:\php");
```

When this statement executes, the directory listing is displayed, and $result contains the last line that was output from the command. If you echo $result, you see something like the following:

```
11 Dir(s)     566,263,808 bytes free
```

The contents of $result with the system function is the last line of the output from the dir command.

Using the exec function

The exec function executes a system command but does not display the output. Instead, the output can be stored in an array, with each line of the output becoming an element in the array. The last line of the output is returned.

Perhaps you just want to know how many files and free bytes are in a directory. You can execute a command without saving the output in an array with the following statement:

```
$result = exec("dir c:\php");
```

The command executes, but the output is not displayed. The variable $result contains the last line of the output. If you echo $result, the display looks something like this:

```
11 Dir(s)     566,263,808 bytes free
```

The output is the last line of the output of the `dir` command. If you want to store the entire output from the dir command in an array, use the following command:

```
$result = exec("dir c:\php",$dirout);
```

After this statement, the array `$dirout` contains the directory listing, with one line per item. You can display the directory listing as follows:

```
foreach($dirout as $line)
{
   echo "$line\n";
}
```

The loop displays the following:

```
Volume in drive D has no label.
 Volume Serial Number is 394E-15E5

 Directory of d:\php

02/25/2004  10:48a    <DIR>          .
02/25/2004  10:48a    <DIR>          ..
02/25/2004  04:30p    <DIR>          dev
02/25/2004  04:30p    <DIR>          ext
02/25/2004  04:30p    <DIR>          extras
02/25/2004  04:30p           417,792 fdftk.dll
```

You can also use the following statements to get specific elements from the output array:

```
echo $dirout[3];
echo $dirout[7];
```

The output is as follows:

```
Directory of C:\PHP
02/25/2004  04:30p    <DIR>          dev
```

Using the passthru function

The `passthru` function executes a system command and displays the output exactly as it is returned. To execute a system command, use the following statement:

```
passthru("dir c:\php");
```

The statement displays the directory listing but does not return anything. Therefore, you don't use a variable to store the returned data because nothing is returned.

The output is displayed in raw form; it is not processed. Therefore, this function can be used when binary output is expected.

Understanding security issues

When you execute a system command, you allow a user to perform an action on your computer. If the system command is `dir c:\php`, that's okay. However, if the system command is `rm /bin/*` or `del c:\*.*`, you won't be happy with the results. You need to be careful when using the functions that execute system commands outside your script.

As long as you only execute commands that you write yourself, such as `dir` or `ls`, you're okay. But when you start executing commands that include data sent by users, you need to be extremely careful. For example, suppose you have an application in which users type a name into a form and your application then creates a directory with the name sent by the user. The user types `Smith` into the form field named `directoryName`. Your script that processes the form has a command as follows:

```
$directoryName = $_POST['directoryName'];
exec("mkdir $directoryName");
```

Because `$directoryName = Smith`, `mkdir Smith` is the system command that is executed. The directory is created, and everybody is happy.

However, suppose the user types `Smith; rm *` into the form. In this case, `$directoryName =Smith;rm *`. The system command that executes is now `mkdir Smith;rm *`. On many operating systems, such as Unix/Linux, the semicolon is the character that separates two commands so that two commands can be entered on one line. Oops! The commands are executed as follows:

```
mkdir Smith
rm *
```

Now you have a problem. The directory Smith is created, and all the files in the current directory are removed.

If you use a variable in a system command, you must use it carefully. You must know where it came from. If it comes from outside the script, you need to check the value in the variable before using it. In the preceding example, you could add code so the script checks the variable to be sure it contains only letters and numbers before using it in the `mkdir` command.

Using FTP

Transferring files from one computer to another happens a gazillion times a day on the Internet. When colleagues on opposite sides of the country need to share files, it's not a problem. A quick transfer takes only seconds, and all parties have the files they need.

Files can be transferred by using your Web server or FTP. Transferring files via your Web server is described in Chapter 11. In this section, I discuss how to transfer files using FTP.

FTP is independent of the Web. You can use FTP to transfer files in a script running in PHP for the Web or in an independent, stand-alone script. FTP allows you to get a directory listing from another computer, or to download or upload a single file or several files at once.

FTP is client/server software. To use FTP to transfer files between your computer and a remote computer, you connect to an FTP server on the remote computer and send it requests.

To use FTP in your scripts, FTP support needs to be enabled when PHP is installed. If you installed PHP for Windows, you don't need to do anything extra to enable FTP support. If you're compiling PHP on Unix/Linux/Mac, and you want to enable FTP support, you can use the FTP support installation option, as follows:

```
--enable-ftp
```

For more information on this and other installation options, see Appendix A.

Logging in to the FTP server

To connect to the FTP server on the computer you want to exchange files with, use the `ftp_connect` function, as follows:

```
$connect = ftp_connect("janet.valade.com");
```

Or, you can connect by using an IP address, as follows:

```
$connect = ftp_connect("172.17.204.2");
```

After you connect, you log into the FTP server. You need a user ID and a password to log in. You may have your own personal ID and password, or you may be using a general ID and password that anyone can use. Some public sites on the Internet let anyone login by using the user ID of anonymous and the user's e-mail address as the password. It's best to put the user ID and password into a separate file and include the file when needed. (See Chapter 8 for more details.)

The ftp_login function allows you to login to an FTP server after you've made the connection. This statement assumes you have your account ID and password stored in variables, as follows:

```
$login_result = ftp_login($connect,$userid,$passwd);
```

If you try to login without establishing a connection to the FTP server first, you see the following warning:

```
Warning: ftp_login() expects parameter 1 to be resource,
         boolean given in d:\test1\test13.php on line 9
```

The warning does not stop the program. The login fails, but the script continues, which is probably not what you want. Because the rest of your script probably depends on your successful FTP connection, you may want to stop the script if the functions fail. The following statements stop the script if the function fails:

```
$connect = ftp_connect("janet.valade.com")
          or die("Can't connect to server");
$login_result = ftp_login($connect,$userid,$passwd)
          or die("Can't login to server");
```

After you login to the FTP server, you can send it requests to accomplish tasks, such as getting a directory listing or uploading and downloading files, as described in the following sections.

Getting a directory listing

One common task is to get a directory listing. The ftp_nlist statement gets a directory listing from the remote computer and stores it in an array, as follows:

```
$filesArr = ftp_nlist($connect,"data");
```

The second parameter in the parentheses is the name of the directory. If you don't know the name of the directory, you can request the FTP server to send you the name of the current directory, as follows:

```
$directory_name = ftp_pwd($connect);
$filesArr = ftp_nlist($connect,$directory_name);
```

The directory listing that FTP sends after the ftp_nlist statement runs is stored in an array, one filename in each element of the array. You can then display the directory listing from the array, as follows:

```
foreach($filesArr as $value)
{
    echo $value\n;
}
```

Downloading and uploading files with FTP

You can download a file from the remote computer with the ftp_get function. The following statement downloads a file from the remote computer after you're logged into the FTP server:

```
ftp_get($connect,"newfile.txt","data.txt",FTP_ASCII);
```

The first filename, newfile.txt, is the name the file will have on your computer after it's downloaded. The second filename, data.txt, is the existing name of the file that you want to download.

The FTP_ASCII term in the statement tells FTP what kind of file is being downloaded. The choices for file mode are FTP_ASCII or FTP_BINARY. Binary files are machine language files. You can determine which file mode you need by examining the contents of the file. If the contents are characters that you can read and understand, the file is ASCII. If the contents appear to be garbage, the file is binary. Graphic files, for example, are binary.

You can upload a file with a similar function called ftp_put. The following statement uploads a file.:

```
ftp_put($connect,"newfile.txt","data.txt",FTP_ASCII);
```

The first filename, newfile.txt, is the name the file will have on the remote computer after it's uploaded. The second filename, data.txt, is the existing name of the file that you want to upload.

When you're finished transferring files over your FTP connection, you can close the connection with the following statement:

```
ftp_close($connect);
```

The script in Listing 13-2 downloads all the files in a directory that have a .txt extension. The files are downloaded from the remote computer over an FTP connection.

Listing 13-2: A Script to Download Files via FTP

```
<?php
 /* Script name: downloadFiles
  * Description: Downloads all the files with a txt
  *              extension in a directory via FTP.
  */
 $dir_name = "data/";
 $connect = ftp_connect("janet.valade.com")
     or die("Can't connect to FTP server");
 $login_result = ftp_login($connect,$userID,$passwd)
     or die("Can't log in");
 $filesArr = ftp_nlist($connect,$dir_name);
 foreach($filesArr as $value)
 {
    if(ereg("\.txt$",$value))
    {
      if(!file_exists($value))
      {
         ftp_get($connect,$value,$dir_name.$value,FTP_ASCII);
      }
      else
      {
         echo "File $value already exists!\n";
      }
    }
 }
 ftp_close($connect);
?>
```

The script gets a directory listing from the remote computer and stores it in `$filesArr`. The `foreach` statement loops through the filenames in `$filesArr` and checks to see whether files have a `.txt` extension. If so, the scripts tests to see whether a file with the same name already exists. If such a file doesn't already exist, the file is downloaded; if such a file does exist, a message is printed, and the file is not downloaded.

Other FTP functions

Additional FTP functions perform other actions, such as change to another directory on the remote computer or create a new directory on the remote computer. Table 13-2 contains most of the FTP functions that are available.

Table 13-2 FTP Functions

Function	*What It Does*
`ftp_cdup($connect)`	Changes to the directory directly above the current directory.
`ftp_chdir($connect, "directoryname")`	Changes directories on the remote computer.
`ftp_close($connect)`	Closes an FTP connection.
`ftp_connect("servername")`	Opens a connection to the computer. *servername* can be a domain name or an IP address.
`ftp_delete($connect, "path/filename")`	Deletes a file on the remote computer.
`ftp_exec($connect, "command")`	Executes a system command on the remote computer.
`ftp_fget($connect,$fh, "data.txt",FTP_ASCII)`	Downloads the file contents from the remote computer into an open file. `$fh` is the file handle of the open file. (See Chapter 12 for more on file handles.)
`ftp_fput($connect, "new.txt",$fh,FTP_ASCII)`	Uploads an open file to the remote computer. `$fh` is the file handle of the open file.
`ftp_get($connect,"d.txt", "sr.txt",FTP_ASCII)`	Downloads a file from the remote computer. `sr.txt` is the name of the file to be downloaded, and `d.txt` is the name of the downloaded file.
`ftp_login($connect, $userID,$password)`	Logs into the FTP server.
`ftp_mdtm($connect, "filename.txt")`	Gets the time when the file was last modified.
`ftp_mkdir($connect, "directoryname")`	Creates a new directory on the remote computer.
`ftp_nlist($connect, "directoryname")`	Gets a list of the files in a remote directory. Files are returned in an array.
`ftp_put($connect,"d.txt", "sr.txt",FTP_ASCII)`	Uploads a file to the remote computer. `sr.txt` is the name of the file to be uploaded, and `d.txt` is the filename on the remote computer.
`ftp_pwd($connect)`	Gets the name of the current directory on the remote computer.

Function	What It Does
`ftp_rename($connect, "oldname","newname")`	Renames a file on the remote computer.
`ftp_rmdir($connect, "directoryname")`	Deletes a directory on the remote computer.
`ftp_size($connect, "filename.txt")`	Returns the size of the file on the remote computer.
`ftp_systype($connect)`	Returns the system type of the remote file server, for example Unix.

Using E-Mail

E-mail is the most widely used application on the Internet. Many PHP applications require the use of e-mail. Applications that allow customers to order products send e-mail messages to customers to acknowledge their orders. When users create a new account, the application sends them e-mail to verify their accounts. When users click the "I forgot my password" link on a login screen, the application sends the users e-mail with their passwords. Applications send monthly newsletters to lists of subscribers. And e-mail has many other uses as well.

PHP provides a function that makes sending e-mail simple. This section tells you how to send e-mail from your application.

Setting up PHP to send e-mail

E-mail is sent by an outgoing e-mail server. To send e-mail, you need access to an outgoing server. If you can send e-mail from your own computer right now, you're using an outgoing server. You just need to tell PHP the name of the outgoing e-mail server so PHP can find it when you send mail from your script.

Your outgoing mail server is typically an SMTP (Simple Mail Transfer Protocol) server. Whether you use a LAN at work, a cable modem at home, or an ISP via a modem, you send your mail with an SMTP server, and the server has an address that you need to know.

You can usually find out the name of your outgoing server through your e-mail software. The e-mail software must know the name of your e-mail server so it can store the name somewhere. Look for the settings for your e-mail software and find the name of your outgoing server. In Outlook Express, you can usually find it by performing the following steps:

1. **Choose Tools⇨Services.**
2. **In the list of services, highlight Internet Email.**
3. **Click Properties.**
4. **Click the Servers tab.**

   You see a field that shows the name of your outgoing mail server.

If you can't find the name of your outgoing mail server, you can ask your e-mail administrator for the name. If you use an ISP, you can ask the ISP. The name is likely to be in a format similar to the following:

```
mail.ispname.net
```

If you're using a Linux/Unix computer connected to a network, the mail server is probably `sendmail`.

With the name of your outgoing mail server in front of you, open `php.ini`. Look for the following lines:

```
[mail function]
; For Win32 only.
SMTP = localhost

; For Win32 only.
;sendmail_from = me@localhost.com

; For Unix only.  You may supply arguments as well (default:
          "sendmail -t -i").
;sendmail_path =
```

Windows users need to change the first two settings. The first setting is where you put the name of your outgoing server, as follows:

```
SMTP = mail.ispname.com
```

The second setting is the return address that is sent with all your e-mail. Change the setting to the e-mail address you want to use for your return address, as follows:

```
sendmail_from = Janet@Valade.com
```

The third setting is for Unix users. The default is usually correct. If it doesn't work, you need to talk to your system administrator about the correct path to your outgoing mail server.

For Unix users: Some paths to `sendmail` that may be correct are `/usr/sbin/sendmail` or `/usr/lib/sendmail`. If your system doesn't use `sendmail`, there is usually a wrapper for the e-mail server you are using. For example, Qmail users may try `/var/qmail/bin/sendmail` or `/var/qmail/bin/qmail-inject`.

You may have to restart your Web server before the e-mail settings in `php.ini` go into effect.

Sending e-mail messages

PHP provides a function called `mail` that sends e-mail from your script. The format is as follows:

```
mail(address,subject,message,headers);
```

These are the values you need to fill in:

- *address*: The e-mail address that receives the message
- *subject*: A string that goes on the subject line of the e-mail message
- *message*: The content that goes in the e-mail message
- *headers*: A string that sets values for e-mail headers

You may set up and send an e-mail message as follows:

```
$to = "janet@valade.com";
$subj = "Test";
$mess = "This is a test of the mail function";
$headers = bcc:techsupport@mycompany.com\r\n
$mailsend = mail($to,$subj,$mess,$headers);
```

The message is sent to the address in the `$to` variable. You can send the message to more than one person by using the following statement:

```
$to= "janet@valade.com,me@mycompany.com";
```

The `$headers` string in this example also sends a blind copy of the message to `techsupport`. You can include more than one header as follows:

```
$header = "cc:tech@mycompany.com\r\nbcc:sales@mycompany.com";
```

Headers are optional. Only the first three parameters are required.

The $mailsend variable contains TRUE or FALSE. However, TRUE is no guarantee that the mail will get to where it's going. It just means that it started out okay.

Sending e-mail attachments

Sometimes you may prefer to send information as an e-mail attachment rather than as an e-mail message. For example, you may want to send the 30-page service contract to all your customers as an attachment, rather than as a 30-page e-mail message.

To send a message as an attachment, you send a mail header instructing that the e-mail be sent as an attachment. The header is as follows:

```
Content-disposition: attachment; filename=test.txt
```

The header tells the e-mail software to send the message as an attachment with the filename of test.txt. The following example shows how to send a short message as an attachment, although it's very unlikely that you'd actually want to do this:

```
$to = "janet@valade.com";
$subj = "Testing an attachment";
$mess = <<< END
This is the test message.
This message should arrive as an attachment.
Let's see what happens.
END;
$headers = "Content-disposition: attachment;
            filename=test.txt\n";
$headers .= "cc:sales@mycompany.com\n";
$mailsend = mail($to,$subj,$mess,$headers);
```

This e-mail message has two headers: the Content-disposition header and the cc header. The headers are written together into one string, stored in the variable $headers. Each header ends with \n. With some e-mail software, to get the same effect you may need to use \r\n at the end.

If you want to send e-mail as an attachment, it's probably because you want to send the contents of a file. To do this, you simply read the file into a variable that you then send as the message. Reading data from a file is discussed in more detail in Chapter 12.

For the purpose of sending e-mail, you can store the read file as one long string. PHP provides the file_get_contents function for that purpose, as follows:

```
$mess = file_get_contents("filename");
```

Listing 13-3 shows a script that sends a text file as an attachment.

Listing 13-3: A Script to Send a Text File As an E-Mail Attachment

```
<?php
 /* Script name: mailTest
  * Description: Sends a text file as an e-mail
  *              attachment.
  */
$filename = "mydata.txt";
$mess = file_get_contents($filename);
$to = "janet@valade.com";
$subj = "Sending mydata as an attachment ";
$headers = "Content-disposition: attachment;
           filename=mydata.txt\n";
if(!$mailsend = mail($to,$subj,$mess,$headers))
{
   echo "Mail not sent\n";
}
else
{
   echo "Mail sent\n";
}
?>
```

This script reads the contents into a string with `file_get_contents`. The header is stored in `$headers`. Then the mail is sent with the `mail` function. An `if` statement tests whether the `mail` function succeeds, printing the appropriate message.

You may want to send another type of file as an attachment, not just a text file. To do this, you need to send headers that tell the e-mail software what type of file you're sending. One such header is the `Content-type` header, which you can send as follows:

```
Content-type: contenttype
```

The content type for plain text is `text/plain`, the type of file in the previous examples. In most cases, `text/plain` is the default. Another type of text file is an HTML file, which has the content type of `text/html`.

Other types of files you may want to send are binary files. For example, image files, audio files, and video files are binary files. Some of the file types for these files are as follows:

```
image/gif
image/jpeg
audio/x-wav
audio/vnd.rn-realaudio
video/mpeg
video/avi
```

You also may want to send application files. Some are text files, and some are binary files. For example, an RTF file is a text file, whereas a Word document or an Excel spreadsheet are binary files. A general type for binary files is `application/octet-stream`. If the file is binary and you're unsure what application generated it, try `application/octet-stream`.

Binary files should be encoded when sent over e-mail, to ensure that they arrive in good shape. PHP provides functions that encode files for you, as follows:

```
$mess = chunk_split(base64_encode($string));
```

The variable `$string` contains the contents of the binary file stored with the `fread` function.

In addition, if you send an encoded file, you need to let the mail software know about that as well, with the following header:

```
Content-Transfer-Encoding: base64
```

The script in Listing 13-4 shows how to send a graphics file (binary and encoded) as an e-mail attachment.

Listing 13-4: A Script to Send a Graphics File as an E-Mail Attachment

```
<?php
 /* Script name: mailGraphic
  * Description: Sends a graphic file as an e-mail
  *              attachment.
  */
$filename = "logo.gif";
$fh = fopen($filename,"rb");
$fileContent = fread($fh,filesize($filename));
fclose($fh);
$mess = chunk_split(base64_encode($fileContent));
$to = "janet@valade.com";
$subj = "Sending an image as an attachment";
$headers = "Content-disposition: attachment;
           filename=logo.gif\n";
$headers .= "Content-type: image/gif\n";
$headers .="Content-Transfer-Encoding: base64\n";
if(!$mailsend = mail($to,$subj,$mess,$headers))
{
   echo "Mail not sent\n";
}
else
{
   echo "Mail sent\n";
}
?>
```

This script encodes the file contents to store in `$mess`. It includes the additional headers needed for transferring information that's not text.

Chapter 14

PHP Extensions

In This Chapter

- Understanding extensions
- Installing PEAR
- Using PEAR packages

The PHP architecture consists of a PHP core and PHP extensions. The *PHP core* provides the basic functionality of the language.

PHP's great flexibility and power depend greatly on its hundreds of functions, which consist of built-in functions and functions available in a PHP extension. Many PHP built-in functions are discussed throughout this book, and Appendix B provides a reference list of many functions. However, many more functions are available in PHP through the use of extensions.

Most PHP functions are contained in the PHP extensions. Extensions broaden the capabilities of PHP. Several core extensions are compiled into PHP and are always there by default. Other standard extensions are included in the PHP distribution, but you must add them to PHP before you can use their functions. PHP database functions are among those included in the PHP distribution that must be activated before they can be used (as discussed in Chapter 12). In addition, many extensions are written and made available by individuals. Many of the best of these are part of *PEAR*, the PHP Extension and Application Repository.

This chapter discusses available extensions and how to get and use them.

Investigating the Basic Extensions

The basic PHP distribution includes several extensions. These are compiled into PHP, and their functions are available for your use. You don't actually need to know about these extensions. You don't need to do anything to activate them; you can just use their functionality. (In fact, if you don't want them, you have to do something to deactivate them, as discussed in Appendix A.) Many of the functions that are made available by extensions are discussed throughout this book.

To determine which extensions are activated in your PHP installation, look at the information that is output by `phpinfo()`. It shows a list of settings for the PHP core, and then it shows the settings for the PHP extensions that are activated. The following list of extensions is activated by default:

- **BCMath:** A math library that has more precision than PHP floating point numbers provide.
- **calendar:** A library that provides functions for converting between various calendar formats, such as Julian, Gregorian, French Republican, and so on.
- **COM:** Provides access to COM objects.
- **ctype:** Functions that check characters, such as checking whether characters are alphabetic characters or punctuation.
- **ftp:** Functions that connect and send requests to an FTP server. Can be used to transfer files between computers.
- **odbc:** Functions for using ODBC databases.
- **pcre:** Functions for Perl-compatible regular expressions.
- **session:** Functions for creating and using PHP built-in sessions.
- **SQLite:** Functions for storing data in flat files using SQL.
- **tokenizer:** Functions that parse PHP code.
- **wddx:** Functions for use with WDDX, an XML-based standard for exchanging data between applications.
- **xml:** A library to parse XML documents.
- **zlib:** A library to read and write gzip-compressed files.

This list shows the extensions that are currently compiled into PHP. However, this list of extensions can change. By the time you read this, the list may be longer or shorter.

If you downloaded and installed Windows binaries for PHP, the preceding extensions were compiled into the binaries. If you compile your own PHP on Unix or Linux, these extensions are included by default. If you want to exclude one of them, you must exclude it when you compile. For example, if you are not using sessions and don't want sessions support compiled into your version of PHP, you need to use an installation option, as described in Appendix A, as follows:

```
--disable-session
```

In general, the built-in extensions are the ones that users are most likely to use. It's rarely wise to exclude any of them.

PHP is included on most Linux computers when purchased and in most Linux distributions when you install the operating system. However, if you are using PHP provided by your Web hosting company and thus didn't install PHP yourself, you can't be sure which extensions were installed. Usually the extensions listed in this section are included, but there are no guarantees. You can find documentation for these extensions in the on-line PHP manual at the PHP Web site.

Taking a Look at Standard Extensions

Many extensions are included in the PHP distribution but not compiled into PHP. That is, you have the necessary files, but support for the extensions is not built-in. You need to activate them before you can use them. Generally, these extensions are needed less frequently than the basic extensions. The PHP developers provide the extensions for your use but don't compile them into PHP to conserve resources.

If you need to use any of the extensions in the PHP distribution, adding an extension to your PHP installation is not difficult. If you compile PHP when installing it, use the installation option for the extension you need. (The installation instructions in Appendix A discuss installation options.) Most Unix and many Linux and Mac users compile PHP at installation. Very few Windows users compile PHP.

If you download and install a binary copy of PHP, rather than compile your own, you can install any of the standards extensions as follows:

1. **Copy the appropriate dll file from the ext subdirectory into your main directory.**

   The ext subdirectory is in a location such as `c:\php\ext`.

2. **Open your `php.ini` file and look for a line similar to the following:**

   ```
   ;extension=php_gd2.dll
   ```

3. **Remove the semicolon at the beginning of the line.**

The following are some of the most popular extensions:

- **Database extensions:** Many people use database extensions. They provide functions for interacting with a specific type of database. As mentioned previously, the ODBC database extension is included in PHP by default. (Database extensions are discussed in Chapter 12.)
- **GD library:** One of the most popular extensions is the GD library. It provides functions so you can output graphics, as well as HTML. You can create and manipulate images in several formats, such as JPEG, GIF, PNG, and others.

  PHP versions since (and including) PHP 4.3.0 include a bundled version of GD, which is preferable to other versions of GD. You can use this bundled version rather than installing an external version of GD. To do this, compile with the installation option `with-gd2`, as described in Appendix A, and do not specify a path to a directory (do not use `=DIR`).
- **PDF extension:** This is a library of functions that allow you to create a PDF document. You can set fonts, write text to the document, and add graphics.
- **cURL:** This library allows you to communicate with many kinds of servers, such as HTTPS, Telnet, FTP, LDAP, and others.

Most extensions provide functions that interact with software libraries. For example, the database extensions provide functions that interact with specific database software. For extensions to work, the software they interact with must be installed. (For example, for the Oracle database extensions to work, the Oracle software must be installed.) On occasion, the software libraries are already installed on your computer. If not, you must download and install the required library. Be sure to look at the documentation in the PHP manual on the PHP Web site for any extension you are considering using. Look for information about the required libraries and where to get them and to see any other specific requirements for the extension. Some libraries are provided in the PHP distribution, so that you don't need to find them and download them yourself. Such libraries are available in the main directory where PHP is installed. For example, MySQL support requires that the library `libmysql.dll` (MySQL 4.0 or earlier) or `libmysqli.dll` (MySQL 4.1 or later) be available. This library is included in the main PHP directory, allowing the mysql and mysqli functions to work correctly.

Table 14-1 provides a list of most of the extensions provided with the PHP distribution, with the exception of the database extensions, which are described in Chapter 12.

In the table, all dll names start with `php_` and are found in the `php/ext` directory. `DIR` is the directory where the software library is installed. If `DIR` is not included, a default is used.

Table 14-1 PHP Extensions

Extension	*Description*	*dll name*	*Install option*
bzip2 Compression	Read/write bzip2-compressed files.	_bz2.dll	--with-bz2=DIR
ClibPDF	Create PDF documents.	_cpdf.dll	--with-cpdflib=DIR
Crack	Test the strength of a password.	_crack.dll	--with-crack=DIR
cURL	Communicate with various types of servers.	_curl.dll	--with-curl=DIR
Domxml	Read/create XML documents.	_domxml.dll	--with-dom=DIR
FDF	Handle forms with PDF document.	_fdf.dll	--with-fdftk=DIR
GD	Output images.	_gd2.dll	--with-gd2
gettext	Native language support.	_gettext.dll	--with-gettext=DIR
iconv	Convert strings between character set encoding.	_iconv.dll	--with-iconv=DIR
IMAP	Manage e-mail.	_imap.dll	--with-imap=DIR
JAVA	Integrate Java support.	_java.dll	--with-java=DIR
LDAP	Access directory servers.	_ldap.dll	--with-ldap=DIR
Multi-byte String	Handle Japanese and (default is Japanese) other characters.	_mbstring.dll	--with-mbstring=LANG
Mcrypt Encryption	Encrypt strings.	_mcrypt.dll	--with-mcrypt=DIR
Mhash	Create check-sums and more.	_mhash.dll	--with-mhash=DIR

(continued)

Table 14-1 *(continued)*

Extension	*Description*	*dll name*	*Install option*
Mime type	Guess the content type.	_mime_magic.dll	--with-mime-magic
Ming for Flash	Create Flash format movies.	_ming.dll	--with-ming
OpenSSL	Provide secure data transfer.	_openssl.dll	--with-openssl=DIR
PDF	Create PDF files.	_pdf.dll	--with-pdflib=DIR
Printer	Write data to printer. Windows only.	_printer.dll	N/A
Shared Memory	Read/write shared memory segments.	_shmop.dll	--enable-shmop
SNMP	Manage SNMP objects.	_snmp.dll	--with-snmp=DIR
Sockets	Low-level interface to socket communication.	_sockets.dll	--enable-sockets
XML-RPC	Write XML-RPC servers and clients.	_xmlrpc.dll	--with-xmlrpc=DIR
XSLT	Extensible Stylesheet Language Transformations.	_xslt.dll	--enable-xslt
Zip Files	Read zip files.	_zip.dll	--with-zip=DIR

At any time, some of these extensions can be removed from the PHP distribution or new extensions can be added.

Using PEAR

PEAR is the PHP Extension and Application Repository, and it maintains a structured library of open source code. The code itself is provided by developers outside PEAR, but PEAR handles the management and distribution of code from the various projects.

PEAR has developed a consistent method of distribution. Code for a project is distributed in packages. Developers who want to contribute an extension or application must conform to standards. They must include specified elements in their packages, such as documentation, and use PEAR coding standards and methods for handling errors. The standard structure makes maintaining code more feasible over the long run. If the developer who is maintaining a PEAR application wins the lottery and goes on a permanent vacation to Tahiti, someone else can assume the maintenance of the abandoned code more easily because its structure and standards are consistent.

Before a project is added to PEAR, it must be accepted. PEAR only accepts high-quality code that conforms to the coding standards. Code contributors must be willing to maintain the code and provide documentation. Code contributors submit their code to the PEAR developers, who must accept it before it is added to PEAR. After it's accepted, the code contributors add it to PEAR and maintain it.

Finding a PEAR Package

According to the PEAR Web site (`http://pear.php.net`), PEAR currently holds 263 packages. Six packages are included with the PHP software when you download it:

- **DB:** Database abstraction layer. Allows you to interact with different databases by using the same set of functions.
- **Net_Socket:** Net Socket Interface. A class interface to TCP sockets.
- **Net_SMTP:** Provides an implementation of the SMTP (Simple Mail Transfer Protocol) protocol using Net_Socket.
- **Mail:** Provides various methods for checking and sending e-mail.
- **XML_Parser:** An XML parser based on PHP's built-in XML extension.
- **PHPUnit:** Used to automate testing of PHP functions and classes.

You can find these PEAR packages in the directory where PHP is installed in `PEAR/packages` or `PEAR/go-pear-bundle`. The packages are in zipped files. You can use the PEAR installer, described in the following section, to install the PEAR package.

Descriptions of all the PEAR packages are available on the PEAR Web site (`pear.php.net`). You can browse through categories to look for packages, or you can search the package database.

Notice two links in the left column of the Web page: List Packages and Search Packages. To browse, click List Packages; you see the following categories:

Authentication
Benchmarking
Caching
Configuration
Console
Database
Date and Time
Encryption
File Formats
File System
Gtk Components
HTML
HTTP
Images
Internationalization
Logging
Mail
Math
Networking
Numbers
Payment
PEAR
PHP
Processing
Science
Streams
Structures
Text
Tools and Utilities
Web Services
XML

If you click a category, you see a page showing all the packages in that category. If you click a package, you see a page showing package information. The dependencies section lists packages that must be installed before this package will run. You also see links to where you can download the package. However, you don't need to download it manually. The PEAR installer will download it for you.

If you click Search Packages, you see a search form that allows you to search for a package by name, category, maintainer, or date. The search results give you a list of links to packages that match your search. If you click one of these links, it takes you to the information page for the package.

The information page provides a short description about the package, which may or may not be enough information to determine whether it's the package you need. You can find more information about the package in the manual. One of the links in the left panel on the PEAR home page is Manual, under Documentation. Clicking this link takes you to the PEAR manual table of contents (after you select a language). Section IV, Packages, has a link for each package category. The category manual page contains documentation for the packages in the category. More package information is available in the manuals, including instructions for using the classes/functions in the package.

You can return to the PEAR Web site home page at any point by clicking the pear in the upper-left corner of any page.

After you have identified the package you want, write down its exact name. You find out how to install it in the following sections.

Setting up PEAR

PEAR includes a package manager that administers PEAR packages. The package manager is included in your PHP distribution. The installer can install, uninstall, and update packages. It maintains a registry of installed packages. It can display a list of available packages, check information about packages, check dependencies, and perform other management tasks.

Setting up PEAR when compiling PHP

If you compiled PHP yourself, the PEAR installer was included, and the six bundled PEAR applications were installed. You can check the PEAR installer by running `pear.php` from your PHP directory. To do this, type `pear`, and a list of options for PEAR is displayed. Alternatively, you can type `pear list-all`, in which case a list of all packages available is displayed. (This process sometimes takes a minute or two because the list is downloaded over the Internet.)

For versions of PHP prior to 4.3.0, the PEAR installer is not installed when PHP is compiled and installed. You can find a script that downloads and installs the PEAR components at `go-pear.org`.

Setting up PEAR on Windows

If you installed PHP using the installer or the zip file, PEAR was not installed. To set up PEAR on Windows, you need to perform the following steps:

1. **Download the PEAR components.**

   You need to download the Windows zip file for manual installation, as described in Appendix A. Then unzip the PEAR directory into the directory where PHP is installed, which is generally a directory such as `c:\php\pear`. If you installed PHP by using the manual installation instructions from Appendix A, all the pieces of PEAR should be there already; you don't need to download them again.

2. **Add the PEAR directory to your include file path.**

   Open `php.ini` and look for the following line:

   ```
   include_path = ".;c:\php\includes;c:\php\PEAR"
   ```

   If the path shown does not include the PEAR directory, add it as shown in this example `php.ini` line.

3. **Download and install the PEAR Installer.**

   Double-click `go-pear.php` (or `go-pear.bat`) in the directory where PHP is installed. The `go-pear` script opens a command prompt window and displays the following:

   ```
   Welcome to go-pear!

   Go-pear will install the 'pear' command and all the files
   needed by it. This command is your tool for PEAR
    installation and maintenance.

   Go-pear also lets you download and install the PEAR
   packages bundled with PHP: DB, Net_Socket, Net_SMTP,
           Mail,
   XML_Parser, phpUnit.

   If you wish to abort, press Control-C now, or press
           Enter:
   ```

   The program asks you a few questions and installs the PEAR installer. It also gives you the option of installing the six bundled packages if you want. When the program is finished, it displays a final message.

The code in the go-pear.bat script includes the following line that sets the path to PHP CLI. In previous versions of PHP, PHP CLI was located in a subdirectory called /cli. If the script line shows the old path, as follows:

```
Set PHP_BIN=cli/php.exe
```

the go-pear script will fail. If so, you can edit the file so the path is correct.

After you finish installing the PEAR installer (and the 6 programs if you chose to install them), you should have a program called `pear.bat` in the directory where PHP is installed. You can test `pear.bat` by running it from the Command

Prompt window. To do this, type `pear`, and a list of options for PEAR is displayed. Alternatively, you can type `pear list-all`, in which case a list of all packages available is displayed. (This process sometimes takes a minute or two because the list is downloaded over the Internet.)

When you use `list-all` with the PEAR installer, it displays a list of all available programs. Remember the name of any program that looked useful for you. You need to know the exact name in order to install the program.

Installing a PEAR package

You install a PEAR package using the PEAR installer (the `pear.bat` program installed in the previous section). You test the installer in the previous section by getting a list of all the packages available. In this section, you find out how to install a package using the PEAR installer.

To install a package, type the following in your PHP directory (`c:\php`):

```
pear install packagename
```

The PEAR installer downloads the package file from the PEAR Web site and installs it. For example, you can install Mail by typing the following:

```
pear install Mail
```

`pear` then displays the following:

```
downloading Mail-1.0.2.tgz ...
...done: 12,287 bytes
requires package 'Net_SMTP'
Mail: dependencies failed
```

This output says that Mail was downloaded. It also tells you that Mail requires Net_SMTP in order to run and that Net_SMTP is not installed. Therefore, it did not install Mail. You need to install Net_SMTP and then install Mail.

After you have installed Net_SMTP and then installed Mail, if you try to install Mail again, the PEAR installer displays:

```
Mail already installed
```

You can get a list of all the PEAR packages currently installed by typing the following:

```
pear list
```

You can update a package with the following command:

```
pear upgrade Mail
```

In this case, the following output is displayed:

```
downloading Mail-1.0.2.tgz ...
...done: 12,287 bytes
upgrade to a newer version (1.0.2 is not newer than 1.0.2)
```

If you try to install without being connected to the Internet, the PEAR installer displays the following message:

```
Connection to pear.php.net:80 failed
```

You can uninstall any package, as follows:

```
pear uninstall Mail
```

The following is displayed:

```
uninstall ok: Mail
```

Using a PEAR package

After a package has been installed, you can use its functions or methods.

Accessing a PEAR package

After a package has been installed, a file with the package name (with a `.php` extension) resides in the PEAR directory. For example, after you install Mail, the PEAR directory contains a file named `Mail.php`. To use a PEAR package, you include that file in your script. For example, you can use the Mail package in your script after you use the following statement:

```
require_once("Mail.php");
```

Use `require_once` to be sure the entire `Mail.php` file is not included more than once. Using `require` causes the script to stop if the `Mail.php` file can't be found.

For the details on using the methods or functions of a package, see the PEAR manual on the PEAR Web site.

DB is one of the most popular PEAR packages. Therefore, I use DB in the next section to demonstrate the use of a PEAR package. I don't provide a comprehensive explanation of the DB package — just a short program to show you the principles of using a PEAR package.

Introducing DB — an example of a PEAR package

DB is a library that allows you to interact with different databases by using the same functions. In Chapter 12, you discover that PHP has several sets of database functions, a different set for each database. Consequently, you use functions such as `mysql_connect` and `pg_connect`. Database access is very simple with database functions.

The problem with using database functions arises if you change your database. Suppose you have your database application humming along using MySQL, and one morning your boss walks in and says, "I just bought Oracle. We need to move all our data into Oracle." Not only must you move all the data, but you must also find all the places in your PHP scripts where you use MySQL database functions and change them all to Oracle functions. Some of the functions may have a different format, and some may have parameters in a different order. This is certain to cause problems for a while.

If you're positive you will never change to another database, you don't need to concern yourself with this specter. However, if there's any possibility of changing your database in the future, you may want to use a database-independent database interface instead. DB is popular for database interaction.

Interacting with a database

Using PEAR DB, you use steps similar to those that are described in Chapter 12 to interact with a database:

1. **Connect to the database**
2. **Send the database a query that tells it to perform an action.**
3. **If information is returned from the query, process the information.**

To connect to a database using PEAR DB, you just provide the parameters, such as the account and password, and the SQL to be executed and tell PEAR DB which type of database it's communicating with. The required information, formatted correctly, is the Data Source Name (DSN). Using the information in the DSN, DB handles the exact syntax. To give DB the necessary information, you can use the following statements:

```
$host = "localhost";
$user = "admin";
$passwd = "secret";
$dbname = "Sales";
$dbtype = "mysql";
$dsn = "$dbtype://$dbuser:$dbpasswd@$host/$dbname";
```

The `$dsn` variable contains the information PEAR DB needs to connect to a database. You can connect to the database as follows:

```
$db = DB::connect($dsn);
```

After you are connected to the database you can send an SQL query as follows:

```
$sql = "SELECT * from Customer";
$result = $db->query($sql);
```

If the query returns data, as the `SELECT` query does, you can access the information using the following DB statement:

```
$row = $result->fetchRow(DB_FETCHMODE_ASSOC);
```

In this statement, the method `fetchRow` returns one row of the results in an associative array with the field names as the keys to the array. You can then use the data in the array in the same way as you use any other array.

As you can see, if you change your database, the only thing you need to change is the value for `$dbtype`. Nothing else in your script needs to be changed. So by doing a little extra work up front, you eliminate the problems created by changing from one RDBMS to another. As of this writing, PEAR DB supports the following types of databases:

- `mysql` (MySQL)
- `pgsql` (PostgreSQL)
- `ibase` (InterBase)
- `msql` (Mini SQL)
- `mssql` (Microsoft SQL Server)
- `oci8` (Oracle 7/8/8I)
- `odbc` (ODBC — Open Database Connectivity)
- `sybase` (Sybase)
- `ifx` (Informix)
- `fbsql` (FrontBase)

To change to another database (say from MySql to Sybase), you can just change `$dbtype = "mysql";` to `$dbtype = "sybase";` and you're done.

Handling errors

As described in Chapter 12, statements that interact with a database can fail. For example, the database software may be down when your script attempts to connect. You want your script to stop when the database interaction fails, and you want to receive an informative message.

DB provides the method isError that you can use to check for errors. The method checks the variable to see whether it is TRUE or an error object. If the variable contains an error object, you can use a method called getMessage to see what the error message is. The following statements show how to use isError:

```
$db = DB::connect($dsn);
if(DB::isError($db))
{
   die($db->getMessage());
}
```

The method isError checks the contents of $db. If $db contains TRUE, the connect function succeeded, and the statements in the if block are not executed. However, if $db contains an error object, the if block executes. In this case, the if block contains a die statement, which displays a message and stops the script. $db->getMessage gets the error message stored in $db. Suppose the information you used in building the DSN included a typo in the database name. The connect statement fails, and the die statement displays the following message:

```
DB Error: no such database
```

Putting it all together

The script shown in Listing 14-1 displays a customer list taken from a database. A script to produce the same output was shown in Chapter 12, using PostgreSQL database functions. The script from Chapter 12 is shown here, in altered form, by using the PEAR DB library.

Listing 14-1: A Script That Displays a Customer List

```
<?php
/* Script name: DisplayCustomer-DB
 * Description: Gets all customer records from a
 *              database and displays the
 *              Customer list in a Web page.
 */
 require_once("DB.php");      # includes PEAR DB classes
 $host = "localhost";
 $dbuser = "admin";
 $dbpasswd = "secret";
 $dbname = "Sales";
 $dbtype = "pgsql";
 $dsn = "$dbtype://$dbuser:$dbpasswd@$host/$dbname";
 $db = DB::connect($dsn);
 if(DB::isError($db))
 {
   die($db->getMessage());
 }
```

(continued)

Listing 14-1 ***(continued)***

```
 $sql = "SELECT * from Customer";
 $result = $db->query($sql);
 if(DB::isError($result))
 {
   die($result->getMessage());
 }
 echo "<html>
    <head><title>Customer List</title></head>
    <body>
    <table width=\"100%\" border=\"0\">\n";
 while($row = $result->fetchRow(DB_FETCHMODE_ASSOC))
 {
    if(DB::isError($row))
    {
       die($row->getMessage());
    }
    echo "<tr>";
    echo "<td>{$row['lastname']}, {$row['firstname']}</td>
          <td>{$row['phone']}</td>";
    echo "</tr>\n";
 }
 echo "</table></body></html>";
?>
```

The output is a list of customer names in the following format:

```
Lastname, Firstname      phonenumber
```

Using PEAR libraries is easy in terms of getting access to them. The PEAR installer installs the package, and you just include it with a `require_once` statement. However, each package has its own functions and classes and methods for accomplishing tasks. In a way, each new package is like learning a new language. The things you know about PHP may not help you at all. Some PEAR packages are documented well in the PEAR manual, online documentation, and books. Other PEAR packages are not documented as thoroughly.

Part V
The Part of Tens

"You ever get the feeling this project could just up and die at any moment?"

In this part . . .

The chapters in this part extend your knowledge of PHP. This part provides hints and warnings to keep in mind while programming and pointers to the mega-information on PHP that is available on the Web. PHP itself is a growing, expanding language. As a PHP programmer, you will grow and expand along with it.

Chapter 15

Ten Things to Look For When Troubleshooting a Script

In This Chapter

- Recognizing common PHP errors
- Interpreting error messages

I guarantee that you will do all the things that I mention in this chapter. You just can't write scripts without making these mistakes. The trick is to train yourself to recognize them, roll your eyes, say, "Not again," and just fix them. One error message that you'll see many times is

```
Parse error: parse error in c:\test.php on line 7
```

This is PHP's way of saying "Huh?" It means that it doesn't understand something. This message helpfully points to the file and the line number where PHP got confused. Sometimes it's directly pointing at the error, but sometimes PHP's confusion results from an error earlier in the script.

Here are ten of the most common errors and how to avoid them.

Missing Semicolons

Every PHP statement ends with a semicolon (;). PHP doesn't stop reading a statement until it reaches a semicolon. If you leave out the semicolon at the end of a line, PHP continues reading the statement on the following line. For example, consider the following statement:

```
$test = 1
echo $test;
```

These statements don't make sense to PHP; it reads the two lines as one statement, so it complains with an error message, such as the following:

```
Parse error: parse error in c:\test.php on line 2
```

This is a very common error. Before you know it, you'll be writing your home address with semicolons at the end of each line.

Not Enough Equal Signs

In a *comparison statement,* in which you ask whether two values are equal, you need two equal signs in a row. Using one equal sign is a common mistake. It's a perfectly reasonable error because you have been using one equal sign to mean *equal* since the first grade when you learned that 2 + 2 = 4. This is a difficult mistake to recognize because it doesn't cause an error message. It just makes your script do odd things, like infinite loops or `if` blocks that never execute. I am continually amazed at how long I can stare at

```
$test = 0;
while ( $test = 0 )
{
   $test++;
}
```

and not see why it's looping endlessly.

Misspelled Variable Names

This is another PHP gotcha that doesn't result in an error message, just odd script behavior. If you misspell a variable name, PHP considers it a new variable and does what you ask it to do. Here's another clever way to write an infinite loop:

```
$test = 0;
while ( $test == 0 )
{
   $Test++;
}
```

Remember, to PHP, `test` is not the same as `Test`.

Missing Dollar Signs

A missing dollar sign in a variable name is really hard to see, but at least it usually results in an error message so that you know where to look for the problem. It usually results in the old familiar parse error:

```
Parse error: parse error in test.php on line 7
```

Troubling Quotes

You can have too many, too few, or the wrong kind of quotes. You have too many when you put quotes inside of quotes, such as this example:

```
$test = "<table width="100%">";
```

PHP sees the second double quote (") — before `100` — as the ending double quote (") and reads the `1` as an instruction, which makes no sense. *Voilà!* Another parse error. The line must be either

```
$test = "<table width='100%'>";
```

or

```
$test = "<table width=\"100%\">";
```

You have too few quotes when you forget to end a quoted string, such as

```
$test = "<table width='100%'>;
```

PHP continues reading the lines as part of the quoted string until it encounters another double quote ("), which may not occur for several lines. This is one occasion when the parse error that points to where PHP got confused is not pointing to the actual error. The actual error occurred some lines previously, when you forgot to end the string.

You have the wrong kind of quotes when you use a single quote (') when you meant a double quote (") or vice versa. The difference between single and double quotes is sometimes important and is explained in Chapter 5.

Invisible Output

Some statements, such as the `header` statement, must execute before the script produces any output. If you try to use such statements after sending output, they fail. The following statements fail because the header message is not the first output:

```
<html>
<?php
   header("Location: http://company.com");
?>
```

`<html>` is not in a PHP section and is therefore sent as HTML output. The following statements work:

```
<?php
   header("Location: http://company.com");
?>
<html>
```

The following statements fail:

```
 <?php
   header("Location: http://company.com");
?>
<html>
```

It's not easy to see, but there's one, single blank space before the opening PHP tag. The blank space is output to the browser, although the resulting Web page looks empty. Therefore, the header statement fails because there is output before it. This is a common mistake and is difficult to spot.

Numbered Arrays

PHP believes that the first value in an array is numbered zero (0). Of course, humans tend to believe that lists start with the number one (1). This fundamentally different way of viewing lists results in us humans believing an array isn't working correctly when it is indeed working just fine. For example, consider the following statements:

```
$test = 1;
while ( $test <= 3 )
{
   $array[] = $test;
   $test++;
}
echo $array[3];
```

No output (or an error notice) results. I leap to the conclusion that there is something wrong with my loop. Actually, it's fine. It just results in the following array:

```
$array[0]=1
$array[1]=2
$array[2]=3
```

and doesn't set anything into `$array[3]`.

Including PHP Statements

When a file is read in by using an `include` statement in a PHP section, it seems reasonable to me that the statements in the file will be treated as PHP statements. After all, PHP adds the statements to the script at the point where I include them. However, PHP doesn't see it my way. If a file named `file1.inc` contains the following statements:

```
if ( $test == 1 )
      echo "Hi";
```

and I read it in with the following statements in my main script:

```
<?php
$test = 1;
include ("file1.inc");
?>
```

I expect the word `Hi` to display on the Web page. However, the Web page actually displays this:

```
if ( $test == 1 ) echo "Hi";
```

Clearly, the file that is included is seen as HTML. To send `Hi` to the Web page, `file1.inc` needs to contain the PHP tags.

```
<?php
if ( $test == 1 )
      echo "Hi";
?>
```

Missing Mates

Parentheses and curly brackets must come in pairs. Opening with a `(` that has no closing `)` or a `{` without a `}` results in an error message. One of my favorite examples of this is when I use one closing parenthesis where two are needed, as in the following statement:

```
if ( isset($test)
```

This statement needs a closing parenthesis at the end. It's much more difficult to spot that one of your blocks didn't get closed when you have blocks inside of blocks inside of blocks. For example, consider the following:

```
while ( $test < 3 )
{
if ( $test2 != "yes" )
{
if ( $test3 > 4 )
{
echo "go";
}
}
```

You can see there are three opening curly brackets but only two closing ones. Imagine that 100 lines of code are inside these blocks. It can be difficult to spot the problem — especially if you think the last closing bracket is closing the `while` loop, but PHP sees it as closing the `if` loop for `$test2`. Somewhere later in your script, PHP may be using a closing bracket to close the `while` loop that you aren't even looking at. It can be difficult to trace the problem in a large script.

Indenting blocks makes it easier to see where closing brackets belong. Also, I often use comments to keep track of where I am, such as

```
while ( $test < 3 )
{
 if ( $test2 != "yes" )
 {
  if ( $test3 > 4 )
  {
   echo "go";
  } # closing if block for $test3
 }  # closing if block for $test2
}   # closing while block
```

Confusing Parentheses and Brackets

I'm not sure whether this is a problem for everyone or just a problem for me because I refuse to admit that I can't see as well as I used to. Although PHP has no trouble distinguishing between parentheses and curly brackets, my eyes are not so reliable. Especially while staring at a computer screen at the end of a 10-hour programming marathon, I can easily confuse `(` and `{`. Using the wrong one gets you a parse error message.

Chapter 16

Ten PHP Resources You Can't Live Without

In This Chapter

- Where to find articles and tutorials
- Where to find code libraries

One advantage of PHP is its growing developer community. Many people use it, and the PHP community is helpful. Many resources are available online. This chapter describes the most useful resources. Remember that you are not alone.

The PHP Web Site

This is the official PHP Web site. Here, new versions of PHP are released for download, and the PHP manual is online. You can find anything that you need to know about PHP here.

```
www.php.net
```

PHP Lists

When you've struggled for days with some recalcitrant code that stubbornly refuses to run, take it to the lists. Hundreds of PHP developers frequent the lists, and these folks know everything. Post a question to a PHP list, and you often have the answer before your finger is off your mouse key. You'll find different lists for different subjects: `php-general`, `php-db`, `php-install`, `php-windows`, and others. You can sign up for the lists on the PHP Web site.

The PHP lists have a lot of traffic. You can easily get more than 100 e-mail messages per day. However, when you are starting with PHP, reading the messages that other coders ask and the solutions that they receive can greatly help you learn PHP. At the very least, subscribe to the announce list to be informed of new versions and important releases. The announce list won't deluge you with e-mail; it only sends a message every now and then.

```
www.php.net/mailing-lists.php
```

Zend

The Zend engine is the core scripting engine of PHP. This Web site is full of information about PHP. You can find tutorials, articles, news, online seminars, and even a PHP job board.

```
http://zend.com
```

PHP Builder

PHP Builder is a Web site containing a variety of resources for PHP coders. You can find news there and a list of useful articles. In addition, PHP Builder has a code library where you can obtain snippets of code or functions for a broad range of uses. You can search for code in such categories as databases, calendars, shopping carts, games, graphics, and many others.

```
www.phpbuilder.com
```

Black Beans

If you could only have one resource, the Black Beans Web site would be a good candidate. Black Beans is a Web site that provides lists of resources. It has links to articles, forums, user groups, tools, and many other resources.

```
www.black-beans.com.br/php_home_eng.htm
```

PHP Beginners

PHP Beginners is a collection of articles on PHP and related subjects. Articles there are oriented specifically toward beginners.

```
www.phpbeginner.com
```

PHP Dev Center

PHP Dev Center is a repository of very good PHP articles and tutorials on subjects from beginners to quite advanced levels. The authors are always knowledgeable.

```
www.onlamp.com/php
```

PHPMac.com

This Web site has articles and instructions for installing and using PHP for the Mac. This information is invaluable and much harder to find than information on PHP for Windows and Unix/Linux.

```
www.phpmac.com
```

PHP Editors

This Web site provides a list of all the editors and IDEs (Integrated Development Environments) that you can use to write PHP scripts. As of this moment, 105 are listed, both free and commercial. The list includes comments from users.

```
http://phpeditors.linuxbackup.co.uk
```

SourceForge.net

SourceForge.net is the largest repository of Open Source code and applications available on the Internet. You can find software for all purposes at this site. You can find software written specifically in PHP by using the following method:

1. **Click the Software Map tab.**
2. **Click Programming Language in the column on the right.**
3. **Click PHP in the column of alphabetically listed programming languages on the left.**

As of today, SourceForge.net shows almost 7,000 projects in PHP.

```
www.sourceforge.net
```

Free PHP Hosting Directory

This site is a list of free Web hosting companies that offer PHP. Hosts are rated up to five stars.

```
www.oinko.net/freephp
```

My Web Site

I provide a Web site where I support my books. There I post the scripts from the book and additional code for download by readers, as well as a list of any necessary error corrections. I also provide PHP news and links to important PHP-related Web sites.

```
http://janet.valade.com
```

Part VI
Appendixes

"Yes, Unicenter has an automated 'Help' function. Why?"

In this part . . .

This part provides the instructions for installing PHP, as well as a complete reference of essential PHP functions. In Appendix B, you can quickly find any function that you need, including functions that I didn't have room to discuss in the book.

Appendix A

Installing PHP

In this Appendix, I describe how to install PHP on the Unix/Linux, Windows, and Mac platforms, both for use with Web sites and with PHP command line interface (CLI). For Web sites, although PHP runs with several Web servers, I discuss Apache and IIS (Microsoft Internet Information Server), which together power almost 90 percent of the Web sites on the Internet. If you need instructions for other operating systems or Web servers, see the PHP Web site (`www.php.net`).

This appendix provides installation instructions for PHP 5. If you are installing an earlier version, the installation may be slightly different; in this case, please read the file `install.txt` that is provided with the PHP distribution.

Installing PHP on Computers Running Unix/Linux

You can install PHP as a partner with Apache for use in Web pages or as a stand-alone interpreter. If you want to use PHP for both Web sites and as a stand-alone language, you need to install PHP with Apache and PHP CLI, which are two separate types of PHP. The instructions below include information for both types of PHP installations — PHP for the Web and PHP CLI.

You install PHP by downloading the source files, compiling them, and then installing the compiled programs. This process isn't as technical and daunting as it may appear. I provide step-by-step instructions in the next few sections. Read all the way through the steps before you begin the installation procedure to be sure that you understand it all clearly. Try to have everything prepared so you don't have to stop in the middle of the installation.

For Linux users only: Many Linux distributions automatically install both Apache and PHP, thus saving you the trouble of installing them yourself. In addition, PHP for Linux is available in an RPM as well as in source files. It may be in RPM format on your distribution CD. However, when PHP is preinstalled or when you install it from an RPM, you can't control the options that PHP is installed with. For example, in these instances, PHP CLI may not have been installed. Or perhaps an RPM doesn't install PHP with support for the database that you plan to use. In addition, an RPM usually enables all the most popular options, so an RPM may enable options that you don't need. And Linux distributions and RPMs are likely to be slightly older versions; they probably don't install the most recent version of PHP that is available. Consequently, the simplest and most efficient way to install PHP may be from the source. If you're familiar with RPMs, by all means feel free to find an RPM and install it. RPMs are available. However, I provide steps for source code installation, not RPMs.

Before installing on Unix/Linux

If you want to use PHP with Apache for your Web site, Apache must be installed. Most Unix/Linux operating systems install Apache by default when the operating system is installed. Before beginning to install PHP, check the following:

- **The Apache version is 1.3.0 or newer.** To check the version, type the following at the command line:

  ```
  httpd --v
  ```

  You may have to be in the directory where `httpd` is located before the command will work.

  Because of security issues with Apache, it is much better to use Apache 1.3.27 or newer.

  PHP with Apache 2 is still considered experimental. For use on production Web sites, it's better to use Apache 1.3 than Apache 2.

- **The Apache module `mod_so` is installed.** It usually is. To display a list of all the modules, type the following:

  ```
  httpd -l.
  ```

  You may have to be in the directory where `httpd` is located before the command will work. The output usually shows a long list of modules. All you need to be concerned with for PHP is `mod_so`. If `mod_so` is not loaded, Apache must be reinstalled using the option `enable-module=so`.

- **The `apxs` utility is installed.** (Or `apxs2` for use with Apache 2.) `apxs` is often installed when Apache is installed. To determine whether it's installed on your computer, you should look for a file called `apxs`, possibly at `/usr/sbin/apxs`. If you can find the file `apxs`, it's installed; if not, it's not. If Apache was installed on Linux from an RPM, `apxs` may not have been installed. Some RPMs for Apache consist of two RPMs: one for the basic Apache server and one for Apache development tools. Possibly the RPM with the development tools, which installs `apxs`, needs to be installed.

Installing on Unix/Linux

To install PHP 5 on Unix/Linux, follow these steps:

1. **Point your Web browser to** www.php.net**, which is the PHP home page.**
2. **Click Downloads.**
3. **Click the latest version of the PHP source code, which is version 5.0.0 as of this writing.**

   A dialog box opens.
4. **Select the option to save the file.**

   A dialog box opens that lets you select where the file is to be saved.
5. **Navigate to where you want to save the source code (for example,** /usr/src**). Then click Save.**
6. **After the download, change to the download directory (for example,** cd-/usr/src**).**

   You see a file named php-, followed by the version name and tar.gz. This file is called a *tarball* because it contains many files compressed into one file using the tar command.
7. **Unpack the tarball.**

   The command to unpack the tarball for PHP version 5.0.0 is the following:

   ```
   gunzip -c php-5.0.0.tar.gz | tar -xf -
   ```

   A new directory called php-5.0.0 is created with several subdirectories.
8. **Change to the new directory that was created when you unpacked the tarball.**

   For example, you can use a command like the following:

   ```
   cd php-5.0.0
   ```
9. **Type the** configure **command:**

   The configure command consists of ./configure followed by all the necessary options. If you are installing PHP for use with Apache, use the following configure command:

   ```
   ./configure --with-apxs
   ```

   You will see many lines of output. Wait until the configure command has completed. This may take a few minutes.

   If the apxs utility is not installed in the expected location, you see an error message, indicating that apxs could not be found. If you get this message, check the location where apxs is installed (find / -name apxs) and then include this path in the with-apxs option of the configure command: —with-apxs=/usr/sbin/apxs.

If you decide to use Apache 2, you need to use `apxs2`.

You may need to use many other options, such as options for the database that you're using or options that change the directories where PHP is installed. These `configure` options are discussed in the section, "Installation Options for Unix/Linux/Mac," later in this Appendix.

10. **Type** `make`**.**

    You will see many lines of output. Wait until it is finished. This may take a few minutes.

    By default, both the CLI and CGI versions of PHP are built. The file `libphp5`.so is built for use with Apache. PHP CLI is named `php` and is located in the directory where php is intalled (e.g. `user/local/php`). If you don't want both versions, you can disable one or the other with a `configure` option, as described in the section, "Installation Options for Unix/Linux/Mac," later in this chapter.

11. **Type** `make install`**.**

    The files are moved to the correct locations. For instance, the Web version of PHP is installed in the directory where Apache is installed (e.g. `/usr/local/apache/libexec/libphp5.so`).

Alternative method for installing with Apache

Occasionally, you can't install PHP using `apxs`. This section provides an alternative method of installation for situations in which `apxs` isn't available or refuses to work. The preceding installation method is easier and usually works fine. This section is just here to provide an alternative in case the first section fails you. Follow these steps:

1. **Point your Web browser to** `www.php.net`**, which is the PHP home page.**
2. **Click Downloads.**
3. **Click the latest version of the PHP source code — version 5.0.0 as of this writing.**

   A dialog box opens.

4. **Select the option to save the file.**

   A dialog box opens that lets you select where the file is to be saved.

5. **Navigate to where you want to save the source code (for example,** `/usr/src/php`**), and then click Save.**
6. **After the download is complete, change to the download directory (for example,** `cd-/usr/src/php`**).**

You see a file named `php-`, followed by the version number and `tar.gz`. This type of file is called a *tarball.*

7. **Unpack the tarball.**

   The command to unpack the tarball for the current PHP version 5.0.0 is as follows:

   ```
   gunzip -c php-5.0.0.tar.gz | tar -xf -
   ```

   A new directory called `php-5.0.0` is created with several subdirectories.

8. **Repeat Steps 1 through 5, but this time, download the Apache source code into the directory where the PHP source code was unpacked.**

   You can find the Apache source code at `httpd.apache.org`.

   For the rest of this example, I use the current version, 1.3.27. By the time you read this, a later version may be available.

   As of this writing, using PHP with Apache 2 is not recommended for a production Web site. Check the PHP Web site before downloading to see whether the recommendation has changed about using PHP with Apache 2.

9. **Unpack the Apache tarball. For the current version, the command is as follows:**

   ```
   gunzip -c apache_1.3.27.tar.gz | tar -xf -
   ```

   Now there are two directories: `php-5.0.0` and `apache_1.3.27`. Each has several subdirectories.

10. **Type** `cd apache_1.3.27`**.**

11. **Type** `./configure`.

    The options do not matter for this command. This is a preliminary configuration of Apache that should be done before you configure PHP. The Apache `configure` will be run again in a later step with the appropriate options. Wait until the `configure` has completed. This may take a while.

12. **Type** `cd ../php-5.0.0`**.**

13. **Type the following:**

    ```
    ./configure --with-apache=../apache_1.3.27
    ```

    If you need to type the `configure` command on two lines, type a \ at the end of the first line.

    You may need to use many other options, such as options for the database that you are using or options that change the directories where PHP is installed. The `configure` options are discussed in the section, "Installation Options," later in this Appendix.

14. **Type** `make`**.**

    You see many lines of output. You will be informed when it is finished running. It may take some time.

15. **Type** `make install`**.**

    This finishes quickly.

16. **Type** `cd ../apache_1.3.27` **to return to the Apache directory tree.**

17. **Type the following command to configure Apache again:**

    ```
    ./configure --prefix=/www
         --activate-module=src/modules/php5/libphp5.a
    ```

    You can type this command on one line. If you type it on two lines, type a \ at the end of the first line. Be sure there is at least one space between the end of one option and the beginning of the next.

18. **Type** `make`**.**

    You see many lines of output. You will be informed when it is finished running. It may take some time.

    The final step depends on whether Apache is already installed on your system or whether this is the first installation of Apache.

19. **For a first installation of Apache, type** `make install`**.**

    If Apache is currently installed and running, do the following:

    a. **Shut down Apache.**

       You can stop the Apache Web server by running a script that was installed on your system during installation. This script is usually called `apachectl`. It may be located in the `bin` directory in the directory where Apache was installed — for example, `/usr/local/apache/bin` or in `/sbin` or in `/usr/sbin`. You also may be able to find it in the directory on your system where startup scripts are located — for example, `/etc/rc.d/init.d`. If you find the script, you can stop the server by typing the name of the script, followed by stop, for example: `apachectl stop`. You may need to be in the directory with the script in order to run it.

    b. **Find the new file named** `httpd` **that you just created in Step 18.**

       This file will be somewhere under the `apache` directory tree that you just created — for example, `/usr/src/php/apache_1.3.27/bin/httpd`.

    c. **Find the existing file named** `httpd`**.**

       This file will be somewhere on your disk, possibly in `/usr/local/apache/bin` or `/sbin` or `/usr/sbin`.

    d. **Copy the new file named** `httpd` **over the old one — that is, replace the old one with the new one.**

TIP

You may want to make a backup copy of the old one before you copy over it.

If you decide to upgrade PHP to a newer version, you must use this installation method. You can't use this method to install now; you'll need it next time.

Installing PHP on Computers Running Mac OS X

With the release of PHP 4.3, you can install PHP on Mac OS X as easily as on Unix/Linux. You can install PHP as a partner with Apache (for use in Web pages) or as a stand-alone interpreter. If you want to use PHP for both Web sites and as a stand-alone language, you need to install PHP with Apache and PHP CLI, which are two separate types of PHP. The instructions below include information for both types of PHP installations: PHP for the Web and PHP CLI.

You install PHP by downloading source files, compiling the source files, and installing the compiled programs. This process isn't as technical and daunting as it may appear. I provide step-by-step instructions in the next few sections. Read all the way through the steps before you begin the installation procedure to be sure that you understand it all clearly and have everything prepared so you don't have to stop in the middle of the installation.

Before installing on Mac

If you want to use PHP with Apache for your Web site, Apache must be installed. Most Mac OS X systems come with Apache already installed. Before beginning to install PHP, check the following:

- **The Apache version is 1.3.0 or newer:** To check the version, type the following on the command line:

  ```
  httpd --v
  ```

  You may have to be in the directory where `httpd` is located before the command will work.

  Because of security issues with Apache, it is much better to use Apache 1.3.27 or newer.

  PHP with Apache 2 is still considered experimental. For use on production Web sites, it's better to use Apache 1.3 than Apache 2.

- **The Apache module `mod_so` is installed.** It usually is. To display a list of all the modules, type the following:

  ```
  httpd -l.
  ```

  You may have to be in the directory where `httpd` is located before the command will work. The output usually shows a long list of modules. All you need to be concerned with for PHP is mod_so. If mod_so is not loaded, Apache must be reinstalled with the --enable-module=so option.

- **The apxs utility is installed.** apxs often is installed when Apache is installed. To determine whether it's installed on your computer, you should look for a file called apxs, usually in the /usr/sbin/apxs directory. If you can find the file apxs, it's installed; if not, it's not.
- **The files from the Developer's Tools CD are installed.** This CD is supplemental to the main Mac OS X distribution. If you can't find the CD, you can download the tools from the Apple Developer Web Site at developer.apple.com/tools/macosxtools.html.

Installing on Mac

To install PHP on Mac, follow these steps:

1. **Point your Web browser to www.php.net, which is the PHP home page.**
2. **Click Downloads.**
3. **Click the latest version of the PHP source code, which is version 5.0.0 as of this writing.**

   A dialog box opens.
4. **Select the option to save the file.**

   A dialog box opens that lets you select where the file is to be saved.
5. **Navigate to where you want to save the source code (for example, /usr/src), and then click Save.**
6. **After the download, change to the download directory (for example, cd-/usr/src).**

   You see a file named php-, followed by the version name and tar.gz. This file is called a *tarball.* The file may have been unpacked by the Stuffit Expander automatically so that you see the directory php-5.0.0. If so, skip to Step 8.
7. **Unpack the tarball.**

   The command to unpack the tarball for PHP version 5.0.0 is the following:

   ```
   tar xvfz php-5.0.0.tar.gz
   ```

   A new directory called php-5.0.0 is created with several subdirectories.
8. **Change to the new directory that was created when you unpacked the tarball.**

   For example, you can use a command like the following:

   ```
   cd php-5.0.0
   ```

9. **Type the `configure` command:**

   The `configure` command consists of `./configure` followed by all the necessary options. The minimum set of options are as follows:

   - **Location options:** Because the Mac stores files in different locations than the PHP default locations, you need to tell PHP where files are located. Use the following options:

```
--prefix=/usr
--sysconfdir=/etc
--localstatedir=/var
--mandir=/usr/share/man
```

   - `zlib` **option:** `—with-zlib`
   - **Apache option:** If you are installing PHP for use with Apache, use the following option: `—with-apxs`.

   Therefore, the most likely configuration command that you should use is

```
./configure --prefix=/usr --sysconfdir=/etc
    --localstatedir=/var --mandir=/usr/share/man
     --with-apxs -with-zlib
```

   You can type the configure command on one line. If you use more than one line, type a \ at the end of each line.

   You will see many lines of output. Wait until the `configure` command has completed. This may take a few minutes.

   If the `apxs` utility is not installed in the expected location, you will see an error message, indicating that `apxs` could not be found. If you get this message, check the location where `apxs` is installed (`find / -name apxs`) and include the path in the `with-apxs` option of the `configure` command: `—with-apxs=/usr/sbin/apxs`.

   If you decide to use Apache 2, you need to use `apxs2`.

   You may need to use many other options, such as options for the database that you're using or options that change the directories where PHP is installed. These `configure` options are discussed in the section, "Installation Options for Unix/Linux/Mac," later in this Appendix.

10. **Type** `make`**.**

    You will see many lines of output. Wait until it is finished. This may take a few minutes.

    By default, both the CLI and CGI versions of PHP are built. The file `libphp5.so` is built for use with Apache. PHP CLI is named `php` and is located in the directory where php is intalled (such as `user/local/php`). If you don't want both versions, you can disable one or the other with a configure option, as described in the section, "Installation Options for Unix/Linux/Mac," later in this chapter.

11. **Type** `sudo make install`**.**

Installation Options for Unix/Linux/Mac

The previous sections give you steps to quickly install PHP. However, PHP can be installed with many options, and you may want to use some of these options during installation. For example, you may want to install PHP with support for the database that you plan to use, such as MySQL or Oracle. Or, all the PHP programs and files are installed in their default locations, but you need to install PHP in different locations. Or you may be planning applications using additional software.

You can use additional command line options if you need to configure PHP for your specific needs. Just add the options to the configure command shown in Step 13 of the Linux/Unix installation instructions or Step 9 of the Mac installation instructions. In general, the order of the options in the command line doesn't matter. Table A-1 shows the most commonly used options for PHP. To see a list of all possible options, type `configure -help` in the directory where PHP is installed.

Table A-1 PHP Configure Options

Option	*Tells PHP To . . .*
`prefix=`*`PREFIX`*	Set main PHP directory to *`PREFIX`*. Default *`PREFIX`* is `/usr/local`.
`infodir=`*`DIR`*	Install info documentation in *`DIR`*. Default is *`PREFIX`*`/info`.
`mandir=`*`DIR`*	Install man files in *`DIR`*. Default is *`PREFIX`*`/man`.
`with-config-file-path=`*`DIR`*	Look for the configuration file (`php.ini`) in *`DIR`*. Without this option, PHP looks for the configuration file in a default location, usually `/usr/local/lib`.
`disable-cgi`	Don't build the PHP CGI binary program.
`disable-cli`	Don't build the PHP CLI binary program.
`disable-libxml`	Disables XML support.
`enable-debugger`	Enable support for internal debugger.
`enable-ftp`	Enable FTP support.
`enable-magic-quotes`	Enable automatic escaping of quotes with a backslash.
`enable-url-includes`	Allow the `include()` function to get files from HTTP and FTP locations, as well as from the `include` directory.

Option	Tells PHP To . . .
`with-msql=DIR`	Enable support for mSQL databases. Default *DIR* where mSQL is located is `/usr/local/Hughes`.
`with-mysql=DIR`	Enable support for MySQL 4.0 or earlier databases. Default *DIR* where MySQL is located is `/usr/local`.
`with-mysqli=DIR`	Enable support for MySQL 4.1 or later databases. No default. *DIR* must be the path to the file `mysql_config` that is installed with MySQL 4.1 or greater. Do not enable both mysql and mysqli.
`with-openssl=DIR`	Enable OpenSSL support for a secure server. Requires OpenSSL version 0.9.5 or later.
`with-oracle=DIR`	Enable support for Oracle. Default *DIR* is contained in the environmental variable, `ORACLE_HOME`.
`with-pgsql=DIR`	Enable support for PostgreSQL databases. Default *DIR* where PostgreSQL is located is `/usr/local/pgsql`.
`with-servlet=DIR`	Include servlet support. *DIR* is the base install directory for the JSDK. The Java extension must be built as a shared dll.
`with-xml`	Enable XML support.

Configuring on Unix/Linux/Mac

PHP has configuration settings that allow you to change some of its behavior. The configuration settings are read by PHP at startup from a file called `php.ini`. The default location where `php.ini` should be located is `/usr/local/lib/php.ini`. However, you can change this default location by using an installation option, as I describe in the previous section. If PHP doesn't find the `php.ini` file in the expected directory, default settings are used.

You may have to copy the `php.ini` file to the correct location. The default file is in the `php` directory called `php.ini-dist`. Copy it by using the following command:

```
cp php.ini-dist /usr/local/lib/php.ini
```

On the Mac, use the following:

```
sudo cp php.ini-dist /usr/local/lib/php.ini
```

You can edit php.ini to change the settings for PHP. In general, the defaults are okay. PHP settings are discussed throughout the book when the settings are relevant to PHP features. For example, you can change the settings in php.ini to control how PHP handles and displays error messages. The error handling settings are discussed in Chapter 4 when PHP error handling is discussed.

If you're using PHP with Apache, you must configure Apache to recognize PHP files. To configure Apache, follow the steps below:

1. **Locate the Apache configuration file, called httpd.conf.**

   It is on your system, possibly in /etc or in /usr/local/apache/conf. On Mac, it is probably located in /etc/httpd. You must edit this file before PHP can run properly.

2. **Add a line to the file that tells Apache to load the PHP module.**

   Find the list of LoadModule statements. You load the PHP module with the line:

   ```
   LoadModule php5_module libexec/libphp5.so
   ```

   Check to be sure that this line is there. If it is not there, add it. If it is there with a pound sign (#) at the beginning of the line, remove the pound sign.

3. **Add a line to the file that tells Apache which files may contain PHP code.**

   Look for a section describing AddType. You may see one or more AddType lines for other software. The AddType line for PHP is

   ```
   AddType application/x-httpd-php .php
   ```

   Look for this line. If you find it with a pound sign (#) at the beginning of the line, remove the pound sign (#). If you don't find this line, add it to the list of AddType statements. This line tells Apache to look for PHP code in all files with a .php extension. You can specify any extension or series of extensions. On Mac, add this line to the bottom of the file.

4. ***Mac only:* If you have been previously running the PHP that came with the Mac, you need to comment out the following lines.**

   ```
   LoadModule hfs_apple_module
   libexec/httpd/mod_hfs_apple.so
   AddModule mod_hfs_apple.c
   ```

   Just add a # at the beginning of each line to make the lines inactive.

5. **Start (if it's not running) or restart (if it is running) the Apache httpd server.**

   You can start or restart the server by using a script that was installed on your system during installation. This script may be apachectl or httpd.apache, and it may be located in /bin or in /usr/local/apache/bin. For example, if the script is called apachectl, you can start the server by typing `apachectl start`, restart it by using `apachectl restart`, or stop it by using `apachectl stop`. On Mac, type `sudo apachectl restart`. Sometimes restarting Apache doesn't change your PHP settings; if your settings didn't change, you must stop the server first and then start it again. In addition, your computer is undoubtedly set up so that Apache starts whenever the computer starts. Therefore, if you're having trouble, you can always shut down and then start your computer to restart Apache.

Whenever you change any of the settings in `php.ini`, you may have to restart Apache before the changes go into effect.

Installing PHP on Computers Running Windows

PHP runs on Windows 98/Me (although it's not recommended) and Windows NT/2000/XP. You can use PHP with your Web server for your Web site (PHP CGI) or you can use PHP as an independent stand-alone scripting language (PHP CLI). The two types of PHP require different executable files. You can install either or both types of PHP software.

There are two ways to install PHP — using the Windows Installer or manually from a Windows `.zip` file. Which one you use depends on what you are planning to use PHP for. Use the following guidelines to choose a method of installation:

- **Windows Installer:** Installs PHP CGI only. Includes built-in support for a selected set of popular functions. This installation includes support for ODBC, which is a method of interacting with some databases, such as MS Access, and for SQLite, a quick easy way to store data in flat files. (See Chapter 12 for a discussion of database use with PHP.) Support is also included for XML, FTP, and COM. PHP CLI is not installed using this method.

  You can use this simpler, faster installation method as long as the following criteria are met:

  - You are using PHP with your Web site and don't need to use PHP CLI independently.
  - You are using PHP for simple HTML or to process forms.
  - You are not using a database or, if you are using a database, you are using ODBC for your database interaction.
  - You are using only the built-in functionality.

- **Manual installation:** All the required files are bundled into a Windows `.zip` file. You download the `.zip` file, unzip it, and place the needed files into the correct locations manually.

PHP includes a lot more functionality than is automatically installed by the installer. If you need to use any of that functionality, then you need to use the manual installation method. For example, if you need to use PHP CLI or if you need to interact with a database other than by using ODBC, you need to install manually. In addition to the built-in functionality of PHP, extensions are available with a great deal of added functionality. If you want to use any of this additional functionality, the necessary files are included in the Windows `.zip` file. For more discussion of extensions and how to install them, see Chapter 14.

Installing PHP CGI with the PHP installer

The following steps install PHP on a Windows computer for use on your Web site but do not install PHP CLI:

1. **Point your Web browser at `www.php.net`.**
2. **Click Download.**
3. **Go to the Windows Binaries section. Click the download link for the installer for the most recent version of PHP (as of this writing, 5.0.0).**
4. **Click the link for a mirror Web site from which to download the file, and then choose the site closest to your location.**

   A dialog box opens.
5. **Select the option to save the file.**

   A dialog box opens that lets you select where the file is to be saved.
6. **Navigate to where you want the file to be downloaded. Then click Save.**

   After the download is complete, you see a file in the download location containing all the files needed. The file is named `php`, followed by the version number and `-installer.exe`. For the current version, the file is named `php500-installer.exe`.
7. **If you're not using IIS or PWS for your Web server and you currently have your Web server running, shut it down.**
8. **Navigate to the directory where you downloaded PHP and double-click `php500-installer.exe`.**

   The installer software starts with the screen shown in Figure A-1.
9. **Click Next.**

   The license is displayed.
10. **Click I Agree to continue.**

    You see a screen in which you can choose the type of installation.

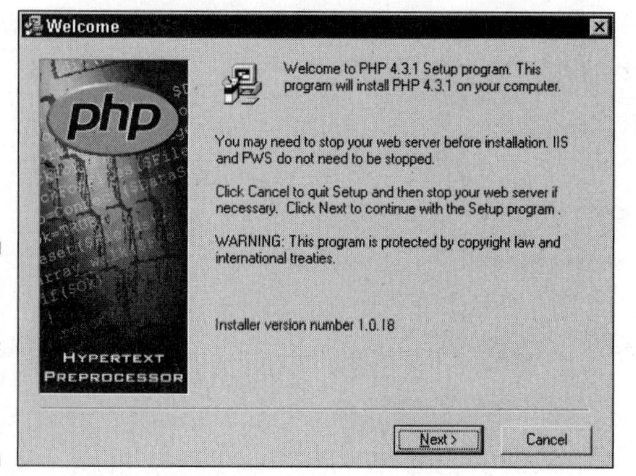

Figure A-1: The opening screen of the PHP installer.

11. **Select Standard and then click Next.**

    You see a screen showing the directory where PHP is to be installed.

12. **If you want to install PHP in the default directory,** `c:\php`**, click Next. If you want to install PHP in a different directory, click Browse, select a directory, and click OK; then click Next.**

    You see a mail configuration screen.

13. **The mail screen has two fields to collect information for use when you send e-mail from a PHP script. If you plan to send email and know the address of your SMTP server or the From address you want to use in your e-mail, enter them now. If you don't know this information, just leave the defaults selected.**

    If you need to, you can change this later by editing the PHP configuration file.

14. **Click Next**

    You see the screen shown in Figure A-2. It shows a list of Web servers that PHP can be installed with.

15. **Select the server that you're using. If the server that you're using is not listed, select None.**

16. **Click Next.**

    You see the Ready screen. The installer is now ready to install.

17. **Click Next to start the installation.**

    You see a confirmation message after PHP 5.0.0 has been installed. Any information that you need is be displayed, such as whether you need to reboot or restart your server. For example, when I selected Apache, I saw the screen in Figure A-3.

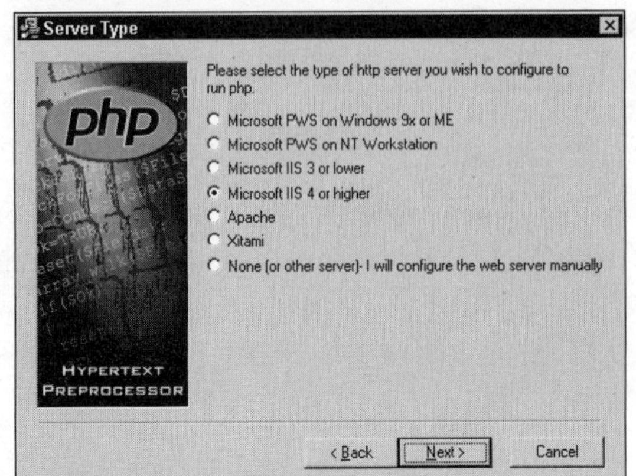

Figure A-2: The Server Type screen in the PHP installer program.

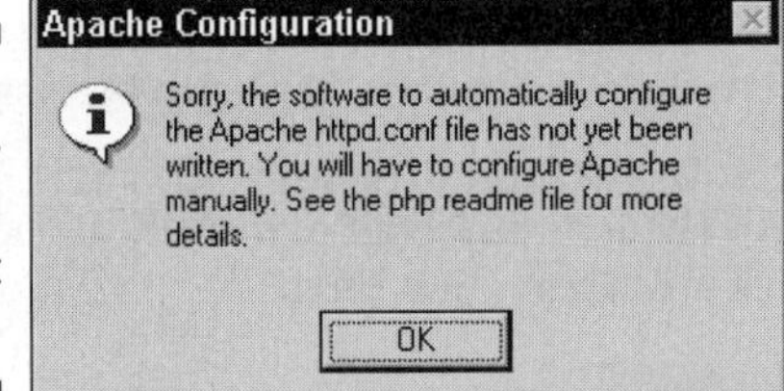

Figure A-3: An installer message about Apache.

This message doesn't mean that Apache was not installed. It just means that it wasn't automatically configured, so I have to configure it myself, as described in the configuration section later in this Appendix. Perhaps by the time that you install PHP, the configuration for Apache will also be an automated process, saving you the trouble.

Installing PHP manually

To install PHP5 manually on Windows, you must first download a zip file that contains all the necessary files for PHP. The following steps show how to install PHP on Windows.

1. **Point your Web browser at** `www.php.net`**.**
2. **Click Download.**
3. **Go to the Windows Binaries section. Click the download link for the zip package for the most recent version of PHP (as of this writing, 5.0.0).**

   If you are familiar with `.bz` format files and know how to uncompress them, download the `.bz` file. It's smaller and faster to download, but not all software can uncompress it.

4. **Click the link for a mirror Web site from which to download the file, and choose the site closest to your location.**

   A dialog box opens.

5. **Select the option to save the file.**

   A dialog box opens that lets you select where the file is to be saved.

6. **Navigate to where you want the file to be downloaded. Then click Save.**

   After the download is complete, you see a file in the download location containing all the files needed. The file is named `php`, followed by the version number and `-win32.zip`. For the current version, the file is named `php5.0.0-win32.zip`.

7. **Extract the files from the `.zip` file into the directory where you want PHP to be installed, such as `c:\php`.**

   If you double click the `.zip` file, it should open in the software on your computer that extracts files from `.zip` files, such as WinZip or PKzip. Select the menu item for extract and select the directory into which the files are to be extracted.

   When you extract all files from the `.zip` file, it may put the contents into a file called `php-5.0.0-win32`. If so, you can just rename it to something more reasonable. For example, you can extract the directory into `c:\` and then rename it to `php`, so your installation is in `c:\php`. `c:\php` is a good choice for installation because many configuration files assume that's where PHP is installed, so the default settings are more likely to be correct.

   It's best not to install PHP in a directory with a space in the path, such as in Program Files/PHP. It sometimes causes problems.

   You now have a directory with several subdirectories that contain the files that you need.

8. **Copy PHP CLI into the directory where you intend to run it. It is currently located in the directory where PHP is installed and is named `php.exe`. You can run it from this directory if you want to.**

Configuring PHP and your Web server on Windows computers

PHP uses a configuration file that you can edit to change some of the behavior of PHP. In addition, if you are using PHP for your Web site, you need to configure your Web server as well.

Configuring PHP on Windows

PHP uses settings in a file named `php.ini` to control some of its behavior. PHP looks for `php.ini` when it begins and uses the settings that it finds.

If you used the Windows Installer, a default php.ini file was installed. If you installed manually, you need to install the php.ini file yourself. A default configuration file php.ini-dist is located in the directory where PHP was installed. Copy this file into one of the following directories, giving it the name php.ini:

- **Windows 98/Me/XP:** windows
- **Windows NT/2000:** winnt

If you have a previous version of PHP installed (such as PHP 4.3), make a backup copy of the php.ini file before you overwrite it with the new one for PHP5. You can then see the settings you are currently using and change the settings in the new php.ini file where needed.

If you're using PHP with the IIS Web server, you need to change one of the default settings. Open the php.ini file in the windows or winnt directory. Find the line:

```
; cgi.force_redirect = 1
```

This setting needs to be changed to 0. Also, the above setting has a semicolon at the beginning of the line, which comments the line so that it isn't active. For IIS, you need to use the following line.

```
cgi.force_redirect = 0
```

In general, the default settings allow PHP to run okay (with the exception described in the previous paragraph), but you may need to edit some of the settings for specific reasons. I discuss settings in the php.ini file throughout the book when I am discussing a topic that may require you to change settings. For example, PHP error handling actions can be changed by settings in the php.ini file. The possible settings and their effects are discussed in Chapter 4.

Configuring your Web server for PHP

Your Web server needs to be configured to recognize PHP files. If you installed with the Windows Installer and your Web server is IIS or PWS, it was automatically configured during the installation procedure (except for IIS 6). If your Web server is Apache or if you used the manual installation procedure, you need to do the configuration yourself.

Configuring Apache

To configure Apache to use PHP, follow these steps:

1. **You configure Apache by editing a file called httpd.conf.**

   You may be able to edit it by choosing Start➪Programs➪Apache HTTP Server➪Configure Apache Server➪Edit Configuration.

If you can't find a menu item at the above location, find the `httpd.conf` file on your hard disk, usually in the directory where Apache is installed, in a subdirectory called `conf` (for example, `c:\program files\Apache group\Apache\conf`). Open this file in an editor, such as Notepad or WordPad.

2. **Your `httpd.conf` file must instruct Apache to send PHP code to the PHP program. Two statements work together to do this:**

   - **`ScriptAlias`:** A `ScriptAlias` statement is used to set up a name for the directory where PHP is installed. Look for `ScriptAlias` statements in the `httpd.conf` file. You may see some for other software. If you do not see one for PHP, add the following:

     ```
     ScriptAlias /php/ "c:/php/"
     ```

     The first argument is the name, and the second argument is what it represents. In this statement, the name `/php/` is used to mean `c:/php/`.

   - **Action:** An `Action` statement is used to tell Apache where to find PHP. If you don't find an `Action` statement for PHP, add the following:

     ```
     Action application/x-httpd-php /php/php-cgi.exe
     ```

     Notice that the `Action` statement uses the name defined in the `ScriptAlias` statement. It locates `php-cgi.exe` in `/php/`, which means `c:/php/`. If you change the `ScriptAlias` statement to say `c:/php27/`, the `Action` statement would then look for `php-cgi.exe` in `c:/php27`.

It's better to use forward slashes. Apache can find the location on Windows okay.

3. **You need to tell Apache which files may contain PHP code.**

   In the `httpd.conf` file, look for a section describing `AddType`. This section may contain one or more `AddType` lines for other software. The `AddType` line for PHP is

   ```
   AddType application/x-httpd-php .php
   ```

   Look for this line. If you find it with a pound sign (#) at the beginning of the line, remove the pound sign. If you don't find the line, add it to the list of `AddType` statements. This line tells Apache to look for PHP code in all files with a `.php` extension. You can specify any extension or series of extensions.

4. **Start (if it's not running) or restart (if it is running) Apache.**

   You can start it as a service on Windows NT/2000/XP by choosing Start➪Programs➪Apache HTTP Server➪Control Apache Server.

   Or you can start it on Windows 98/Me by choosing Start➪Programs➪Apache Web Server➪Management.

Sometimes restarting Apache doesn't change the settings; if your settings didn't change, you must stop it first and then start it. In addition, your computer is undoubtedly set up so that Apache starts whenever the computer starts. Therefore, if you're having trouble, you can always shut down and then start your computer to restart Apache.

Configuring IIS manually

If you installed PHP with the Windows Installer and are using IIS 5 or before, IIS was automatically installed. However, if you installed PHP manually, you need to configure IIS. In addition, if you installed PHP with Windows Installer and are using IIS 6/Windows Server 2003, IIS was not totally configured, so you need to perform the steps in this section.

To configure IIS to work with PHP, follow these steps:

1. **Enter the IIS Management Console.**

   You should be able to enter by choosing Start➪Programs➪Administrative Tools➪Internet Services Manager or Start➪Settings➪Control Panel➪Administrative Tools➪Internet Services Manager.

2. **Right-click your Web site (such as Default Web Site).**
3. **Select Properties.**
4. **Select the Home Directory tab.**
5. **Click the Configuration button.**
6. **Choose the App Mappings tab.**
7. **Click Add.**
8. **In the Executable box, type the path to the PHP interpreter: for example,** `c:\php\php-cgi.exe`**.**
9. **In the extension box, type** `.php`**.**

   This will be the extension that is associated with PHP scripts.

10. **Select the Script Engine check box.**
11. **Click OK.**

Repeat Steps 6–10 if you want any additional extensions in addition to `.php` to be processed by PHP, such as `.phtml`.

Appendix B

Useful PHP Built-in Functions

PHP is as powerful as it is because of its many functions. This Appendix is a reference to the most useful functions.

Some of the functions are discussed at various places in the book; some are not. If the function is discussed in the book, its definition includes a chapter reference where a more complete description can be found.

Array Functions

This section describes built-in functions that work with arrays.

array

Creates a new array. (See Chapter 6.)

Format: `$array = array(key=>value,key=>value,key=>value,...);`

array_count_values

Creates an array that contains a count of the values in the original array.

Format: `$array_out = array_count_values($orig_array);`

For example, suppose that `$orig_array` contained the following:

```
$orig_array[a] = John
$orig_array[b] = Mary
$orig_array[c] = John
$orig-Array[d] = Jose
```

Then `$array_out` would contain the following:

```
$array[John] = 2
$array[Mary} = 1
$array[Jose] = 1
```

array_diff

Returns $array_out with elements from *$array1* that are not present in any other of the specified arrays (*$array2*, *$array3*, and so on). (See Chapter 6.)

Format: `$array_out = array_diff($array1,$array2,$array3 . . .);`

array_intersect

Creates an array that contains the elements that are the same (rather than different) in two or more arrays. (See Chapter 6.)

Format: `$simArray = array_intersect($array1,$array2, . . .);`

array_keys

Creates an array containing all the keys in the $orig_array. If search_key is included, only keys that match search_key are in the new array.

Format: `$array_out = array_keys($orig_array,"search_key");`

For example, suppose that $orig_array contained the following:

```
$orig_array[a] = CA
$orig_array[b] = OR
$orig_array[c] = TX
```

Then $array_out would contain the following:

```
$array_out[0] = a
$array_out[1] = b
$array_out[2] = c
```

Suppose that search_key= OR, as in the following:

```
$array_out = array_keys($orig_array,"OR");
```

Then $array_out would contain the following:

```
$array_out[0] = b
```

array_merge

Merges two or more arrays together. If more than one element has the same non-numeric key, only the last value for the key is added to the output array. (See Chapter 6.)

Format: `$bigArray = array_merge($array1,$array2, . . .);`

array_merge_recursive

Merges two or more arrays. If more than one element has the same non-numeric key, an array with all the values for the key is added to the output array. (See Chapter 6.)

Format: `$bigArray = array_merge($array1,$array2, . . .);`

array_pop

Removes and returns the last element in an array.

Format: `$element = array_pop($orig_array);`

array_push

Adds the specified element(s) to the end of the array. Returns the new size of the array.

Format: `$new_size = array_push($orig_array,"el1","el2","el3");`

array_reverse

Reverses the order of the items in `$orig_array`.

Format: `$array_out = array_reverse($orig_array);`

array_search

Searches an array for a value. If *`value`* is found, key is returned.

Format: `$key = $array_search("value",$orig_array);`

array_slice

Creates a new array that contains a subset of an existing array. Puts *number* of elements, beginning with *`start`*, into `$subArray`. (See Chapter 6.)

Format: `$subArray = array_slice($orig_array,start,number);`

array_sum

Adds all the values in an array. (See Chapter 6.)

Format: `$sum = array_sum($orig_array);`

array_unique

Removes duplicate elements from an array. (See Chapter 6.)

Format: `$array_out = array_unique($orig_array);`

arsort

Sorts an array by value in reverse order. (See Chapter 6.)

Format: `arsort($orig_array);`

asort

Sorts an array by value, keeping the original keys. (See Chapter 6.)

Format: `asort($orig_array);`

compact

Creates an array from the specified variables (`$var1`, `$var2`, and so on). The variables can be strings or arrays.

Format: `$array_out = compact($var1, $var2, . . .);`

count

Returns the number of elements in the array. (See Chapter 6.)

Format: `$size = count($orig_array);`

current

Returns the value of the array element where the pointer is currently located. (See Chapter 6.)

Format: `$value = current($array);`

end

Moves the pointer to the last element in an array and returns the value. (See Chapter 6.)

Format: `$value = end($array);`

explode

Creates an array containing substrings of a string. The specified separator, `sep`, which is generally something like a comma or a tab, divides the string into substrings. (See Chapter 6.)

Format: `$array_out = explode("sep",$string);`

extract

Creates a set of variables, one for each element of an array. The key for the element is used as the variable name. (See Chapter 6.)

Format: `extract($array);`

implode

Builds a string containing the values of all the elements in an array, separated by the specified separator. (See Chapter 6.)

Format: `$string = implode($array,"sep");`

in_array

Searches through the values in an array for a specified *value*. Returns TRUE or FALSE.

Format: `$bool = in_array("value",$array);`

key

Returns the key of the array element where the pointer is currently located.

Format: `$key = key($array);`

key_exists

Checks an array to see whether it contains an element with the specified key. Returns TRUE or FALSE.

Format: `$bool = key_exists("key",$array);`

ksort, krsort

Sorts the array by key. `ksort` sorts in ascending order, and `krsort` sorts in reverse (descending) order. (See Chapter 6.)

Format: `ksort($array); krsort($array);`

natsort, natcasesort

Sorts an array by value in natural order. The order of the results is n1, n2, n12, n25, rather than n1, n12, n2, n25 in the usual sort. The function `natcasesort` works the same way but is case-insensitive.

Format: `natsort($array); natcasesort($array);`

next

Moves pointer in array to next element. (See Chapter 6.)

Format: `next($array);`

prev

Moves pointer in array to previous element. (See Chapter 6.)

Format: `prev($array);`

range

Sets up an array with elements spanning a range of values. Possible ranges can be numerical (such as 1–10 or 10@nd1) or alphabetical (such as a–m or m–a).

Format: `$array_out = range(start,end);`

reset

Moves pointer to the first element in an array. (See Chapter 6.)

Format: `reset($array);`

sizeof

Returns the number of elements in an array. (See Chapter 6.)

Format: `$size = sizeof($array);`

sort, rsort

Sorts array by value. `sort` sorts in ascending order, and `rsort` sorts in reverse (descending) order. (See Chapter 6.)

Format: `sort($array); rsort($array);`

Date and Time Functions

This sections contains functions that work with date and time values.

checkdate

Checks whether date is valid. Returns TRUE or FALSE.

Format: `checkdate(month,day,year);`

date, gmdate

Converts a Unix timestamp into a formatted date. The function `gmdate` returns Greenwich Mean Time. (See Chapter 5.)

Format: `$formatted_date = date("format",$timestamp);`

getdate

Creates an array from a Unix timestamp, each element containing part of the array, such as seconds, minutes, month, day of the year, and so on.

Format: `$array_date = getdate($timestamp);`

localtime

Creates an array of values related to your local time, such as seconds, minutes, day of month, and so on.

Format: `$array_date = localtime($timestamp);`

microtime

Returns time in seconds and microseconds since January 1, 1970.

Format: `$time_out = microtime();`

mktime, gmmktime

Returns a Unix timestamp. `gmmktime` uses Greenwich Mean Time. (See Chapter 5.)

Format: `$timestamp=mktime("hrs","min","sec","mo","da","yr");`

time

Returns the Unix timestamp for the current time. (See Chapter 5.)

Format: `$timestamp = time();`

File System Functions

This section contains functions for use with your file system.

basename

Returns the filename from a full path. (See Chapter 13.)

Format: `$filename = basename("`*`path`*`");`

chdir

Change to a different directory. (See Chapter 13.)

Format: `chdir("`*`pathtodirectory`*`");`

chgrp

Changes the group for a file.

Format: `chgrp("`*`pathtofile`*`","`*`group`*`");`

chmod

Changes the permissions of the file.

Format: `chmod("pathtofile","octalnumber");`

chown

Changes the owner of a file.

Format: `chown("pathtofile","newowner");`

closedir

Closes the directory pointed to by the directory handle `$dh`. (See Chapter 13.)

Format: `closedir($dh);`

copy

Copies a file, resulting in two copies of the file. (See Chapter 13.)

Format: `copy("oldfilename","newfilename");`

dirname

Returns the directory from a path. (See Chapter 13.)

Format: `$directory_name = dirname("path");`

dis_total_space

Returns the number of bytes of total space on the disk.

Format: `$space = disk_total_space("path");`

disk_free_space

Returns the number of bytes of free (unused) space.

Format: `$free = disk_free_space("pathtodir");`

fclose

Closes an open file pointed to by the file handle `$fh`. (See Chapter 12.)

Format: `fclose($fh);`

feof

Returns TRUE when the pointer reaches the end of the file. (See Chapter 12.)

Format: `feof($fh);`

fgetc

Returns one character (the current character) and moves the pointer to the next character in the file.

Format: `$char = fgetc($fh);`

fgetcsv

Reads a line of no longer than *length* from a file and returns it as an array, breaking it into elements at the specified separator, *sep*. (See Chapter 12.)

Format: `$array_out = fgetcsv($fh,length,"sep");`

fgets, fgetss

Reads a line from file of no longer than *length*. Does not return the end-of-line character. `fgetss` also strips tags from line. (See Chapter 12.)

Format: `$line = fgets($fh,length); $line=fgetss($fh,length);`

file

Reads a file and returns an array with one line per element. (See Chapter 12.)

Format: `$array_lines = file($fh);`

file_exists

Checks whether a specific file exists. Returns TRUE or FALSE. (See Chapter 13.)

Format: `$bool = file_exists("pathtofile");`

fileatime

Returns the time that the specified file was last accessed. (See Chapter 13.)

Format: `$timestamp = fileatime("pathtofilename");`

filectime

Returns the time that the specified file was created. (See Chapter 13.)

Format: `$timestamp = filectime("pathtofilename");`

filemtime

Returns the time that the specified file was last modified. (See Chapter 13.)

Format: `$timestamp = filemtime("pathtofile");`

fileowner

Returns the user ID of the owner of the file. (See Chapter 13.)

Format: `$userID = fileowner("pathtofile");`

fileperms

Returns the file permissions for the file.

Format: `$perms = fileperms("pathtofile");`

filesize

Returns the file size in bytes. (See Chapter 13.)

Format: `$size = filesize("pathtofile");`

filetype

Returns the file type, such a file or directory. (See Chapter 13.)

Format: `$type = filetype("pathtofile");`

flock

Locks a file so that no one else can access it until it's unlocked. (See Chapter 12.)

Format: `flock($fh,mode);`

fopen

Opens a file and returns a pointer to the specified file. (See Chapter 12.)

Format: `$fh = fopen("pathtofile","mode");`

fputs

Writes text to a file. Alias for `fwrite`. Returns the number of bytes written to the file or FALSE if the function fails. (See Chapter 12.)

Format: `$result = fputs($fh,"text",length);`

fread

Reads *number* of bytes, unless it reaches the end of the file first, from a file. (See Chapter 13.)

Format: `$file_content = fread($fh,number);`

fscanf

Reads text from a file and returns a formatted string. (See the format and syntax for `sprintf` in Chapter 13.)

Format: `$string = fscanf($fh,"format",$v1,$v2, . . .);`

fseek

Moves the file pointer, depending on the next two parameters. The value specified in `num` is a number of characters. You can set `mode` to `SEEK_SET` (moves to `char in position num`), `SEEK_CUR` (moves `num` characters forward from current position), or `SEEK_END` (moves `num` characters back from the last character).

Format: `fseek($fh,num,mode);`

fwrite

Writes *`text`* to the file indicated by `$fh`, stopping at *`length`*. Specifying *`length`* is optional. (See Chapter 12.)

Format: `$bytes_written = fputs($fh,"text",length);`

getcwd

Returns the path to the current directory.

Format: `$current_directory = getcwd();`

getlastmod

Returns the last modification date of the current script.

Format: `$timestamp = getlastmod();`

is_dir

Checks whether the specified path is a directory. (See Chapter 13.)

Format: `$bool = is_dir("pathtodir");`

is_file

Checks whether a specified file is a regular file, rather than a directory or special system file. (See Chapter 13.)

Format: `$bool = is_file("pathtofile");`

is_readable

Checks whether a specified file is readable. (See Chapter 13.)

Format: `$bool = is_readable("pathtofile");`

is_uploaded_file

Checks whether a specified file was uploaded via Web server form.

Format: `$bool = is_uploaded_file("pathtofile");`

is_writable

Checks whether a specified file is writable. (See Chapter 13.)

Format: `$bool = is_writable("pathtofile");`

link

Creates a hard link to *path* at *newpath*.

Format: `link("path","newpath");`

mkdir

Creates a new directory. The value specified in *mode* is permissions in octal form.

Format: `mkdir("pathtonewdir",mode);`

move_uploaded_file

Moves a file from its temporary upload directory to a permanent file. (See Chapter 11.)

Format: `move_uploaded_file("filename","pathtodestination");`

opendir

Opens a directory. Returns a pointer to the open directory. (See Chapter 13.)

Format: `$dh = opendir("pathtodir");`

passthru

Executes a system command and outputs the result. (See Chapter 13.)

Format: `passthru("systemcommand");`

pathinfo

Creates an array with information about a path. The array contains three elements: `dirname`, `basename`, and `extension`.

Format: `$array_dir = pathinfo("pathtodir");`

readdir

Reads one filename from the open directory. (See Chapter 13.)

Format: `$filename = readdir($dh);`

readfile

Reads a file and outputs the contents. Can handle a URL.

Format: `$numberOfBytesRead = readfile("pathtofile");`

rename

Renames a file. (See Chapter 13.)

Format: `rename("oldfilename","newfilename");`

rewind

Sets a file pointer to beginning of the file referred to by `$fh`.

Format: `rewind($fh);`

rmdir

Removes a directory. (See Chapter 13.)

Format: `rmdir("pathtodir");`

tempnam

Generates a unique filename with a specified prefix in the directory.

Format: `$filename = tempnam("pathtodir","prefix");`

tmpfile

Creates a temporary file with a unique name, opens it with write privileges, and returns a pointer to the open file.

Format: `$fh = tmpfile();`

touch

Sets the modification date of a file. If *time* isn't specified, it sets the date to the current time. If the file does not exist, it's created.

Format: `$bool = touch("pathtofile",time);`

umask

Sets the default permissions to *mask* and returns the previous mask. The previous defaults are restored at the end of the script.

Format: `$old_mask = umask(mask);`

unlink

Deletes a file. (See Chapter 13.)

Format: `unlink("pathtofile");`

HTTP and Mail Functions

This section contains functions related to HTTP headers and mail functions.

get_browser

Returns an object containing information about the user's current browser or about the browser name if specified.

Format: `$string = get_browser("name");`

get_meta_tags

Creates an array, each element of which is a name attribute for any meta tags found in a file.

Format: `$array_tags = get_meta_tags("pathtofile");`

header

Sends an HTTP header to the Web server. (See Chapter 10.)

Format: `header("HTTPformattedheader");`

mail

Sends e-mail from a PHP script. (See Chapter 13.)

Format: `$success = mail("to","subj","message","headers");`

parse_url

Returns an array, each element of which is a part of the URL, such as host, path, port, user, and so on.

Format: `$array_url = parse_url("url");`

setcookie

Creates a cookie. (See Chapter 10.)

Format:
`setcookie("name","value",exp,"path","domain",is_secure);`

Mathematical Functions

This section contains functions that perform mathematical operations. There are many more functions for advanced math that are not listed in this section, such as `cos` for cosine, `tan` for tangent, and `pi`.

abs

Returns the absolute value of *number*.

Format: `$absolute = abs(number);`

bindec

Converts *binary* to a decimal value.

Format: `$number_decimal = bindec(binary);`

exp

Returns the constant *e* raised to the power specified in *exponent*.

Format: `$number = exp(exponent);`

floor

Rounds *float* to the next lower integer.

Format: `$int = floor(float);`

hexdec

Converts *hex* (a number in hexadecimal form) to decimal.

Format: `$number_decimal = hexdec(hex);`

log

Returns the natural log of *number*.

Format: `$log = log(number);`

log10

Returns the base-10 logarithm of *number*.

Format: `$log10 = log10(number);`

max

Returns the largest number found in an array or a list of numbers.

Format: `$num_large = max($array);` or `$num_large = max(num1,num2, . . .);`

min

Returns the smallest number found in an array or a list of numbers.

Format: `$num_min = min($array);` or `$num_min = min (num1,num2, . . .);`

number_format

Formats a number with specified decimal (*dec*) and thousands separators (*thous*). The default is a standard decimal point (.) and a comma (,) for the thousands separators. (See Chapter 5.)

Format: `$formatted = number_format(number,"dec"',"thous");`

octdec

Converts a number in octal form to decimal form.

Format: `$number_decimal = octdec(octal);`

pow

Returns *number* raised to *power*.

Format: `$result = pow(number,power);`

rand

Returns a random number between *min* and *max*.

Format: `$number_rand = rand(min,max);`

round

Rounds `number` to the nearest number with the specified number of decimal places.

Format: `$result = round(number,dec);`

sqrt

Returns the square root of *number*.

Format: `$square_root = sqrt(number);`

srand

Seeds the random number generator with *seed*.

Format: `srand(seed);`

PHP Options and Information Functions

This section contains functions that work with PHP options and information.

getenv

Returns the value of an environmental variable.

Format: `$environment_value = getenv("envvarname");`

getlastmod

Gets the time that the current script was last modified.

Format: `$timestamp = getlastmod();`

ini_get

Gets the value for a configuration option.

Format: `$string = ini_get("option");`

ini_set

Sets the value of a configuration option. (See Chapter 4.)

Format: `ini_set("option","setting");`

phpinfo

Outputs information about your PHP version and settings. (See Chapter 2.)

Format: `phpinfo();`

phpversion

Returns the current PHP version.

Format: `$version = phpversion();`

putenv

Sets an environments variable. The value indicated in *`setting`* is usually in the form *`name=value`*.

Format: `putenv("setting");`

String Functions

This section contains functions that work with strings.

addslashes

Escapes single quotes, double quotes, backslashes, and `\0` in strings.

Format: `$string_escaped = addslashes("string");`

base64_encode, base64_decode

Encodes/decodes a string of base-64–coded characters, usually binary data. (See Chapter 13.)

Format: `$string_encoded = base64_encode("string");`

chop

Truncates blank spaces at the end of a string.

Format: `$chopped = chop("string");`

chr

Returns a single ASCII character for the number code.

Format: `$char = chr(code)`

count_chars

Creates an associative array out of a string. Each element has a character as a key, and the value is the number of that character in the string. This function has some options for only returning characters with count 0 or with nonzero and others. Default, when no options is specified, is all characters.

Format: `$array = count_chars($string,option);`

echo

Outputs a list of one or more items. (See Chapter 3.)

Format: `echo item1,item2,item3, . . .`

ereg, eregi

Searches a string for *pattern*. The function `eregi` works the same but is case-insensitive. (See Chapter 7.)

Format: `$bool = ereg("pattern",$string);`

ereg_replace, eregi_replace

Searches a string for *pattern* and replaces *pattern* with *newchar*. Ereg_replace is case-sensitive; `eregi_replace` is not. (See Chapter 7.)

Format: `$newstring = ereg_replace("pattern","newchars", $string);`

explode

Creates an array. Each element is part of the string, split at *sep*.

Format: `$array_out = explode("sep",$string);`

htmlentities

Converts HTML entities to special characters in a string.

Format: `$string_out = htmlentities($orig_string);`

htmlspecialchars

Converts special characters to HTML entities, such as `&` to `&`.

Format: `$string_out($string);`

implode

Joins every element in an array into a string, separated by *sep*.

Format: `$string_out = ($array,"sep");`

nl2br

Inserts a <br /> before all new line characters (\n) in $string.

Format: `$string_out = ($string);`

ord

Returns the ASCII value of the first character in the string.

Format: `$integer = ord("string");`

parse_url

Creates an associative array. Each element is part of the URL.

Format: `$array = parse_url($url);`

print

Outputs *item*, where *item* can be a string, a number, or a variable.

Format: print *item*;

printf

Outputs a string formatted according to *format*. (See Chapter 5.)

Format: `printf("format",arg1,arg2,arg3, . . .);`

split, spliti

Creates array. Each element is part of a specified string, split based on the regular expression *pattern*. Split is case-sensitive; spliti is not.

Format: `$array = split("pattern",$string); $array = spliti("pattern",$string);`

sprintf

Returns a string formatted according to *format*. (See Chapter 5.)

Format: `$string = sprintf("format",arg1,arg2,arg3 . . .);`

str_pad

Returns a string that is padded to make it *number* long. The character specified by *pad* is used to pad the string.

Format: `$string_out = str_pad($string,numberh,"pad");`

str_repeat

Returns a string that contains `$string` repeated *`number`* times.

Format: `$string_out = str_repeat($string,number);`

str_replace

Finds all instances of *`oldtext`* in `$string` and replaces them with *`newtext`*.

Format: `$string_out = str_replace("oldtext","newtext",$string)`

strchr, strrchar

The function `strchr` returns part of string from *`char`* to end of `$string`, and `strrchar` returns `$string` from *`char`* to start of string.

Format: `$string_part = strchr($string,"char");`

strcmp, strcasecmp

Compares two strings on alphabetical and numerical order . Returns @@n1 if *`str1`* is less, 0 if two strings are equal, or +1 if *`str1`* is greater. `strcmp` is case-sensitive; `strcasecmp` is not.

Format: `strcasecmp($str1,$str2);`

strcspn

Returns the position of the first occurrence of *`char`* in `$string`.

Format: `$int = strcspn($string,"char");`

strip_tags

Removes HTML and PHP tags from string. The value *`allowed`* is optional and specifies tags that should not be stripped. (See Chapter 10.)

Format: `$string_stripped = strinp_tags($string,"allowed");`

strlen

Returns the number of characters in `$string`. (See Chapter 7.)

Format: `$length = strlen($string);`

strpos, strrpos

`strpos` returns the position of the first occurrence of *`char`* in `$string`. `strrpos` returns position of last occurrence of *`char`* in string.

Format: `$integer = strpos($string,"char"); $integer = strrpos($string,"char");`

strspn

Returns the length of the substring in `$string` that matches *text*.

Format: `$length = strspn($string,"text");`

strstr, stristr

Returns part of `$string` from the first occurrence of *char* to end of `$string`. Strstr is case-sensitive; `trichar` is case-insensitive.

Format: `$str_part = strstr($string,"char"); $str_part = strstr($string,"char");`

strtolower, strtoupper

Converts `$string` to lowercase or uppercase.

Format: `$string_lower = strtolower($string);`

strtr

Converts *from* characters in `$string` to characters in *to*.

Format: `$string_out = strtr($string,"from","to");`

substr

Returns a substring of `$string`. Starts at *start* and reads *number* characters.

Format: `$substring = substr($string,start,number);`

substr_replace

Replaces a substring with *newtext*. Starts at *start* and reads *number* characters.

Format: `$string_new = substr_replace($string,"newtext",start,number);`

trim, ltrim, rtrim

Removes whitespace characters from `$string`. The `trim` function removes from beginning and end; `ltrim` removes from beginning; `rtrim` removes from end.

Format: `$string_new = trim($string);`

ucfirst

Converts first character in `$string` to uppercase.

Format: `$string_new = ucfirst($string);`

ucwords

Converts first character of each word in `$string` to uppercase.

Format: `$string_new = ucwords($string);`

wordwrap

Inserts end-of-line character (`\r\n`) into `$string` every *length* characters.

Format: `$string_out = wordwrap($string,length);`

Variable Functions

This section contains functions that work with variables.

empty

Tests whether the variable specified is empty. (See Chapter 7.)

Format: `$bool = empty($varname);`

get_defined_classes

Creates an array containing the names of all the classes in the script, including those in included files.

Format: `$array_classes = get_defined_classes();`

get_defined_constants

Creates an associative array of all the constants.

Format: `$array_constants = get_defined_constants();`

get_defined_functions

Creates an array with names of all functions.

Format: `$array_functions = get_defined_functions();`

get_defined_vars

Creates an array of all variables.

Format: `$array_vars = get_defined_vars();`

isset

Checks whether variable is set. (See Chapter 7.)

Format: `$bool = isset($varname);`

print_r

Outputs contents of a variable. (See Chapter 4.)

Format: `print_r($varname);`

putenv

Sets an environmental variable as specified by *`setting`*. *`setting`* is usually *`name=value`*.

Format: `putenv("`*`setting`*`");`

serialize

Converts data into a string containing binary data. Used to store data in a file or database. The specified variable can be any type, including an object or a function.

Format: `$string_ser = serialize($variable);`

unserialize

Converts serialized data back to its original form.

Format: `$variable = unserialize($string_ser);`

unset

Removes a variable. (See Chapter 4.)

Format: `unset($varname);`

var_dump

Outputs contents of a variable. (See Chapter 4.)

Format: `var_dump($varname);`

Index

• Symbols •

• D •

• G •

• H •

• L •

• M •

• N •

• O •

• P •

• T •

• U •

• V •

• W •

• Z •

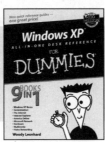

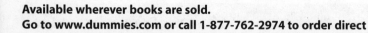